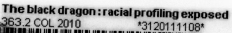

The Black Dragon

Racial Profiling Exposed

award-winning investigative journalist

Joseph Collum

author of Brady's Run

Jigsaw Press
Sun River, Montana

For information mailing address: Editor, Jigsaw Press, 784 US Hwy 89, Vaughn, Montana, 59487.

ISBN: 978-1-934340-77-6
LCCN: 2009937065

Proudly published in the United States of America.

For the missing pieces of your reading puzzle...

Jigsaw Press
www.jigsawpress.com

To my sons
Peter, Simon, Spencer and James Collum

Acknowledgments

I owe thanks to so many people it's hard to know where to begin. First must be my publisher and editor M.L. Bushman of Jigsaw Press, who asked to publish *The Black Dragon* after publishing my first novel, *Brady's Run,* and whose always expert editing helped me whip the manuscript into final form.

Thanks to William H. Buckman, the civil rights attorney who I believe is one of the true heroes of the fight against racial profiling and who gave me generously of his time. His colleagues Jeffrey Wintner, Justin Loughry, Fred Last, and Wayne Natale were also incredibly helpful.

A great number of present and former New Jersey State Troopers were also exceedingly accommodating, including Kenneth Ruff, Darryl Beard, Greg Sanders, Glenn Johnson, Victor Cooper, Justin Dintino, Fred Martens, Emblez Longoria, Vincent Belleran, Arnie Abrams, Sam Davis, Gary Gibson, Amy Johnson, John Hogan and Paul McLemore, as well as a host of others, some of whom spoke to me anonymously.

Thanks to attorneys Peter Neufeld, Linda Kenney Baden, Jack Arseneault, Robert Galantucci, Francis Hartman, Renee Steinhagen, former New Jersey Attorney General Robert Del Tufo, as well as public defenders Sheri Woliver and the late Walter Marvin, and the New Jersey American Civil Liberties Union. Rutgers University Law professors Frank Askin and Alfred Slocum were also very giving of their time and information.

Thank you also to attorneys Scott Weber of Patton Boggs, and Douglas Wheeler and Albert Porroni of the State of New Jersey

Legislature. And to Senator William Gormley and Reverend Reginald Jackson, whose moral authority helped force the State of New Jersey to finally face its transgressions. My old high school classmate and now forensic specialist Dennis Letendre was extremely helpful checking my description of crime laboratory procedures.

I also want to thank a number of authors, including: General H. Norman Schwarzkopf for the rich and invaluable depiction of his father and the founding of the New Jersey State Police in *It Doesn't Take A Hero,* written with Peter Petre, published by Bantam Books; Angus Kress Gillespie and Michael Aaron Rockland for *Looking for America on the New Jersey Turnpike,* Rutgers University Press; Leo J. Coakley for *Jersey Troopers,* Rutgers University Press; John Starks, author of the excellent *Troopers Behind the Badge;* John Hogan for his book *Turnpike Trooper;* and the late Johnnie L. Cochran, Jr. for *A Lawyer's Life.*

My gratitude to a litany of my fellow journalists and publications that produced a deep cache reporting on racial profiling and the issues that fostered it, including *The New York Times, New Jersey Monthly Magazine, PBS Frontline, The Newark Star-Ledger, The Bergen Record, The Philadelphia Inquirer, New York Daily News, New York Post, Asbury Park Press, The Times of Trenton, and Camden Courier-Post.*

And my great thanks to my former employer WWOR-TV, which for a decade-and-a-half afforded me the immeasurable pleasure and honor to practice the art of investigative journalism in the world's preeminent news market, and particularly my former bosses Tom Petner and Will J. Wright. And thank you to my friends and superlative former producers, Gary Scurka and Barbara Gardner, without whom this story would not have been possible.

Above all, I want to thank my wife Donna, who never uttered a discouraging word during all the years it took me to complete this marathon and who has brought to my life nothing but joy.

Introduction

The Black Dragon is the culmination of twenty years of work that began for me in 1989. At the time, I was an investigative reporter chasing a story about the practice that was to become known as racial profiling. The Oxford English Dictionary defines racial profiling as *"selection for scrutiny by law enforcement based on race or ethnicity rather than on behavioural or evidentiary criteria."*

Racial profiling is a vestige of the Jim Crow America most of us associate with Alabama, Mississippi and the Deep South. I saw it with my own eyes as a white child growing up in the 1950's and '60s in Fort Lauderdale, Florida. I recall realizing at a young age that there was something inherently wrong with the fact that 'Coloreds' or Negroes, as black-skinned people were commonly referred to then, were prohibited from bathing at the city beaches where I swam, or drinking from the water fountains in the supermarket where my mother shopped, or eating at most restaurants that my family and I were free to enter as we pleased. I remember being horrified at the images on television of black civil rights marchers attacked by dogs and fire hoses in Selma and Birmingham. Of adults vilifying Dr. Martin Luther King Jr. as a "communist" for his non-violent protests. Of King being murdered. And a country in flames. It's hard to explain to young people today how raw and bitter relations between the races were when I was young.

Of course, racial relations have vastly improved since then, yet America is still not the *Promised Land* that Dr. King spoke of the day before his murder. Racial inequity, though greatly diminished, unfortunately does still exist in America—as evidenced by the contents of this book.

As an adult, I came to the conclusion that racism is a direct result of ignorance. Not stupidity, but ignorance. Even after the desegregation of schools and restaurants and beaches, blacks and whites in our country have lived in largely separate worlds. I believe that divide is responsible in great part for the ignorance between the races and, consequently, the racism that still exists in the United States.

Much of my career in journalism has been dedicated to rooting out racial injustice, from private companies preying on poor and uneducated minorities to school systems methodically denying proper educations to economically disadvantaged minority children. Consequently, I—unlike many white Americans—had the good fortune to spend a lot of time with people who don't look like me. I covered stories in the poorest wards of Houston, the crime-ridden neighborhoods of Newark, and the most blighted sections of Bedford-Stuyvesant, Brooklyn. And the single most important lesson I learned from those experiences is that—black, white, brown, yellow, or red—we are all the same. The overwhelming majority of us want to be safe and prosperous, live good lives and see our children do well.

By the time I moved to the Northeast in 1987 to work as an investigative reporter at a television station covering New York City and New Jersey, I—like many white Americans—believed that decades of progress had finally eradicated most of the ugly practices of America's past.

Yet, when my colleagues and I began looking into a story we'd been tipped off about—that something terrible was happening on the New Jersey Turnpike—we discovered a secret and cynical system at work that harkened back to the worst of our country's racial yore. In essence, a Race War was being waged under the banner of the War on Drugs. As we subsequently found, this war was an illegal campaign fought by an elite police agency in collusion with prosecutors, judges, and elected officials who seemed perfectly content to attack one societal problem by violating the most basic rights of tens of thousands of their fellow citizens and led some to brand New Jersey *"the Mississippi of the 1990s."*

Our initial reports presaged a much wider awareness of racial profiling. By the late 1990s, profiling had become such a titanic issue, not only in New Jersey but throughout the United States, that I felt compelled to write the story of how and where the practice was born. (Little did I know at the time that, as *The Oxford English Dictionary* later informed me, I had actually coined the term *racial profiling.*) But I didn't write *The Black Dragon* only because I helped light the fuse. Rather, because it is such an incredible story, truly an epic saga, filled with heroes and villains and all of the raw emotions that race evokes in America.

This book recounts a dark chapter in the history of American race relations. It does not paint a pretty picture of what happened in the Garden State, including more than a decade of cover-up of racial profiling that reached to the highest levels of government. However, I would be remiss if I did not report that, in the years after *The Black Dragon* concludes in 2002, the State of New Jersey and its Division of State Police finally took steps to eradicate the problem.

In 2005, New Jersey became the first state in America to prohibit racial profiling and require every police officer within its borders to undergo intensive instruction on profiling and protecting citizen rights. Jersey also became one of only two states in the nation to make racial profiling a criminal offense. In addition, in 2009 the State Police successfully met the dictates of a consent decree with the U.S. Justice Department and was removed from federal monitoring.

As for me, shortly after spending September 11, 2001, and the days immediately thereafter at Ground Zero, I left the world of journalism to begin writing this book. I am fortunate to have had access to a prodigious treasure trove of information, including approximately 200,000 documents, hundreds of hours of sworn testimony, and interviews with many, many dozens of individuals (please see *Acknowledgments*).

One other thing. Because I personally played a fundamental role in the story, I was faced with the awkward task of writing about myself, which I had never done before and chose to do here in the third person, a vanity for which I hope readers will forgive me. I sincerely hope what follows does justice to the amazing story of *The Black Dragon*.

—*Joseph Collum*—

"*The greatest dangers to liberty lurk in insidious encroachment by men of zeal, well-meaning but without understanding.*"
—Justice Louis Brandeis "*Olmstead v. United States*"

Prologue

THE NEWS TRAVELED FAST. By midnight word had spread from Netcong to Red Lion to Bass River. The entire Outfit knew something had happened. Something bad.

The next morning the headlines splashed across the front pages were all the chatter in courthouses around the state. When names leaked out, insiders volunteered their utter lack of surprise.

"He was a time bomb waiting to go off," someone said.

A collective shudder shot through the ranks of the *crime dogs*. They'd always feared something like this. In hindsight, it was bound to happen sooner or later. What astounded them, though, was that this case seemed so textbook: A carload of *johnnies,* out-of-staters, in a rental vehicle. And they tried to escape. Tried to run the *diggers* down, for God's sake!

The needles all pointed to one conclusion: the *johnnies* were dirty. Absolutely had to be! Then to find nothing! Incredible! It made no sense.

A sickening notion began to grip the organization. War drums had been beating for years; that was nothing new. They'd always been able to fend off the enemy, hold the fort. But this was different. This was exactly the kind of thing that could blow a hole in the ramparts.

This was trouble.

Chapter 1

THE NEW JERSEY TURNPIKE was the most important highway in America in the 1980s, the nation's most heavily traveled road, with 200 million cars, trucks, and buses logging more than 4 billion miles a year. It was also the main thoroughfare to and from the greatest city in the world.

At its northern extreme, the Jersey Turnpike was a 12-lane monster, a reeking, shrieking gasoline alley dissecting a twilight zone of refineries, toxic swamps and fire-breathing smokestacks. The panorama was one of raw power. On one side, jumbo jets roared into Newark Airport; on the other, legions of giant blue cranes perched like robotic praying mantis plucking containers from mammoth cargo ships at Port Elizabeth. Endless lines of railroad tankers, boxcars, and hundreds of miles of twisting pipes lined its perimeters. At rush hours so many vehicles gushed from tributary roads the Turnpike became a surging river of metal rushing toward its Niagara in the distance—the Empire State Building, the World Trade Towers, New York City.

The Turnpike retraced an ancient trail blazed thousands of years before by the Hackensackee Indians through a region they called *"Scheyichbi"*—*"land bordering the ocean."* Colonists adopted the native path. George Washington and his rag-tag Continental Army battled the British along the same route that eventually became the main artery for stagecoach lines linking the infant nation's business hubs of New York and Philadelphia. Railroads followed. Then the automobile sealed New Jersey's destiny as *the* corridor state of the northeast.

By the 1940s, endless convoys of cars and trucks had the state gagging on their fumes. Bold action was required and in 1949 the pastoral peace of rural South Jersey was shattered by bulldozers and hot tar. A blacktop spine was carved through cranberry bogs and asparagus fields that soon stretched the length of the state. *Time Magazine* hailed it as *"The Miracle Turnpike,"* a 117-mile engineering marvel, designed and built in a breathtaking two years, a monument to America's can-do spirit.

The finest road ever constructed for its time, the Turnpike was a wide, straight, muscle-bound conveyor belt for speed. At 75 miles per hour, the five-hour marathon between Philadelphia and New York became a lickety-split two-hour sprint. The roadway wasn't friendly or pretty; no flowers, trees, or hospitality centers. Service plazas were bleak yet functional, designed for travelers to gas up, make a pit stop, gobble a burger at Bob's Big Boy, and hit the road again.

The highway was owned and operated by a monolithic institution called the New Jersey Turnpike Authority, a public entity which answered to no one, made its own regulations and ruled with an iron glove. No stopping, no picture taking, and not even diplomatic immunity was recognized. Ambassadors and foreign dignitaries, presuming themselves impervious to the law, were routinely caught zooming down the Turnpike at 100 miles per hour only to be shown to the nearest exit and banned from the highway.

By the 1980s, the Authority was collecting nearly $200 million dollars a year in tolls. And a basketful of that money ended up in the coffers of the New Jersey State Police which, for a stipend of almost $20 million a year, dedicated an entire 187-member unit—Troop D— exclusively to the Turnpike.

Troop D called itself "Dog troop," but the "D" could well have denoted *danger.* Five state troopers had been killed on the highway since it opened in 1951—three shot to death and two run down. Dozens more were seriously injured by guns and cars.

Turnpike troopers weren't beat cops; they had no constituency, no friendly drive-by waves from local soccer moms, ministers or mailmen. The Turnpike was a city on wheels—a long, mobile city with a daily population of more than a half million and all the mischief attendant to a major metropolis. Those who traveled it were potential ne'er-do-wells and, over time, an unwavering principle evolved among members of the New Jersey State Police. That troopers were more than just glorified traffic cops, but true crimebusters. The big road could be an excellent venue to catch criminals, outlaws, real desperados, particularly narcotics traffickers.

So, during the late 1960s the troopers began making a number of drug arrests. Curiously, though, the vast majority of their prey looked strikingly similar—young, white, long-haired men, many of them college students from nearby schools like Rutgers University in New Brunswick.

In 1970, a Rutgers Law School professor and civil rights attorney named Frank Askin filed a federal lawsuit accusing the State Police of violating the Fourth Amendment to the U.S. Constitution by systematically targeting long-haired travelers for highway stops and searches. Askin claimed 95% of the searches were fruitless and asked the court to issue an injunction to stop the practice. The case dragged on for years, in large part due to a hostile U.S. District Court Judge Robert Shaw, who Askin privately described as a "judicial troglodyte."

After three years of courtroom maneuvers Judge Shaw reluctantly held a trial that was supposed to last days, but stretched on for six months and 67 witnesses. Most of the testimony came from long-haired hippie-types like Ron Greenblatt, who had a full beard and flowing hair down to his waist.

Greenblatt had recently played the role of Jesus Christ in a film about the crucifixion. Before that he'd been a student at Rutgers. Greenblatt testified he had been stopped and searched by troopers 13 times. When asked if he was angry at the State Police he said: "I forgive them, for they know not what they do."

Before Judge Shaw could render a verdict, he died suddenly of a heart attack. The case was transferred to another federal judge, John J. Kitchen, who upon assignment remarked: "This case killed Judge Shaw; it's not going to kill me." Two weeks later Kitchen dropped dead. A third judge was forced to recuse himself due to ill health. Finally, the case was assigned to Judge Curtiss Meanor, who found Askins' evidence disturbing.

"The district court's extensive findings of fact reveal what can only be described as callous indifference by the New Jersey State Police for the

rights of citizens using New Jersey roads," the 3rd Circuit Court of Appeals wrote, pointing out in a footnote that Judge Meanor was still alive and well.

But by 1975 the U.S. Supreme Court had issued a ruling that blocked federal courts from intervening in the operations of local and state police departments and Meanor reluctantly declined to give the injunctive relief Askin sought. The six year battle to rein in alleged State Police harassment of motorists came to naught, a lost opportunity that would reverberate over the next two decades.

When the *Great Drug War* of the 1980s was launched, the State Police were ready. New York City was the drug capital of America, which meant—coming or going—most illicit narcotics would likely be transported through New Jersey by way of the Turnpike. The State Police would be America's front line troops in the war and their battlefield would be the long, mighty asphalt colossus troopers called *The Black Dragon.*

Chapter 2

1921 WAS A VERY GOOD YEAR. Babe Ruth hit 59 home runs; Rudolph Valentino starred in *The Sheik;* Albert Einstein was awarded the Nobel Prize for Physics; and Jack Dempsey knocked out Jacques Carpentier in the first $1 million prizefight. Then, on December 5th, a blizzard roared through the northeast United States, covering the Atlantic states in a shroud of snow.

In New Jersey, the arctic wind whistling through the capital city of Trenton was not enough to prevent an historic ceremony from playing out on the steps of the gold-domed State House. In a biting cold, 81 men lined up side-by-side dressed in French blue tailored jackets with gold trim, olive doughboy jodhpurs, Sam Browne belts, and tan knee boots. Some sat on horses and wore cavalry hats. Others straddled big Harley-Davidson motorcycles and wore stiff-crowned caps with peaks raked sharply over their eyes. A distinctive triangular badge adorned the breast of each man, inscribed with the words *"Honor—Duty—Fidelity."* As snow swirled, a brawny figure slowly made his way down the line, greeting and saluting every man.

Until this day, none of the 81 had ever worn a lawman's badge. A collection of butchers, farmers, fishermen, and soldiers, they were the first members of the New Jersey State Police and the imposing man in front of them was giving each his marching orders. The horsemen were dispatched south to rural hamlets and villages where the roads were mostly dirt and the farm population sparse. The motorcyclists were sent north where at least some paved roads existed.

9

Their leader was remarkably young. Herbert Norman Schwarzkopf had been born 25 years earlier in Newark, New Jersey, the only child of German immigrants. His father Julius, a jeweler, wanted his son to have a fine education, so young Norman went off to West Point. He was not only a diligent student, but also starred on the football field, captained the polo team, and was the Military Academy's heavyweight boxing champion. Schwarzkopf graduated in 1917 at the height of the Great War and was sent to France.

At the Battle of Marne, after 50 days of bitter combat, Capt. Schwarzkopf was caught in a cloud of mustard gas and knocked out of action. After the armistice, because he spoke German, he was appointed provost marshal, police chief, mayor, and civil judge of an occupied German farming town.

When Schwarzkopf returned to the United States he was detailed to the cavalry in El Paso, Texas, to guard the U.S.-Mexican border. But in 1920, Julius Schwarzkopf became crippled by arthritis and his son was forced to resign from the military and return to Newark, where he became his family's sole supporter.

At that moment, New Jersey was a state in siege. Bandits and bootleggers were operating with impunity. Only large cities had police protection. No one was immune. A.D. Rider, the renowned "Cranberry King" of South Jersey, was ambushed by 10 masked men who shot him, his daughter, and brother and made off with a large cash payroll. In Springfield, a party of 18 wealthy gentlemen leaving the exclusive Baltusrol Golf Club was jumped and robbed by gunmen laying in wait. Newspapers carried daily accounts of the disorder. On June 16, 1921, *The New York Times* reported:

"The seizure near Andover, N.J. of a truck loaded with valuable silks and the wanton killing of a motorcyclist by a masked band of highwaymen in broad daylight calls attention once more to the failure of local authorities to protect the users of much-traveled roads in that state. The ruffians who shot the chance-comer on his way to work and flung his body into a brook were as blood-thirsty and callous as human nature ever is. It is high time authorities bestirred themselves and spent something for protection. Unless all the country townships of the state arouse themselves, it will be advisable for travelers for pleasure and on business to arm and be ready to defend themselves."

Prominent citizens began banding together in vigilante groups. Trucks traveled in heavily guarded convoys. There was a growing cry for a State constabulary. But the primary roadblock was New Jersey's Governor Edward I. Edwards, whose métier was not law and order. A product of the nefarious Hudson County Democratic machine of political boss Frank Hague, Edwards had won election crusading against Prohibition and pledging to make New Jersey "wetter than the Atlantic Ocean."

Edwards harshly opposed a State constabulary, but in March 1921 lawmakers overruled him and voted to create the Division of State Police. Ironically, they gave Edwards authority to hand pick the first State Police chief. The most likely candidate was assumed to be Lt. Thomas Broadhurst, a Hague flunky from the Hudson County Boulevard Police. Instead, the eccentric governor surprised everyone. Among the forty applicants was a friend of his son. John Edwards had fought in France alongside Herbert Norman Schwarzkopf and the younger Edwards urged his friend to apply. In his meeting with Schwarzkopf, the governor asked:

"What are your credentials for this job?"

"I'm a West Point graduate, I've had experience in the military, and I'm a good organizer."

"What are your politics?" the governor asked.

"I don't have any," Schwarzkopf said. "I've never voted in an election in my life."

Eschewing his own allegiances, Governor Edwards decided he didn't want a State Police Superintendent beholden to the unsavory political machine that had spawned him. Schwarzkopf was tough, honest and enterprising, and, despite his youth, Edwards saw in him the kind of natural leader needed to build a law enforcement organization from the ground up. It was a bold, inspired choice. Schwarzkopf turned out to be perfect for the job.

"A man of honor," his son, General H. Norman Schwarzkopf Jr., recalled decades later in his autobiography, *It Doesn't Take A Hero*. "He would teach me the simple rule he lived by: No matter what happens, no matter how bad a situation is, no matter what you think the consequences will be, you tell the truth. An honorable man does not lie. A Schwarzkopf does not lie."

Above all, Schwarzkopf was a leader.

"When you are called to lead, lead," he would say in his measured, commanding voice. "And when you take leadership, do the right thing."

A chain smoker who was constantly firing a Zippo to his ever-present Camel cigarettes, State Police Superintendent Schwarzkopf cherished every facet of sculpting his new force. Applications poured in from 1,600 men, which he whittled to just 116 candidates who were called to report to Sea Girt, New Jersey. On September 1, 1921 they were issued olive denims and assigned to tents that would be their homes for three ruthless months.

The first State Police Academy was pure military. Schwarzkopf worked his trainees relentlessly, seven days a week without respite. Every morning they ran five miles in formation. Schwarzkopf devised a series of equestrian exercises, teaching the men to ride and care for their horses. The most challenging of these were the Monkey Drills, a stunt contest that included recruits standing astride a galloping team of horses. He brought in law enforcement experts from the Pennsylvania State Police and Royal Canadian Mounted Police. And by December, the original 116 recruits had been pared to 81. They were administered the oath of office as the first New Jersey State Troopers.

To distinguish his men from other police, Schwarzkopf commissioned his father Julius to design a triangular badge rather than a star or shield, with three stars, one in each corner, signifying the State Police motto: *"Honor, Duty and Fidelity."* Each trooper was awarded a badge with a number that would be his for perpetuity. Schwarzkopf wore Badge Number One.

The superintendent called the State Police his "Outfit," and molded it to reflect military values. Troopers lived in barracks and worked 10 day shifts followed by a 24 hour leave, "if possible." Marrying without Schwarzkopf's permission was grounds for immediate dismissal.

"From the day I was old enough to understand words until the day he died," said General Schwarzkopf (who, seven decades after his father founded the State Police, led the U.S. military as commander of Desert Storm) "my father talked about his dream for this organization. He wanted the New Jersey State Police to be superbly qualified policemen. Super cops! Absolutely incorruptible, without any political allegiance, committed to selflessly serve all the people of New Jersey. Bootleggers would offer him bribes to keep his troopers off certain roads so they could take their contraband through. Pop always approached the job like the western sheriff who says to the bad guy: 'Get out of town by sundown.' A gang would be moving into town and he'd take a couple of troopers, big gorillas, and pay the leader a visit. He'd say, 'You do not want to move into Red Bank. Let me explain to you what's going to happen to you if you do.'"

Banditry and crime waned under Schwarzkopf. In 1932, he became internationally renowned when his Outfit solved the *Crime of the Century*, the kidnapping-murder of aviator Charles Lindbergh's infant son in Hopewell Township. The State Police investigation led to the capture, conviction, and execution of Bruno Richard Hauptmann. The State Police developed a reputation as one of the elite law enforcement organizations in the country and Schwarzkopf set the standard for all future State Police Superintendents. Although he retired in 1936, his colossal shadow would always loom over the organization.

"Shortly before he died, while driving down the parkway," General Schwarzkopf recounted, "he passed a state trooper on the side of the road. He waved. He always waved. He said, 'I never pass a state trooper without waving at him, and there has never been a time when the state trooper didn't wave back.' But this particular time, he was dying of cancer; he sat up, waved, the trooper waved back. He sat up a little straighter and said, 'Son, that's my Outfit.'"

On December 5, 1921, in the blinding snow, the young Schwarzkopf stood before his Outfit of 81 men, 61 horses, 20 motorcycles, one automobile, and a truck, and read "General Order Number One," which became the foundation of the New Jersey State Police:

"The force, individually and collectively, should cultivate and maintain the good opinion of the people of the State by a steady and impartial line of conduct in the discharge of its duties, and by clean, sober and orderly habits, *and by a respectful bearing to all classes.*"

Chapter 3

Around 10 o'clock on Sunday night, September 27, 1987, Nate Jones was listening to jazz and enjoying the remains of a pleasant autumn weekend as he steered his metallic blue Mercedes Benz 380 SL along the dark highway. The Friday before, Jones had driven from his home in Trenton, New Jersey, south to Washington, D.C. to visit his son, Nate Jr., a law student at Howard University. He was proud of Nate. For the Jones family, it was another step up the ladder of success.

Jones' wife Barbara had stayed home for the weekend, and father and son had spent some quality time together. As Sunday evening approached, Jones hugged Nate Jr. and left the capital, pointing his Mercedes north on Interstate 95. He drove through Maryland and Delaware, then over the Delaware Memorial Bridge into New Jersey, keeping his speedometer at about 60 mph.

A half hour from Trenton, red flashing lights began bursting like fireworks in Jones' rearview mirror. *What the heck did I do wrong?* he wondered. *I can't believe this!* He eased the Mercedes onto the shoulder of the highway and, seconds later, two New Jersey state troopers walked up to his car, one to the driver's door, the other on the passenger side.

"What did I do, Officer?" Jones said. "Why did you stop me?"

"Where are you coming from, sir?" one trooper responded.

"Why am I being stopped, Officer? I don't think I was speeding."

The trooper neglected his queries to ask Jones where he was heading.

"I'm on my way home. I live in Trenton, and I will tell you my family is expecting me soon. Why am I being stopped?"

"Sir, I need to see your license, registration, and insurance," the trooper said.

"I keep my papers in the trunk. I don't feel safe keeping them in the convertible."

"Please get out of the car and open the trunk."

Jones persisted. "Officer, I'm asking you again, what am I being stopped for?"

"Sir, if you continue to ask me questions like that I'm going to have to arrest you."

"Arrest me for what? What have I done?"

Jones believed he already knew what he'd done. He was a black man driving an expensive car, factors he was well aware police often viewed with suspicion.

Nonetheless, Nate Jones hardly fit the profile of a criminal. At 54 years old, he was gray-haired and rotund, the principal of a public elementary school. Yet, he suspected the only thing these two troopers saw was a black man driving a Mercedes Benz.

"Get out of the car and open your trunk," one trooper ordered.

Jones relented and climbed out of the Mercedes and walked to the rear of his vehicle, the State Police cruiser's headlights and flashing red strobe illuminating the darkness. Before he could unlock the trunk, the second trooper stepped up to Jones.

"Have you been using drugs, sir?" he said.

"That's a ridiculous question," Jones said.

"Are you involved in drugs?"

Jones didn't smoke cigarettes, drink alcohol and had never taken an illegal drug and was offended by the question. More bothersome, though, was the trooper's menacing tone. Jones had been trained for confrontations like this. During the 1970s he'd served as president of the Trenton NAACP and led marches, protests, and boycotts. He'd been schooled by the NAACP in the tenets of Mahatma Gandhi and Martin Luther King Jr., particularly with regard to not antagonizing the police, never putting yourself or others in explosive situations, and always remaining calm and peaceful. Jones made sure to keep his composure and give the troopers clear, precise answers.

"No, officer, I am not involved in any drug activity," he said. "And I still want to know why you're doing this."

"I told you if you don't stop asking me that I'm going to arrest you."

"But I have a right to know why I'm being stopped."

Suddenly, one of the troopers grabbed Jones by the wrists and led him to the front of the State Police cruiser.

"Lean over the hood and put your hands behind your back," he commanded. Jones felt handcuffs close around his wrists as the second trooper took the car keys from his hand.

"What are you doing? Why are you doing this?"

"I told you. You're under arrest," the trooper said.

The NAACP hadn't prepared Jones for anything like this. He was locked in the back seat of the police car. The troopers opened the Mercedes trunk and began combing through its contents. They found Jones' license, paperwork, and $200 in cash.

"Why are you hiding so much cash in your trunk?" a trooper asked.

"I keep it there in case of emergency," Jones said.

"It's not for drugs, is it?"

"No, it's not for drugs," Jones answered calmly.

The troopers spent nearly an hour ransacking the automobile while Jones waited. Finally they locked the Mercedes, got into their car and drove away with him in the back seat, under arrest for obstruction of justice and resisting arrest.

Chapter 4

KENNY RUFF PULLED HIS CAR INTO Newark Station May 7, 1988 and was instantly engulfed in a maelstrom of noise and motion. The barracks was at the gateway to Newark International Airport where several major roads merged into a massive bottleneck. Hundreds of cars and trucks were crawling bumper-to-bumper through the toll plaza as DC 10's shrieked low overhead. Ruff was awestruck. The Jersey Turnpike! The Black Dragon! For a young cop looking to test his mettle, this was the most demanding highway in America.

Ruff was a tall, strapping man, resplendent in his blue uniform trimmed with gold. He climbed a single flight of stairs to the second floor and was buzzed into a lobby where a New Jersey State Police logo adorned the wall. Shift change was in progress and dozens of troopers were coming and going. One sat at the radio desk just inside the door, a bank of computers behind him, and beyond that the station commander's office, the squad room, gym, detective bureau, locker room, interrogation room, breathalyzer room, and kitchen. There was also a lock-up cell filled with detainees. Ruff noticed he had something in common with them. They all had black skin.

Kenny Ruff had grown up only a few miles away from this very spot. Crestmont Homes was one of Newark's worst housing projects, a foreboding vertical tenement where men pissed, vomited, and shot heroin in the stairwells when they weren't drinking wine and shooting craps in front of the cemetery across the street. Failure was on constant display. Ruff was the third of five children abandoned by their father when Kenny was six years old. His mother, Elizabeth Ruff, was an iron-willed woman who kept her brood on a tight leash. The Ruff kids were inside early every night and in church every Sunday. Kenny spent most of his free time playing baseball. As he got older, though, most of his friends quit playing ball and started hanging out with the drunks and junkies. Elizabeth Ruff saw the writing on the wall and, when Kenny reached 7th grade, she moved her family to East Orange, a few miles from Newark, but a world apart. Ruff finished high school and went to Bloomfield College, where he played baseball and graduated with a degree in criminal justice. His goal was to become a New Jersey State trooper.

At that moment, the State Police was trying to extricate itself from a federal court order in effect since 1975, a time when only 13 of the organization's 1,800 troopers were black. The court had ordered the department to dramatically increase its minority troopers. But, a decade later, that mandate still had not been satisfied and the Outfit was desperately trying to entice African-Americans to join up, advertising in newspapers, on billboards, bus benches, and recruiting at primarily black schools. In September 1986, Ruff entered the State Police Academy. Of the 150 candidates in his class, 21 were black or Hispanic, including Ruff, Darryl Beard and Greg Sanders.

Beard was a big, affable 19-year-old from Queens who'd never dreamed of being a cop. He went away to college in Pennsylvania with a fuzzy notion about getting a high tech education. Then one day a State Police recruiter showed up on campus and painted an intriguing picture of an organization with boundless opportunity for excitement, advancement, and a starting salary of $25,000 for those with the steely resolve to become a trooper. On a lark, Beard took the exam and passed. He mulled it over for awhile and, to the surprise of his family, friends, and even himself, he quit college and signed on with the State Police.

Greg Sanders was a short, oval-faced, bespectacled man who looked and spoke like a chemist, which, in fact, he was for a New Jersey petroleum testing laboratory. The only problem was he hated chemistry. At age 22, Sanders knew he didn't want to spend the rest of his life stuck in a lab pouring gasoline from one test tube to another. He wanted to do something interesting with his life, something with diverse possibilities. He saw a State Police ad touting opportunities for minorities and it stirred something inside him.

Sanders, Ruff, and Beard arrived at Sea Girt the same day, sixty-five years after Herbert Norman Schwarzkopf's first class of recruits. The State Police Academy was the most grueling police school in America; some said tougher than U.S. Marine Corps boot camp. Located on 165 acres near the Jersey Shore, Sea Girt was all about pushing recruits to their limits. The regimen no longer included Schwarzkopf's equine exercises or the Monkey Drills, but candidates had to complete long daily distance swims, do hundreds of push-ups, run three-and-a-half miles, and train in boxing, judo, firearms, high-speed driving, accident investigation, traffic law, constitutional law, juvenile justice, psychology, sociology, first aid, typing, English grammar, and take a weekly spelling test. Everything was spit and polish, with daily inspection at 6:30 a.m., meals eaten in silence, and lights out at 10 p.m.

Recruits were indoctrinated into State Police culture and taught to put great stock in the Blue and Gold. *"We are the best,"* was the message, and they were proud to be part of the best. Being a trooper meant being a member of an elite brotherhood, the New Jersey State Police "family." Only the strong survived. Fewer than ten percent of applicants were accepted and typically only half of a class's recruits graduated. Ruff, Beard and Sanders were young and in excellent physical condition and made it with little difficulty. Their futures seemed bright.

Only one dark cloud loomed on the horizon. The three men noticed an apparent disparity in the way minorities were treated. Blacks and Hispanics seemed to be criticized more than whites, were passed over for assignments like squad leader, and got more than their fair share of the worst chores, like guard duty, washing cars, pulling grass from sidewalk cracks, and fetching cartons of milk for instructors. But the recruits didn't dare complain. They knew if they grumbled, they'd be gone.

On January 15, 1987, after 100 days at the academy, the three friends stood with classmates in the vast War Memorial Auditorium in Trenton decked out in their blue and gold uniforms, visors pulled low over their eyes, heads tilted back, chins jutting out. They filed to the stage and saluted the Superintendent.

"Welcome to the family of the New Jersey State Police," he said. "You are now a member of the most elite."

Each received the prize they'd toiled for so long and arduously: a shiny, triangular, brass badge inscribed with the number that would remain theirs for perpetuity. Then, in unison, they filled the hall with a refrain they'd been chanting for 100 days: "We don't know what you've been told! All we want is the Blue and Gold!"

The new troopers were assigned to barracks around the state. Ruff was sent to Netcong in rural northwestern New Jersey where he worked hard and accumulated a cluster of kudos. *"I could have frozen to death,"* wrote a doctor Ruff had rescued from his stalled car during a heavy snowstorm. A prosecutor praised his testimony in a trial to State Police supervisors. *"You have a right to be proud of this young trooper."*

A year later, Ruff, Beard and Sanders were reunited at Flemington Station in central New Jersey, a country outpost where the main job was arresting drunk drivers and investigating collisions between cars and deer. By then each had learned a lot about being policemen. And, while they loved the job, they'd also detected some alarming omens. Sanders was told by a supervisor: "If you want to get involved in the criminal program, *think dark!"* Ruff found a cartoon in his mailbox depicting a white shoe salesman with his arm around a black man with the caption: *"You wanted to see something in a black loafer?"* Another was a questionnaire entitled *"Employment Application for Jesse Jackson's Staff."*

> *"Yo' Momma's Name:*
> *Yo' Fava's Name (if known):*
> *Marital Status: Common Law__ Shacked Up__ Other__*
> *Sources of Income: Theft__ Relief __ Welfare__*
> *Place of Birth: Charity Ward__ Cotton Patch__ Back Alley__*
> *Zoo__*
> *How Many Children By: 1ˢᵗ Wife__ 2ⁿᵈ Wife__ Neighbor's Wife__*
> *Shack-ups__*
> *State Your Greatest Desire in Life (Other Than a White Woman):"*

Ruff complained to his lieutenant about the literature and was stunned by his response.

"You guys are thin-skinned martyrs," he said.

Being a new trooper, Ruff let it go. As was the case at the academy, he knew if he was branded as someone who cried "racism," his career could be injured, perhaps irreparably.

Then, in May 1988, Ruff, Beard and Sanders received exciting news. They were being transferred to Newark. That meant the Turnpike—where the action was. The young troopers saw it as a gold mine of opportunity and that night they celebrated.

A few days later, they arrived for duty. The squad commander, Sgt. Walter Zukowsky, held roll call in the kitchen. As the squad took seats around a long table, Beard noticed something on the wall labeled the *"Ha-Ha Board"* pinned with jokes and cartoons. His eyes were drawn to a sketch of a black man tied to the roof of a car surrounded by several white men holding guns. The caption read: *"Hunting Season."*

Zukowsky introduced the new troopers and talked about the dense traffic and high stress the yearlings would face on the Turnpike. Compared to Newark, he said, other stations were like country clubs.

To Kenny Ruff, this new sergeant seemed like a personable guy and he sensed he'd like Zukowsky. Then he made an odd remark.

"I don't know how all this is going to turn out," he said.

Ruff was confused by the comment.

"Excuse me, sir," he said. "What do you mean by that?"

"What I mean," Zukowsky said, "is I've never had this many blacks on my squad. I don't know how to treat you guys."

Ruff, Beard and Sanders looked at each other but didn't pursue it. Afterwards they retreated into the locker room and talked amongst themselves.

"What's up with this? Is he serious?"

"It sounds like Jim Crow back in the '40s."

"Wow, this is scary stuff!"

Chapter 5

WITH THE EXCEPTION OF HERBERT Norman Schwarzkopf, no two men made a more profound impact on the New Jersey State Police than Clinton Pagano and Justin Dintino. Both joined the Outfit the same year—1952—yet the two were polar opposites.

Pagano was charming and polished; Dintino plainspoken and uncultivated. Pagano kept a sleek automatic strapped to his ankle; Dintino's beat-up revolver was usually stuffed in his briefcase. Pagano mingled with VIPs, while Dintino preferred grilling Mafia dons. As a former Marine, Pagano was a natural fit for the organization's military countenance; Dintino never served in the armed forces and was not enthralled by the marching, the saluting, the *"yes, sirs"* and *"no, sirs."*

Yet, both men excelled as few others. Pagano began his career as a motorcycle trooper and climbed rapidly through the ranks, becoming a car theft investigator and detective. What separated Pagano from the rest, though, were his consummate political skills. He had a knack for getting close to the high and mighty, jockeying his way into jobs as a driver and aide to New Jersey's Attorney General. More significantly, he became the State Police representative to the office of Essex County's powerful prosecutor, Brendan Byrne.

Dintino, on the other hand, had no use for politics or politicians. The thing he cared most about and displayed a flair for from his earliest days as a trooper—when he arrested a Bible salesman who, in his spare time, robbed banks—was solving crimes. Dintino was a natural born sleuth.

In the 1960s, New Jersey was a snake pit of corruption. Graft was as common as spots on dice. Despite Schwarzkopf's early success against gamblers and bootleggers, Jersey had become a sanctuary to gangsters like Lucky Luciano and Carlo Gambino, who had scores of gluttonous mayors, judges and cops feeding like swine at their troughs. Even the State Police wasn't immune. In 1967, *Life* magazine published an exposé called *"The Brazen World of Organized Crime,"* which quoted an FBI wiretap of a pow-wow between three crime bosses grumbling about a high-ranking State Police official they were paying to protect gambling operations. The greedy bastard wanted his $7,000 a month kickback doubled.

Dintino was a young investigator when he got his first glimpse of State Police protection of racketeers. He'd been raiding race horse parlors and numbers operations in small towns between Atlantic City and Philadelphia. After a plentitude of arrests, a major from headquarters paid him a visit. The major hadn't made a gambling arrest in South Jersey for years, yet he chewed out Dintino in front of his entire squad for encroaching on his turf.

To some inside the State Police that became Dintino's badge of honor. Particularly David B. Kelly, the tough, crusty World War II hero—winner of two Silver Stars, two Bronze Stars, and a Purple Heart—who was appointed Superintendent in 1965. Kelly quickly took bold steps to disinfect the Outfit. Shortly after assuming control, he put together a secret Intelligence Unit composed of a small cadre of handpicked agents, Dintino among them. Existence of the team was kept hush-hush, lest Kelly's plan be crushed by the crooked politicos he hoped to put out of business. For months the new squad met in the basement of the Superintendent's home to surreptitiously plot their attack.

Dintino was assigned to chart the Philadelphia Mafia family of Angelo Bruno, who controlled vice in South Jersey. The young detective began stalking the crime boss night and day, doggedly following him around Philly, the Jersey Shore and points in-between, as Bruno collected booty from his bookmaking and numbers rackets. Before long, Dintino was the pre-eminent authority on Philadelphia's syndicate.

Kelly's cloak-and-dagger operation soon identified seven organized crime families with an army of 3,500 foot soldiers openly doing business in New Jersey. They controlled gambling, loan sharking, labor unions, garbage and construction, and had a cavalcade of police and elected officials in their pockets.

When Kelly finally went public, the dossier his men put together was so stunning that unscrupulous officeholders were too busy scrambling for cover to try to quash the Superintendent's initiative. Kelly announced formation of an Organized Crime Task Force—the first of its kind in America. Staffed by 50 investigators, the elite squad signaled a sea change in New Jersey and the State Police. A throng of gangsters and parasitic politicians went to jail and the Outfit was transformed from a corrupt highway patrol into the most sophisticated state investigative agency in the country. By the early 1970s, Dintino was captain in charge of organized crime investigations and one of the most respected mob experts in the United States.

Pagano's career was also in steep ascent. He reached the rank of captain and was placed in charge of the State Police Narcotics Bureau. Pagano and Dintino were never close, though they sometimes crossed paths, mainly at black tie state functions. Pagano rubbing elbows with Jersey's power brokers, Dintino on duty making sure some mobster didn't walk in uninvited and get his picture taken shaking hands with an unsuspecting governor.

Then, in 1975, New Jersey's new governor Brendan Byrne anointed his old protégé, Clinton Louis Pagano, ninth Superintendent of the State Police. It was a stunning and disputatious pick. Only a captain and relatively low on the State Police food chain, Pagano had leapfrogged a long column of majors vying for the top spot, like a common bishop vaulting the College of Cardinals to become Pope. The promotion bothered and bewildered many in the Outfit, including Dintino.

Pagano seemed to be the antithesis of the great Schwarzkopf—bantam-sized, no college degree, and nearly twice the age the legendary founder had been when he assembled the State Police.

But Pagano was not to be underestimated. Physically disciplined, he didn't smoke, ran several miles a day, and, at 47, had the physique of a man half his age. Perpetually polite, always impeccably dressed, Pagano had piercing blue eyes, a magnetic personality, and before long revealed himself to be a capable, charismatic, stalwart leader. By the late-1980s, he'd become the most powerful Superintendent in State Police annals, regarded with a mix of fear and respect as the *"J. Edgar Hoover of New Jersey."*

Dintino knew Pagano was no slouch and considered him a good cop. But his failure to support the new Superintendent could have meant the end of his career as New Jersey's leading Mafia fighter. Ever the politician, though, Pagano had a genuine talent for turning adversaries into allies. Instead of demoting Dintino, he kept him at the helm of Intelligence.

Pagano was a man who saw the world in black and white, good and bad, right and wrong. If he had a sworn enemy it was crime and he attacked with missionary zeal. But, as Superintendent, his true genius was manipulating the system in favor of the State Police. He was particularly adroit at getting others to pay the Outfit's bills. Pagano turned troopers into high-priced rent-a-cops, collecting tens of millions of dollars annually from state agencies like the Turnpike Authority and Garden State Parkway Authority, charging $100,000 per year for each trooper assigned to the roads. In 1977, when casinos came to Atlantic City, Pagano raked in the first big jackpot. Invoking the specter of the ultimate poltergeist—La Cosa Nostra—he insured every gambling house from Baltic Avenue to the Boardwalk would be staffed by a platoon of troopers—at a hefty fee. Rather than mob stoppers, though, troopers became glorified bouncers for the gaming industry, tossing more drunks and loud-mouthed losers out of casinos than gangsters. But the revenue kept State Police coffers flush with cash.

By the late 1980s, Pagano was overseeing a $160 million empire and the most comprehensive law enforcement organization in America. Under his stewardship, the Outfit grew to 2,700 troopers who not only watched over highways and casinos, but guarded the Governor, Attorney General and Chief Justice of the Supreme Court; patrolled waterways; regulated alcohol; protected nuclear plants; supervised emergency management; ran crime labs; trained police dogs; weighed trucks; maintained a fleet of helicopters and an army of scuba divers; and tested racehorse urine.

And as Pagano's domain grew, so did the aura surrounding him. He instilled fear in criminals and politicians alike, though in New Jersey it was often difficult telling the two apart. A legend persisted that Pagano—like J. Edgar Hoover—kept secret files on prominent state figures, an intimidating prospect for lawmakers. How could they deny funding requests to a man who might have dossiers on their drug habits or sexual peccadilloes? There was no proof Pagano actually used embarrassing information, but the perception was real.

"They were all afraid," a state official told New Jersey Monthly Magazine, "and he allowed them to be afraid."

Most of all, Pagano was keeper of the flame ignited by Schwarzkopf. The State Police was Pagano's family. His brothers Girbert and Lester were also troopers (Lester was killed in a car crash in the line of duty). And woe to the trooper who betrayed family. Pagano kept a quotation hanging on his office wall, the same quote the FBI's Hoover had in his office.

"If you work for a man, in heaven's name, work for him: speak well of him and the institution he represents. As long as you are part of the institution, do not condemn it. If you do, the first high wind that comes along will blow you away and you probably will never know why."

Chapter 6

THE SAVORY AROMAS OF PIZZA, CHOP SUEY, AND fried chicken mingled in the hot night air of Queens, New York on July 12, 1987. The sidewalks along Farmer's Boulevard were bustling with pedestrians and fast food joints were doing brisk business when a white Cadillac screeched to a halt in front of Ho-Ho's Kitchen just as six people walked out carrying bags of hot Chinese food. Gunbarrels poked from the car windows, flames spat and two people collapsed.

Minutes later the same Caddy pulled up to a video arcade a few blocks away. Witnesses thought they heard firecrackers. Six people were hit this time. A man took off running but a gunman chased him down and he died, lying on dirty concrete in a pool of his own blood. Police blamed the drive-by shootings on rival crack gangs.

"Living in this neighborhood is like playing Russian roulette," a local resident told *The New York Times*.

New York had been enjoying a respite from the drugs and violence that had dominated the city during the 1970s when Leroy "Nicky" Barnes controlled narcotics. Barnes was a flamboyant, self-educated ex-junkie who—under the tutelage of Mafia boss "Crazy Joey" Gallo—became known as the "King of Harlem." He posed for the cover of *The New York Times Magazine*, which dubbed him "Mr. Untouchable." Barnes was the real life Superfly, a black Al Capone who owned so many fancy cars the FBI's round-the-clock surveillance team couldn't keep track of him. He created "The Council," a black La Cosa Nostra that controlled heroin in the northeast United States, and once threw a gangster's ball at the Time-Life Building, the epicenter of midtown establishment. "Council" members wore black corsages. But Barnes couldn't stay Teflon forever and, in 1978, the Feds sent him away to prison for life.

With Barnes gone, Gotham's wave of drug violence ebbed and the homicide rate was actually shrinking for the first time in a decade. But that ended in 1984 when, almost in the blink of an eye, New York exploded into another era of lawlessness. The fuse was lit by a new high-octane concoction called *crack*. Demand for coke had been fading and prices were plummeting. Then some resourceful entrepreneur in the Caribbean whipped up the recipe for a cheap, new super-cocaine that produced an amazing high that one user likened to "having 100 orgasms at once."

Crack was first detected in the New York metropolitan area in December 1983. At the time, its primary consumers were white professionals and middle-class suburban kids from Long Island, New Jersey and affluent Westchester County. But at $2.50 a vial, crack quickly made its way into poor neighborhoods. By early 1984, the drug hit Harlem and spread from there like shock waves from a nuclear blast. Police tracked its progress almost block by block as it swept from 125th Street near the Apollo Theater and Cotton Club south to Alphabet City on Manhattan's lower east side. And with crack came a new groundswell of carnage. After a five year decline in murder, blood began running in the streets again. This time there was no Nicky Barnes, no Mr. Big, no general. Instead, 18-year-old lieutenants commanded platoons of 13-year-old street soldiers who hawked drugs on corners like Coney Island carnival barkers. Neighborhoods became dusk-to-dawn drug bazaars.

"These junkies are like cockroaches," one neighbor complained. "They never stop."

Crack transformed urban America's cultural landscape. On schoolyard playgrounds, kids quit playing hopscotch and invented a new game—the winner the one who found more empty crack vials. Yet, the most devastating impact was on women.

Poor black and Hispanic men had long been vulnerable to the seductions of alcohol and heroin while women kept the fabric of innercities from ripping apart. But crack decimated the matriarchal order and, almost overnight, the number of drug-addicted females in New York doubled. In 1986, the city experienced a 250% increase in babies born addicted to drugs. Thousands of mothers abandoned their newborns in hospitals. New York City's foster child population jumped from 16,000 in 1985 to nearly 50,000 by 1990.

The crack conflagration leapt from city to city. U.S. News & World Report compared it to a medieval plague. Newsweek called crack *"The Most Addictive Drug Known to Man."* Time dubbed it *"Issue of the Year."* The biggest jolt came June 17, 1986, when crack killed 22-year-old college basketball icon Len Bias.

Bias wasn't some depraved junkie; he was a charismatic, clean-cut young African-American man with everything to live for, a model for every black child in the nation. The tragedy ignited an anti-drug inferno that politicians stoked with a vengeance.

"Crack is killing a whole generation of children," President Ronald Reagan announced.

Congress didn't need a weatherman to know a storm was brewing. Democrats acted with dizzying speed to prove they were tougher on drugs than Republicans. A process that normally took months or years was accomplished in a few days.

"We held no hearings, consulted no judges or prosecutors. It was all driven by politics," Eric S. Sterling, then-counsel to the U.S. House Judiciary Committee, told PBS's *Frontline.*

At a breakneck pace, Congress made epic revisions in narcotics codes and, in the process, turned the Drug War into a Race War. Despite lofty pledges to target kingpins, the Anti-Drug Abuse Act of 1986 set out draconian penalties aimed squarely at small-time crack dealers and addicts—most of them black and Latino. Prison sentences for crack were 100 times harsher than for powdered cocaine, the upscale white man's drug. First offenders caught with five grams of coke received probation while five grams of crack earned a minimum five years in prison.

The bulls-eye had been painted on the backs of minorities. And the message was not lost on New Jersey's Governor Tom Kean.

"Illegal narcotics is the Number One enemy of the 1980s," Kean said. "I want zero tolerance for drugs in New Jersey. We insist—no more drugs."

New Jersey enacted a sweeping manifesto called SNAP—State Narcotics Action Plan—a declaration of war on everyone from pot heads to bigtime traffickers. SNAP called for development of "drug courier profiles" and an aggressive Highway Drug Interdiction Program designed to take advantage of New Jersey's historic role as a corridor state.

The cocaine to make crack was coming from Colombia. Smugglers there paid $1,500 a kilo and flew it to the Bahamas, loaded it onto high-speed boats for Florida, then drove it north to New York City, where the same kilo fetched $15,000.

But, to reach the Big Apple, traffickers had to travel through New Jersey, which meant driving up the Jersey Turnpike where a gauntlet of State Police lay in wait under the command of their field general, Clinton Pagano.

"The plan for a drug-free New Jersey is achievable," Pagano declared, "provided every trooper and every citizen lends a hand."

Chapter 7

LATE ON A SUNDAY IN MARCH OF 1989, Valerie Taylor began the long drive from New York City to her home in Washington, D.C. Her three children were already asleep. Daughter Tekia, 13, was up front next to her mom while her younger brother and sister were dreaming in the back. They'd spent a pleasant weekend visiting Valerie's sister in the Big Apple.

Taylor was an attractive African-American in her 30s who'd grown up in New York and—except for the four hour drive—loved coming back to see her family. She crossed the Hudson River on the George Washington Bridge and drove onto Interstate 95, which she would follow all the way home. But just a couple of miles down the road, without warning, lights flashed in her rearview mirror.

Taylor glanced at her speedometer. She was driving only a few miles over the 55-mile per hour speed limit. But, as she eased onto the highway shoulder, her stomach tightened with anxiety at the realization she was back on the Jersey Turnpike. Seconds later a state trooper was at her window.

"Do you know you were speeding?" he said.

"No, I didn't," Taylor said.

"Can I see your license and registration, please?"

Taylor fished the license from her pocketbook, then reached over and began rummaging through the glove box for the registration. A second trooper appeared at the passenger window and shined a flashlight into the car.

"I'm sorry, officer, I can't seem to find the registration," Taylor said. "This is my husband's car. He's got my car."

The trooper said, "Don't you know, Miss Taylor, it's illegal to operate a motor vehicle in the state of New Jersey without a registration?"

Taylor couldn't believe it was happening again. A few months earlier she and her husband, Malcolm, were driving home after a visit to New York. Malcolm and their youngest child were asleep when Valerie pulled into a Turnpike service plaza for gas and coffee. On her way back to the car, a state trooper had stopped her and started asking questions about where she'd been and where she was going. Taken aback by the impromptu inquisition, she'd answered him nonetheless. Then he asked her to open the trunk. Taylor was shocked.

"Why do you want to search my car?"

"Is there something in your car you're hiding?" he asked.

"No, I'm not hiding anything."

"Well, if there's nothing to hide, why don't you let me take a look?"

"I didn't do anything for you to have to search my vehicle."

After awhile, the trooper left without forcing the issue further, but it had been a chilling encounter and Taylor drove south determined to get out of New Jersey as quickly as possible. Malcolm had warned her about the Garden State. He drove the Turnpike frequently on business trips and had been stopped by troopers several times. He was never given a ticket, but was interrogated each time and his car had been searched twice. Malcolm shrugged off the incidents with a laugh.

"Basically, it was because I was black and it was Jersey," he said. But on this night Valerie was alone and the situation was anything but funny.

"Where are you coming from?" the large, broad-shouldered trooper asked.

"The city. We've been visiting my sister and doing some shopping."

"Where are you going?" he said, leaning into the car, a hand on his gun.

"Home," she said. "Washington, D.C."

The passenger door suddenly opened and the inside light went on, waking Tekia. The second trooper shined his flashlight around the interior of the car.

"I've got sleeping babies in here," Taylor said. "I don't appreciate you searching inside my car with my kids in here."

"Could you please step out of the car?" the trooper said.

It was a chilly night but Taylor reluctantly exited the vehicle. In the blinding glare of headlights racing by it was difficult to see the trooper's face. He ordered her to follow him to the rear of the car. Through the back window she could see the other trooper shining his flashlight into Tekia's face. Valerie was afraid.

"Please open the trunk, ma'am," the big trooper said, standing over her.

"Why?"

"I want to look inside."

"There's no reason to search my car."

"Are you refusing to let me search your car?" he said.

"I didn't do anything wrong. You have no reason to search me."

"Ms. Taylor, you are driving without a registration. If you don't open the trunk I will have your car impounded. I will have you arrested and your children will be left out on the side of the highway."

Taylor felt trapped. She knew that to resist would be trouble. Reluctantly, she opened the trunk and began pulling out everything, including her baby's wet diapers.

"These are dirty underwear!" she said, holding them up under the trooper's nose. "These are clean clothes. These are receipts from the shopping we've done."

"Is that all you have?" the trooper said. "Are you sure you were visiting your sister?"

"Well, I don't feel I have to answer these questions. I let you search the trunk. You harassed me and my children. Now you're going to tell me that I'm lying?"

Eventually, the troopers wrote Taylor a warning and let her go. As she drove south on the Turnpike, her blood began to boil. Taylor knew the State Police had been looking for drugs. And she had no problem with them trying to stop narcotics traffic. But she also believed she'd been stopped and searched for one reason—because she was black. *There has to be a better way,* she thought.

Chapter 8

"PULL THEM OUT OF THE CAR," the white Trenton cop shouted to his partner.

Paul McLemore, a black man, was sitting behind the wheel. Another black man was next to him and a third was passed out drunk in the back seat.

"Don't do that," McLemore said, reaching for his gun as the policemen opened the door.

McLemore's mind was racing and he quickly formulated a mad plan. If these cops tried to force him and his passengers out of the car, he would kill them. He'd fire two bullets into the pig standing next to him, then two more into the cop on the passenger side. When they were dead, he would drive down East State Street, turn left on Broad Street, make a right at Perry Street, and go straight to *The Times of Trenton* and spill his guts:

"Hey, man, you got two cops lying out on the street. I just blew them away because they was trying to play cowboys and nigger with me and I beat them to the draw."

In November 1969, McLemore was a Molotov cocktail about to erupt in a blaze of glory. A tall, rock-hard man with an Afro hairdo, a mustache and a 9-millimeter automatic pistol in a shoulder holster under his black leather jacket, that evening he'd strutted into the Tuxedo Club, a watering hole for bourgeois black men in Trenton. Two celebrities were at the Tuxedo, militants from Oakland, California, the Mecca of black radicalism—Elijah Turner, of the Black

34

Panther Party, and Paul Cobb, from C.O.R.E., the Congress for Racial Equality. Turner and Cobb were the real deal. They were out on the west coast with Huey Newton and Eldridge Cleaver, challenging the police, opening schools, and spreading the word that blacks didn't have to take the white man's shit anymore. The head of the local NAACP introduced McLemore to the Californians.

"This is the most militant nigger in town," he said. "And he's a state trooper!"

Paul McLemore was not only a New Jersey State Policeman. He was the first black trooper in State Police history. A former Marine from Buffalo, McLemore moved to New Jersey after being discharged and took a job at a plastics factory in Paterson with a white Marine buddy named Johnny Smars. Then, one day Smars announced he'd had enough of factory work.

"I'm going to join the state troopers."

"Who the hell are the state troopers?" McLemore asked.

"They're the guys that ride around with the boots and britches. I'm gonna take the exam. Why don't you come, too?"

"I'm not going to be no cop, man."

"Oh, these guys aren't just cops. They're special. It'll be like the Corps again."

The next day McLemore drove with Smars to Parsippany, took the exam and passed with flying colors. He was sworn in October 2, 1961—almost 40 years to the day after Herbert Norman Schwarzkopf founded the organization. But the lily-white State Police did not greet its first Negro with open arms.

New troopers were generally assigned to stations near their homes. McLemore was detailed to State Police headquarters 78 miles from Paterson. The quasi-military State Police lived in barracks, usually bunking two or three to a room. But McLemore slept alone.

Over time, he got a bird's eye look at how troopers treated other blacks. He was assigned to New Jersey's farm belt where thousands of migrant workers flocked every spring from the Deep South to pick potatoes, peaches and all manner of produce. They lived in labor camps far off the beaten path where troopers were the only law and migrants believed they were all-powerful. State cops often drove chronic troublemakers across the state line and told them they'd been deported and

not to return to Jersey. McLemore once accompanied a white trooper
to a call on a farm worker who'd beaten his wife.

"What the hell did you do, Henry?" the other trooper said.

"I'm sorry, boss."

"You ain't supposed to be doing that."

"Yes, sir, I know. It ain't gonna happen again."

"You're damned right it ain't gonna happen again," the trooper
said. "I'm splitting you and her up. I hereby declare you divorced. Get
out of here and don't come back."

It was common for McLemore to hear Rev. Martin Luther King
referred to by fellow troopers as "Martin Luther Coon." McLemore
was never called "nigger" to his face, but troopers routinely applied
the term to civilians. "Those niggers are crazy," he'd hear, "present
company excepted." As white troopers got to know him, they'd say:
"Paul, you're a credit to your race," as if it were a compliment.

Despite it all, McLemore loved being a trooper and figured
putting up with the bigotry was the price he had to pay to do
something he cherished. Then, at two o'clock on the morning of
July 12, 1967, his telephone rang with the call that would change his
life forever.

"Get your riot gear and report to Hightstown. They're going crazy
up in Newark."

Newark was burning. A local cop had shot a black cab driver and
touched off a major riot. The State Police rode into town like a cavalry
to the rescue and black residents cheered. Finally, order would be re-
stored. But, instead, the rioting grew worse. Troopers began raiding
and destroying black-owned businesses. The economic devastation was
overwhelming, something Newark would never get over.

At one point, McLemore was part of a cordon of police lined up
in the street with M-1 rifles as hundreds of bystanders screamed curses
at them. Suddenly a little black kid broke through the police line and
ran up to McLemore, the only black man in uniform.

"You silly motherfucker," the boy said. "Do you realize how stupid you look?"

McLemore looked down at the boy, stunned. He didn't know what
to say. A Newark cop saw the boy taunting him.

"You little black bastard! How'd you get in here?" he said.

"Fuck you, pig!" the kid said.

The cop put his shotgun under the boy's chin and led him off as he yelled back at McLemore. "You're still a silly looking motherfucker! You pig! You ain't even got the balls to shoot!"

It was a defining moment in McLemore's life. He realized this child had had more guts than he ever did. This mere boy was willing to die defying his white oppressors while he, a big strong man, stood by in his uniform with his guns and bandoliers crisscrossing his chest, as twenty-six people died—most of them black, most of them killed by police. McLemore felt ashamed and haunted by Newark and that kid. He began reading about black oppression. Everything from Frederick Douglas to Malcolm X to Stokely Carmichael to Eldridge Cleaver's *Soul On Ice*. And the more he read, the more hostile he became.

After the riots, McLemore was transferred to State Police Community Services. His assignment was to gather intelligence on black radicals. But he refused. Instead he wrote detailed reports explaining the roots of racial discontent. He grew a mustache and an Afro and eventually came to the conclusion that the only way blacks were going to overcome the tyranny of their white nemeses was by force. That was his state of mind when he walked into the Tuxedo Club and met the celebrity radicals.

"The most militant nigger in town—and he's a state trooper!"

The radicals from Oakland couldn't believe McLemore was a cop. But as the night went on and the rhetoric escalated they found their beliefs were almost identical. McLemore was enamored with the men. They were on the front lines in the fight against the white man. They closed the Tuxedo that night and McLemore offered to drive them to their hotel in his unmarked State Police car. On their way, they were stopped by the two Trenton cops. Paul Cobb was sitting in the front passenger seat; Elijah Turner was unconscious in back. McLemore showed the cops his State Police ID.

"You're a trooper?" one of the cops said.

"That's what it says," McLemore said.

"Don't get wise with me."

"Look, leave me alone. By the way, why did you stop me?"

"You cut me off."

"You are a liar," McLemore said.

"Who are you calling a liar?"

"You."

One word led to another and then the cops said they wanted to check out his car.

"Why?" McLemore said.

"We want to know who these people are in your car."

"It's none of your business, officer. This is a State Police vehicle."

"Well, we want to know who these people are. Get out of the car."

As the cop opened the passenger door McLemore grabbed his pistol, thinking: *Lord, I don't want to go out like this but if they touch anybody I'm going to blow them away.*

"Don't do that," he said.

Everything stopped. No one knew what to do next.

"Maybe we ought to call a street sergeant," one cop said finally.

"That's a good idea," McLemore quickly agreed.

The incident effectively ended McLemore's career. He was already viewed with growing alarm inside the State Police. When superiors discovered he'd gotten into a confrontation with police while chauffeuring a couple of black militants in his troop car, he was court-martialed and sent to State Police Siberia, working the graveyard shift in the teletype room at headquarters.

McLemore decided to get out. While he worked all night, he started going to school during the day, earning his bachelor's degree, then a law degree at the University of Pennsylvania. It took him seven years to break free but, on October 2, 1976, McLemore retired from the New Jersey State Police, exactly 15 years after becoming the first black trooper.

He would not be the last.

Chapter 9

IT DIDN'T TAKE KENNY RUFF AND DARRYL BEARD long to realize something was rotten at Newark Station. They were witnessing some alarming conduct, not by criminals, but fellow troopers.

One summer night at about two in the morning, Ruff and Beard were riding together on the Turnpike. Manhattan twinkled to their left. To their right the shadow of a malodorous heap of garbage known as *Mount Trashmore* rose like a giant tumor from the swampy Jersey meadowlands.

They spotted a car on the roadside with its emergency lights flashing and pulled up behind the two-door sedan with South Carolina license plates. Three black men were standing behind it. As the troopers approached, they seemed to shrink back in fear.

"What's the problem?" Beard asked. "Do you need a tow truck? Are you out of gas?"

"We don't have no keys," one of the men said.

"What do you mean you don't have keys?" Ruff said. "How'd you get out here?"

"We was driving and two of your guys stopped us. They searched the car and when they didn't find nothing the guy just took the keys and threw 'em in the marsh."

"What do you mean they threw your keys in the marsh?" Ruff said.

"They just threw the keys out there," he said, pointing into the darkness.

Ruff and Beard looked at each other. They could see the car had
been searched. The trunk was a jumble of unzipped bags with clothes
still sticking out of them. The men didn't have money for a locksmith
so the troopers drove them to a service plaza to call for help. Afterwards, they wondered whether someone would make up a story like
that. They decided it fit in with things they'd seen since they arrived
at Newark Station. The black troopers had gotten a quick initiation.

"We operate by the 20-20 rule," they'd been told by senior troopers.
The *20-20 rule* was an informal agreement among State Policemen at
Newark that each trooper would issue 20 traffic tickets and 20 warnings per month, no more, no less. "And you better not write more than
that," one trooper warned, "or shit happens."

It turned out some troopers viewed traffic enforcement as a nui-
sance that took time away from their real priority, which was making
drug arrests and finding the *mother lode*.

"You can teach a monkey to write a ticket," a trooper said. "A
digger's got to work."

On his third night at Newark, Ruff was assigned to ride the midnight shift with a trooper named Nicholas Monticello. Monticello
reminded Ruff of Sylvester Stallone in *Rocky*, a big, muscular man,
six feet two inches tall, handsome, with a deep voice and cool de-
meanor. Ruff was 24 and Monticello wasn't much older. He'd been
a Turnpike trooper only 13 months but, in *'pike talk*, he was already
one of Newark Station's biggest *crime dogs*.

Monticello parked his cruiser at the U-turn at mile marker 111.8,
perpendicular to the road. Ruff later testified that the trooper turned
on his spotlight and shined it eye-level at cars whizzing past. A few
minutes later a 1983 Chevrolet drove by and Monticello took chase.
Their cruiser didn't have radar and Ruff didn't know why they were
pursuing the car but, being the new guy, he didn't ask. About a mile
down the Turnpike, Monticello turned on his overhead lights and
pulled over the Chevy. The three occupants were black. Monticello
ordered them out of the car and patted them down. He found a bag
filled with vials of crack cocaine on the backseat passenger. It wasn't
until the prisoners were in the back of the State Police cruiser, Ruff
later said, that Monticello radioed the station that he was in the process of stopping a vehicle.

Afterwards, Ruff received a letter of commendation from the Attorney General for the "outstanding arrests." But he took no pride in it. As far as he was concerned it had been a bad stop. Ruff believed the travelers were singled out for one reason—their color.

Ruff also noticed a mysterious argot being spoken by troopers on the radio. It didn't resemble any language he'd ever been taught and he soon realized troopers were using a code. One day he heard a trooper call in a stop of "a carload of johnnies."

What's a johnnie? he wondered. He drove past the scene and saw the trooper searching a car. The occupants were sitting on the guard-rail. They were black. *I don't believe this,* he thought.

Ruff, Beard, and Greg Sanders were dismayed to discover an entire vocabulary of jargon employed by the *crime dogs* when they talked about black motorists. "Nigger" wasn't commonly used over the radio, but blacks were referred to as "johnnies," "mutts," and "democrats." A vehicle with several black occupants was a "load of coal." "C.B." and "Charlie Bravo" were cipher for "colored boy." A white and black in the same car was a "salt and pepper team."

"They don't even give us credit for being able to put two and two together," Sanders said. "They think saying 'johnnies' skates right over our heads."

The coin of the realm for Turnpike troopers was PRAs—Patrol Related Arrests. If a trooper wanted to get ahead he had to "bring in the bodies." Translation: make drug arrests.

The "tree theory" was a key component of Turnpike metaphysics. If a trooper shook enough *trees* something was bound to fall out. The more cars they searched, the more arrests they'd make. And making arrests was their obsession.

"How many PRA's did you make?" was the most frequent question heard at the station. One trooper kept a computer program to track who was in line for the ultimate honor of "Trooper of the Year." When a drug arrest was made at another station he'd call to find out who got the collar, how many "bodies," and the quantity of the "grab."

Not all troopers were profilers. Some—white and black—made one or two arrests a month, just to keep the bosses off their backs. But Ruff, Beard, and Sanders flatly refused to play the PRA game. And it cost them. Ruff was passed over for special training school.

"Why'd you send that guy to specialist school?" he once asked Sgt. Zukowsky.

"He goes out there and does the job. He makes PRAs," the sergeant replied.

"I'm investigating accidents and handling calls. Because he's making arrests he gets a higher job?"

"Yes."

The three black troopers violated the 20-20 rule their very first month on the Turnpike, each of them writing more than 30 traffic tickets. White troopers reacted as if they'd spit in their faces. Ruff was confronted by a tall thin trooper.

"I can see it already," he said. "We're supposed to be writing 20 tickets and you come out here and think you're going to change things, like you want to take over."

"Only twenty tickets?" Ruff said. "And everyone else can speed? It makes no sense."

"You think you can run things the way you want to run them?" the other trooper shouted.

"Get out of my face with this nonsense." Ruff said heatedly.

"I'm telling you, shit happens."

"Are you threatening me?"

Ruff was about to invite the trooper out behind the station when other troopers stepped between them. Later, he told Beard and Sanders what had happened.

"We almost came to blows over traffic tickets," Ruff said, incredulous. "We're not welcome out here."

The next month Ruff wrote 60 tickets. The war was on at Newark Station.

Chapter 10

CLINTON PAGANO WAS NEW JERSEY'S *Narco Avenger.* The war on drugs was the epic law enforcement battle of the 1980s and the ex-Marine attacked it like John Wayne storming Iwo Jima. No cop in America was itching for the fight more than Pagano and no one was better prepared. In the years leading up to the crack epidemic, his Highway Drug Interdiction Program had cultivated an army of human bloodhounds.

Troopers had developed an uncanny knack for sniffing out drug runners from among the hundreds of thousands of vehicles hurtling along the Jersey Turnpike daily. They were arresting thousands of travelers a year, seizing tons of narcotics, and millions in drug money. No police force did it better. Yet it had only been a preamble of what was to come.

The State Police image was defined by a photograph on the cover of SNAP—the State Narcotics Action Plan—showing a man with his hands pressed against a car being frisked by a trooper at the foot of the Delaware Memorial Bridge.

"The objectives of this plan are to increase enforcement action at the drug consumer level. Increased enforcement emphasis will be placed on Patrol Related Arrests."

Pagano pounded the message home to troopers in speeches, private conversation, and a series of messages printed in the State Police in-house newsletter, *The Triangle,* written in his own hyperbolic, peculiarly elliptical "Pagano speak."

"President Theodore Roosevelt first declared war on narcotics in 1907 and we continue in the trenches of the longest standing battle in the history of our nation," he wrote. *"Our efforts in the drug enforcement area and the implementation of the State Police Plan for Action stand shoulders above any agency."*

Troopers responded in different ways. Detectives went after drug traffickers the old fashioned way—dogged investigation, surveillance, developing sources, and orchestrating elaborate stings. Narcotics Bureau Lt. Frederick Martens set up a fictitious radio station at a State Police barracks called *WNJSP* and assigned a Latino detective to pose as a disc jockey named Paco, who hoodwinked a coke merchant into delivering a kilo of cocaine.

"It was easier getting cocaine than a pizza pie," Martens said.

But conventional detective work demanded time and resources. The State Police was now an agency of "bean-counters." It had been part of the organization's DNA since the 1950s, when then-Sergeant David B. Kelly was assigned the task of modernizing the State Police. He was sent to business school where he learned new management systems. When Kelly became Superintendent a decade later he embedded them in the Outfit.

Kelly championed good detective work—as demonstrated by his creation of the Organized Crime and Intelligence units—but he also wanted barometers to evaluate road troopers—charts, graphs, and statistics. He developed systems like *indexing,* which measured a trooper's arrests and summonses versus his patrol hours. Troopers who wanted to get ahead had to produce numbers. And supervisors who wanted to take the fast track to HQ had to brandish sharp spurs and ride their people hard. Those who didn't were dead wood. One of the first to embrace Kelly's number-crunching mindset was Joseph Babick, who the Superintendent rewarded in 1970 by promoting to captain of Troop "A" at the south end of New Jersey. Babick was 6 feet 3 inches tall and 230 pounds, loud, heavy fisted, a big man with big ambitions. And he knew how to play the numbers game. The embodiment of that philosophy arrived on Babick's doorstep in 1971 in the form of a wiry young trooper named Andrew Mastella.

Mastella was smart, enterprising, and hungry. He wasn't content patrolling the rural back roads of South Jersey chasing stray cows and delivering drunk farmers home to their wives. Criminal arrests separated the stars from the lesser lights and Mastella burst onto the scene like a supernova.

He invented the art of *bridge sitting*. The Delaware Memorial Bridge at the south end of New Jersey was like a giant funnel that drug runners had to pass through to get to or from New York City. A single trooper posted at the foot of the bridge could pick off more smugglers in one week than a squad of undercover narcs could in a month. It was all about numbers.

To justify a stop a trooper needed only to observe a traffic violation and, because almost all drivers were committing some infraction, nearly every car was subject to being stopped. The object wasn't traffic enforcement, but drugs. If a trooper stopped 20-to-30 vehicles per 8-hour shift, that was 400-to-500 stops per month, 6,000-to-7,000 per year. If he hit paydirt on only one percent of his stops he could make 60-to-70 arrests a year, the kind of numbers the bean-counters at HQ loved. The kind of numbers that could turn a trooper into a hero.

By the time Pagano took over as Superintendent, Mastella was generating big numbers, a big reputation and a cocky swagger. And Pagano ate it up. They talked on the telephone almost every day, Mastella sitting in the middle of the squad room, feet up on his desk, smoking a cigarette, talking loud enough for everyone to hear him kibitzing with the Colonel himself, bragging about his latest exploits, laughing and joking like they were best buddies, at times whispering, giving the exchange an air of import. Pagano would fly to Woodstown in a State Police helicopter and take his young star to lunch. The relationship bordered on father-son, which some troopers resented. While Mastella sat at the bridge currying Pagano's favor, they were doing the grunt work, chasing the fugitive cows, cleaning up accidents, investigating burglaries. A Woodstown detective made a pin map showing the scores of arrests at the bridge versus unsolved crimes everywhere else. It was quickly torn down. Drug arrests were the new gold standard.

Mastella became Pagano's poster boy for the ideal trooper. In 1977 the Superintendent rewarded his prodigy with the coveted Red Ribbon as Trooper of the Year. The award became Pagano's most brilliant psychological masterstroke. Every September at the State

Police banquet in Atlantic City—in front of 2,700 State Policemen, their families, and New Jersey's political elite—Pagano would single out one trooper. It was the State Police equivalent of winning the Heisman Trophy. The crimson bar marked a trooper as a breed apart. It meant promotions, choice assignments, and higher pay. And time after time, Pagano's handpicked choice for Trooper of the Year was the man who made the most drug arrests. The message couldn't have been more explicit. Troopers who yearned to be superstars needed to make drug arrests, make them big, and make them often.

Mastella remained king of highway drug interdiction. After riding Cocaine Alley to glory in 1977 he had another stellar year in 1984, seizing more than 100 pounds of cocaine and a half-ton of marijuana. Pagano again crowned him Trooper of the Year, the first man to win the award twice. He became a nationally renowned expert. The U.S. Drug Enforcement Administration recruited him to spread the interdiction gospel to police throughout the United States. But Mastella's greatest influence was as role model to a new generation of State Police young guns. He knew the magic formula for becoming a hero and shared it. Mastella called his team the *"Gotcha Squad"* and hung a poster in the station with a running tally of drug arrests and narcotics seized. It became a motivational tool for raw troopers who—like their idol—became "bridge sitters," too.

Chief among them was James Campbell, who Pagano ordained Trooper of the Year in 1985 after he seized 170 pounds of coke, 145 pounds of marijuana, and arrested 44 travelers. But Campbell was just warming up. On January 25, 1986, he stopped a pick-up truck on Cocaine Alley and found 522 pounds of cocaine worth $13 million. He won the coveted Red Ribbon for the second year in a row.

The craving to be Trooper of the Year erupted into a feeding frenzy. Troopers began stalking the Jersey Turnpike like mongeese hunting cobras, chalking up astonishing numbers. In 1985, they seized 353 pounds of cocaine. In 1986, they quintupled that total—*by the end of March*. In 1987, Turnpike troopers more than doubled the previous year's totals, arresting 4,067 people, grabbing $10 million in narcotics, and $2 million in "drug-tainted" cash. By 1988, arrest totals reached vertiginous heights. The State Police were snaring nearly 840 narcotics violators a month—a 154% increase over the year before.

"The amount of drug money being seized is mind-boggling," trumpeted *The Triangle.*

Pagano began describing State Police narcotics detection techniques as "science" as he raced around the state posing with stone-faced troopers standing next to stacks of cocaine and cash. Praise poured in from the FBI and DEA. *High Times,* a magazine catering to the drug culture, published an alert called *"T'pike Trippers Hot Tips,"* advising readers to avoid the Jersey Turnpike. U.S. Rep. William J. Hughes, of South Jersey, praised Pagano on the floor of Congress.

"Mr. Speaker, I rise today to call special attention to one of the most successful law enforcement operations now in place in the United States. The results of this drug operation have been staggering. It's the result of a sophisticated intelligence operation now regarded as the model program for the entire country. Colonel Pagano and the many people working for him have made a major contribution to our efforts to stem drug trafficking in the United States."

Trooper exploits were widely chronicled in gushing newspaper profiles. *"Duty, for the steadfast James Campbell, is maintaining order on the back roads in Salem County,"* reported *The Bergen Record. "Duty becomes adventure when this Trooper of the Year nails a cocaine runner slipping over the state line from Delaware."*

The vast majority of trooper arrests weren't traffickers, but people caught with small quantities, sometimes no more than a marijuana joint. Yet, Pagano made no apologies.

"The user, the minor, casual user, the guy with one joint, is just as much at fault as the guy who brings in 100 kilos of cocaine. They all are equally guilty," he wrote.

But thorny questions began to crop up. What was the State Police secret to success? How were troopers able to pick out cars carrying drugs from the half-million vehicles traversing the Turnpike daily? There were whispers the "science" of interdiction was more than good police work. Rumblings of a profile to target drivers based on race or ethnicity. The State Police bent over backwards to assure the public they weren't running roughshod over citizen rights.

"There's no profile," Trooper Campbell told an interviewer. "We're not allowed to stop someone because of the way they look, because that would be discrimination."

Chapter 11

Justin Dintino didn't buy into the Highway Drug Interdiction Program. He didn't believe the drug problem could be solved by randomly stopping cars. Despite a few high profile busts, most arrests involved picayune quantities of narcotics. Even more troubling to Dintino was the sharp rise in complaints from motorists claiming their rights were being violated.

Dintino had a thing about the Constitution. When he ran the Organized Crime Bureau he set up strict guidelines to protect civil liberties, even of gangsters. After discovering State Police mob intelligence files were teeming with so-called "green sheets," unsubstantiated rumor, gossip and innuendo, he stopped all investigations and for two months he and his investigators performed a massive review of every file, purging all information that could not be authenticated. It was an extraordinary step later emulated by police agencies around the country. Dintino also co-authored, with detective Frederick Martens, a book entitled *Police Intelligence Systems in Crime Control: Maintaining a Delicate Balance in a Liberal Democracy*, a treatise on preservation of civil rights.

"*Domestic intelligence systems could, if not properly regulated and controlled, result in the erosion of a liberal democracy,*" Dintino and Martens wrote. "*Law enforcement, an institution of power, must develop workable, rational, and above all, just policies.*"

Dintino was also concerned that fledgling troopers were being given free reign on the Turnpike.

There once was a time when State Policemen weren't deemed ready for the Black Dragon until they had at least three years experience. But with so many veterans now assigned to Atlantic City casinos, the Turnpike had become the province of troopers still wet behind the ears. Pagano was telling them to go out and fight the Drug War, but nothing was said about citizens' rights. The Superintendent wasn't blatantly ordering troopers to violate the Constitution, but he wasn't telling them not to, either.

Dintino's concern was reinforced when Cornelius Sullivan, the prosecutor from Burlington County in South Jersey, visited him with a stack of reports from Turnpike drug arrests. They were like carbon copies, in each case troopers using nearly identical justifications for searching vehicles. Sullivan said he suspected State Policemen were making pretext stops simply to search for drugs. Dintino brought the prosecutor in to see Pagano, who was not happy to hear the accusation. He made no commitment to investigate, but did make a veiled threat to take his troopers out of Sullivan's county. Later, Dintino told Pagano he should talk directly to the troops about civil rights.

"Justin, you're right," Dintino said Pagano told him, and promised to address the issue. But he never did.

Despite Dintino's misgivings, he had come to appreciate much about Clint Pagano. By the early 1980s the Superintendent had made Dintino his right-hand man. Thanks to Pagano's support of the Organized Crime Bureau, Dintino was renowned as one of America's pre-eminent authorities on the Mafia. He traveled the country giving lectures and served six years as chairman of the national Law Enforcement Intelligence Unit. Ronald Reagan appointed him to the prestigious *President's Commission on Organized Crime* and Dintino was photographed in the Oval Office shaking hands with the Gipper.

But the more attention Dintino got, the more jealous Pagano grew. Dintino sensed he felt threatened his Number Two might someday vie for the Superintendent's job. Pagano vowed to never again let one of his men become more prominent than himself.

The longer Pagano reigned as Superintendent, the more his power increased and Dintino began to see a metamorphosis. His first five years at the helm, Pagano was relaxed, concerned about citizen rights, and troopers could come into his office, sit down, and discuss anything with him. The second five years Dintino noticed what he called the *Hoover mentality* setting in—*"I'm the Colonel and what I say goes."* His last five years Pagano became what Dintino considered "a little dictator." His power was at its zenith. People were afraid of him. The State Assembly gave him anything he wanted. He felt invincible—and he was.

Then his supremacy was threatened. A logjam had developed at the top of the State Police totem pole. Too few senior troopers were retiring, blocking the upward mobility of younger troopers. The 2,000 member trooper's union began lobbying for mandatory State Police retirement at age 55. If approved, Pagano would be forced to retire.

"Justin, this bill is age discrimination at its worst," Pagano told Dintino. "I'm opposed to it 100 percent."

Pagano wanted to meet with older troopers to begin fighting mandatory retirement. But Dintino smelled a skunk. He was an accomplished poker player and had a talent for reading people. Pagano was a shrewd man and Dintino suspected he might be trying to create a political storm in order to cut a deal for himself.

Dintino didn't personally care about the bill. He planned to retire at 55 anyway. With his sterling reputation he'd already received several high-paying job offers. His children were entering their college years and a job in the private sector combined with his State Police pension would allow him to pay for their schooling and live comfortably.

Nonetheless, Dintino—ever the loyal trooper—did as Pagano asked. He called together a group of majors who were happy to hear the Colonel was in their corner. They formed a group called SPAAD—State Police Against Age Discrimination—which Dintino agreed to lead.

"Sounds like you're on the right track, Justin," Pagano said. "Go to it."

The next day Pagano told Dintino to hop into a State Police helicopter and the two men flew to North Jersey to lobby an influential state senator. The Superintendent did all the talking and, as he spoke, it dawned on Dintino that Pagano had been busy behind the scenes on mandatory retirement for some time. It reinforced his gut feeling Pagano was scheming something. Despite his growing wariness, Dintino continued to lead SPAAD. Senior troopers chipped in $500 each to retain a prominent attorney to press their case. Notorious for having deep pockets and short arms, Pagano didn't contribute, but he was enthusiastic.

"That's great, Justin!" Pagano said. "He's a tremendous lawyer."

Then, suddenly, the troopers' union agreed to amend its mandatory retirement demand. One person would be exempted: the Superintendent. Pagano didn't immediately abandon SPAAD, but his tune changed. He began to see the wisdom behind mandatory retirement. Finally he came out in full support of the age law.

Senior troopers were flabbergasted. The sense of betrayal was enormous. There were recriminations and confrontations and the schism between Pagano and his top officers was detailed in the press. It was an ugly time inside the State Police. The whole mess took a year and a half to play out but, in the end, Pagano had too much clout. He came out smelling like a rose while senior troopers were left with mud on their faces, old men trying to hang on too long. It was a masterful Machiavellian stroke. In one fell swoop Pagano saved his job *and* eliminated the one man who might have eventually dethroned him.

Justin Dintino quietly retired in 1985, ending a 33-year career. The ramifications of his exit would take years to become manifest. No one in the State Police possessed a portfolio to equal his. Even Pagano couldn't ignore Dintino's reputation and moral authority. He was the one man who could stand up to the Superintendent and challenge him on issues like Turnpike stops and the abrogation of rights. The day he walked out the door, he took with him any semblance of a check-and-balance system at State Police HQ.

Chapter 12

NOT ALL BLACK TROOPERS WERE LOATH to target dark-skinned motorists. From the day in 1986 when Kenneth Wilson entered the New Jersey State Police Academy, the message was drummed into his head: State troopers were number one in drug enforcement and they expected to remain number one.

Educated at Valley Forge Military Academy and an Army reservist, Wilson came to the State Police with a military mind-set. He was gung-ho to be an undercover narcotics cop and eventually an instructor at the Academy. Instructors were the guys with the big arrest records. Wilson planned to build a reputation of his own.

"Do you have a problem stopping blacks?" a veteran trooper asked on his first assignment.

"I'll do whatever it takes," Wilson said.

"Look for young black males in late model cars with out of state tags, especially rental tags, traveling southbound," the trooper instructed.

Wilson soon became a *digger*, conducting drug searches at every opportunity, looking in ashtrays, in trunks, under seats. He learned the art of writing reports designed to hold up in court. For instance, if he found marijuana in a closed ashtray, some sharp defense lawyer might cross-examine him about his *probable cause* to open it. But if his report *implied* the ashtray was open and the marijuana in plain view, questions about *probable cause* go away.

Instructors from the Drug Interdiction Training Unit taught Wilson little tricks of the trade, like driving up close behind a car, which tends to cause drivers to swerve, giving the trooper an excuse to stop. He never missed Wednesday night softball when troopers at the Fort Dix barracks bought a keg of beer and got together to play and then, after the game, sat around drinking and chattering about work. Being a junior trooper, Wilson looked at the confabs as learning opportunities. One night a senior trooper uttered a term he'd never heard before—"profile." When Wilson asked what he meant by it he could feel a chill in the air. Then someone spoke up. "That word is taboo. Don't ever say that."

The young trooper knew his best chance to make his reputation was by riding the Black Dragon. He got his wish just 19 months after pinning on the badge. Assigned to the Turnpike's East Brunswick barracks in Central Jersey, he was like a kid at a carnival. Wilson soon identified who was making drug arrests and quizzed them about how they did it. He learned to park his cruiser perpendicular to the highway in order to better see if occupants of passing cars were white, black or Hispanic. At night he learned to *spotlight,* aiming his cruiser's sidelight into traffic at eye level, the beam like a split second flashbulb that revealed the color of people in the cars.

"You have to be patient," a trainer told him. "Just sit and wait for the right car. It'll be there. It can take minutes; it can take hours."

Coaches told Wilson he would have to "step on" 20 to 30 innocent drivers for every arrest he made. The ACLU and others were starting to bellyache about Constitutional violations on the Turnpike. To prevent the bleeding hearts from getting the fodder they needed to substantiate their assertions, Wilson was tutored not to call in every stop, a flagrant breach of State Police rules, but eliminating a potentially pesky paper trail. When searches were conducted, the brass at HQ had ordered troopers to get signed consent-to-search forms. Trainers schooled Wilson on techniques for getting driver's signatures.

"You were weaving out there. Are you tired?"

"No I'm not tired," was a typical response.

"You haven't been drinking, have you?"

"Oh, no, I haven't had anything to drink," they'd say.

"You don't have alcohol in the car, do you?"

"No."

"Do you mind if I have a look?"

"No, go right ahead."

"Well, can you sign this form for me first? This is standard operating procedure."

"Okay."

Before long, Wilson was averaging five arrests every month. But he was not content. Other guys were making more collars and knocking down bigger drug loads. Wilson wanted to *"keep up with the Jones's."* He decided he would only stop drivers who fit the profile. Caucasians could speed past him or weave on the highway, and he wouldn't stop them unless they looked drunk. Otherwise, it was a waste of time. Unless they were black, like him, the chances were slim they would be in possession of the one thing he was looking for—drugs.

Chapter 13

SHERI WOLIVER WAS NEVER QUITE SURE if it was Pam's long legs and short skirts, or Marsha's sultry smile, or even her own petite figure and fizzy personality. All she knew was that the macho young state troopers liked to talk to her, confide in her, tell her secrets, even though she was the enemy.

Woliver was a Deputy Public Defender in Warren County in the northwest corner of New Jersey. Far from the smokestacks, grime and gridlock of urban centers 50 miles to the east, Warren was the state's most picturesque county, a quaint collection of small towns, farms, ranches and breathtaking vistas. The Appalachian Trail ran through it and, in 1988, locals were less concerned about crime than they were a growing black bear population. The killing fields of New York City seemed a world away. Warren County was 95% white and the odds were overwhelming that if a crime was committed, a Caucasian did it.

That's what was bugging Sheri Woliver. The vast preponderance of her clients were white for every category of crime but one—State Police drug arrests on Interstate 80, which were almost exclusively of blacks like McArthur Toney and Frank Cavott. On February 11, 1988, Toney, 42, and Cavott, 65, drove across the Jersey state line on I-80 on the last leg of an 800-mile trip from Chicago to New York City. Within minutes, Trooper R.S. Gaugler stopped them for speeding.

"Something seemed wrong," the trooper reported. *"The driver was observed to be extremely nervous. Passenger Cavott was observed making furtive movements."*

Gaugler searched the car and found $24,000 in U.S. currency, a .22 caliber revolver, bottles of prescription pills, and several glassine bags. He arrested Toney and Cavott and seized the cash as "drug money." When the case landed on her desk, Woliver was elated. She'd been hankering for a fight with the State Police.

Woliver grew up in Long Island, New York, the child of activist parents. During the 1960s they harbored political radicals on the run from the law. Mark Rudd, leader of Students for a Democratic Society, lived in her family's basement for weeks while the FBI hunted him for alleged bombings. Sheri, the most conservative member of her family, gained a measure of respect when she helped take over the school administration building at Binghamton (N.Y.) University in protest over student funding cutbacks. She called her mother from the president's office and proudly announced: "Mom, I'm wearing bell bottoms and a black arm band." Woliver's mother frowned on her daughter becoming an attorney. She didn't trust lawyers. For that matter, neither did Sheri. She considered them sneaky and deceitful. But she loved Public Defenders. They were true believers.

The drug cases coming off Interstate 80 were Woliver's most persistent frustration. She was convinced troopers were targeting minority drivers and, in the process, violating the 4th Amendment.

"*It is my belief,*" she wrote in her motion on behalf of Toney and Cavott, "*that the constitutional protections against unreasonable search and seizures are being violated by the New Jersey state troopers' discriminatory practices.*"

It was the first time a defense attorney formally accused the State Police of racially motivated traffic stops. And the reaction was swift.

"New Jersey state troopers do not discriminate in their highway enforcement," Clinton Pagano said.

But Woliver knew different. She had impeccable sources about racial targeting—the troopers themselves. One reason may have been Pam Brase, an attractive young defense attorney who handled cases for the Public Defender's Office. Brase was tall and had long, shapely legs which she often showcased in short skirts. Another reason may have been Marsha Wenk, an assistant Public Defender who also happened to be young and very pretty, with blonde hair, bright blue eyes, and a captivating smile. Woliver, in her early 30s, wasn't chopped liver, either. All three were smart, excellent lawyers. Wenk was fiery and often got embroiled in heated debates with troopers. Woliver would take them aside and say: "Don't worry, she's young!" Then she and Brase would sit down with them on a bench in the graceful old Warren County courthouse and yak. To Woliver the troopers—with their crewcut hair, bulging necks, and V-shaped torsos—were cookie-cutter cops who spent way too much time in the gym, but not the scary monsters they sometimes seemed. They liked to joke and flirt and could actually be charming, in a frisky, arrogant sort of way. Yet, the lady lawyers seemed to cast a spell over the troopers, who talked and talked and talked.

"Sheri, how can you represent people with drugs in their cars?" they'd say.

"Because I grew up believing in the Constitution," she'd say.

The troopers spoke candidly. Sure, they said, they went after minorities. Why not? They're the ones with the drugs! It was exasperatingly clear to Woliver that the troopers felt above the law. They were fighting the good fight. The Constitution wasn't even on their radar screen. Plus, the more they violated the law, the more they were rewarded. At the same time, though, troopers were calling Woliver with inside information. One told her it was futile to subpoena records because of "ghost stops," troopers stopping and searching motorists and, if they found nothing, *"kicking 'em in the ass and letting 'em go,"* leaving no paper trail.

Woliver met troopers clandestinely at an I-80 rest area where they described how they were trained to target blacks but conceal it by misreporting their race. She used the information to shape her court motions.

"The Fourth Amendment of the U.S. Constitution was designed to protect citizens from law officers acting in an arbitrary and discriminatory fashion," she wrote. *"It appears state troopers are now violating the letter and spirit of the Constitution by basing their stops on New Jersey roads on the race of the occupants of a vehicle."*

In the end, the State did something that would, in time, become a familiar pattern. They made Toney and Cavott an offer they couldn't refuse—one year's probation in return for pleas of no contest. By plea bargaining, the State short-circuited the racial targeting claim.

Even so, after Toney and Cavott pled, Woliver consolidated several I-80 drug cases under one umbrella: *State v. Kennedy.* Curtis Kennedy had a lengthy criminal record and prosecutors refused to settle with him. But Woliver's approach, while ahead of its time, was embryonic and, even she later admitted, "a little goofy." She ultimately failed, yet her joust with State Police would prove to be a vital stepping stone. The frailty of her evidence prompted the courts to set ground rules, which later became a roadmap for other attorneys.

"*We would have been more comfortable,*" an Appellate Court decision said, "*had the Public Defender been precise in estimating the racial composition of those who exceed the speed limit on Route 80 and those who are arrested by the State Police for that offense. (Nevertheless) the Public Defender's survey raises disturbing questions concerning whether, as defendants claim, members of minority groups are being targeted.*"

Unbeknownst to Woliver, she and her alluring colleagues had blazed the first steps on a long, arduous trail, the end of which would take more than a decade to reach.

Chapter 14

THE JERSEY TURNPIKE WAS BECOMING A SCARY PLACE. It wasn't just the stops and searches, but some of the troopers. They looked like Incredible Hulks from Muscle Beach training for a *Mr. Turnpike* contest. Ninety-eight-pound weaklings were morphing into gargantuans overnight.

Inside the organization it was no secret some troopers were injecting *magic juice*. Needles and syringes were found at Newark Station. At least one trooper was fired for selling steroids. Anabolic cocktails were notorious for triggering 'roid rage and many believed it was no coincidence the Outfit was seeing a spike in brutality complaints.

State Police were no strangers to claims of violence. In the spring of 1988 two troopers were sent to federal prison for the beating death of a Turnpike driver. The victim was a white man arrested for drunk driving. He'd kicked out the back window of a State Police cruiser sending a stocky trooper named Harry Messerlian into a frenzy.

Messerlian bashed the man's head with a steel Kel-Lite flashlight and the victim fell into a coma and died. The case was revealing because of the State Police response.

"What scared us," federal prosecutor Bruce Merrill told New Jersey Monthly Magazine, "was that the State Police were perfectly willing to cover it all up."

Clinton Pagano testified as a character witness for Messerlian and helped raise money for his defense. He also launched a vitriolic attack against the U.S. Justice Department.

"There is no excuse for the way in which the federal prosecutors treated many of our members during their investigation," Pagano wrote to his troops in August 1988. *"I'll go to my grave believing those two troopers were not guilty of the charges against them."*

The signal to troopers was that headquarters would defend them against brutality complaints, even as the number of allegations was rising.

One month after Pagano's statement, the graveyard shift at East Brunswick barracks erupted in an orgy of violence. The night began like any other. Troopers were patrolling a 50-mile stretch of Turnpike from Exit 7 north to Exit 12. Trooper John Andryszcyk was working the radio when a call came in on a hit-and-run. The driver was a short, roly-poly, down on his luck white guy with scraggily brown hair named Kenneth Lowengrub. Stoned out of his mind, Lowengrub had a pocketful of illegal pills when he rammed into the back of another car and fled before being arrested by Troopers Steven Waldie and Gary Tornquist. Lowengrub later claimed Waldie handcuffed him, put him in the squad car and began jabbing him in the stomach with his night stick.

At about the same time, a few miles down the Turnpike, Trooper Robert Henig stopped a car containing two black men—Stacy Brown and Christopher Moore—who had just bought two ounces of cocaine in New York. It didn't take Henig long to find the dope.

"Where'd this coke come from?" the trooper asked Brown.

"I don't know nothing about no drugs," Brown said.

Henig, he said, punched him in the ribs. The men were brought to the East Brunswick barracks and booked for drug trafficking. Brown gave Henig—a former college All-American wrestler—a phony name. Moore said the trooper got madder and madder until he finally picked up Brown, lifted him over his head, and slammed him to the ground. The black men were then put in a holding cell with Lowengrub, whom they later testified was ordered by a trooper to pee in a cup. When he couldn't, the trooper slapped him. Lowengrub started screaming and cursing, for some reason directing his ire at Henig, who had nothing to do with his arrest.

Trooper Andryszcyk said later that he watched from the radio desk as Henig unshackled Lowengrub and led him down the hall. After a few seconds Andryszcyk said he heard thuds coming from an office that sounded like someone being punched.

A black trooper named William Sweeney had just entered the barracks when he, too, heard what he later described as "punching sounds." Sweeney walked over and, he said, saw Henig propping a white man up against a wall, repeatedly punching him in the stomach. Henig and Sweeney were by far the biggest *crime dogs* on the Turnpike, and archrivals in a neck-and-neck race for Trooper of the Year. Sweeney said Henig beat the white man so hard the walls began to vibrate. Suddenly the man bolted from the office and bent over, holding his stomach. Sweeney grabbed him and put him back in the holding cell.

The next morning, Lowengrub was taken to the Middlesex County Adult Correction Center. Harriett Condora, a jail nurse, noticed he was crouched over, his skin ashen, and was taking short, rapid breaths.

"Two troopers beat the shit out of me," Condora said Lowengrub told her.

The nurse pressed her fingers into his abdomen and found it was rock hard. She knew that meant it was probably gorged with blood. Condora turned to Karlton Crawford, a black trooper who transported Lowengrub from the State Police barracks to the jail.

"He needs to be taken to the E.R. right away," she said.

At Robert Wood Johnson Medical Center in New Brunswick, Dr. Stanley Trooskin quickly diagnosed a lacerated spleen. The prisoner was bleeding internally and Trooskin estimated he'd lost a quart-and-a-half of blood, about one-fourth of his entire supply. When the doctor began emergency surgery, Lowengrub was near death.

Chapter 15

DR. ELMO RANDOLPH MIGHT AS WELL HAVE been waving a red cape at a bull when he splurged on a sporty new gold BMW 325I low-rider with small thin tires and gold rims. From that point on, rarely did a week go by that the young African-American dentist wasn't stopped by troopers while traveling on the Turnpike between his home in Bergenfield and his office in East Orange. Usually at the *fishing hole* at mile-marker 118 where Interstate 95 merged with Interstate 80 about two miles from the George Washington Bridge.

Fishing holes were U-turns marked "For Official Use Only," and were intended as emergency turnarounds for tow trucks and State Police cars. But for troopers, they were also perfect places to sit and wait for the *mother lode.* When roll call ended at Newark Station, troopers would climb into their cruisers and head out to one of many fishing holes. The 118 U-turn was the most popular. Traffic was always heavy. Radar didn't work because the angle was too severe, so speeders weren't easy to detect. But that didn't matter for some troopers whose primary interest was the skin color of drivers. Race could easily be discerned parking perpendicular to the highway and looking directly at cars as they whooshed around the bend. At night troopers shined spotlights.

Darryl Beard learned about the fishing holes shortly after arriving at Newark Station. Troopers had a loop. They'd start at the 118-U, wait for a car to pass that caught their attention, and stop it. If they came up empty, they proceeded south to the 113-U and repeated the process, then the 111-U, and finally the 109-U. Then they circled back and started over. His first week at Newark, Beard rode with a white trooper, thinking excitedly, *Wow, I'm on the big road.* They parked at the 118 fishing hole and watched for a few minutes as cars zipped past. Before long the other trooper said: "Good stop," and took off. A short distance down the highway, he stopped a car, ordered the driver out of the vehicle and interrogated him. Then he questioned the passengers, searched the car and, finding no contraband, let them go with only a warning. He never explained why it was a "good stop," but Beard did notice the occupants were black.

For Elmo Randolph, being stopped at mile marker 118 became a ritual. It happened so often he started getting paranoid. As he drove around the bend he tried to not look *suspicious,* whatever *suspicious* looked like. He agonized over whether to wear a hat, sunglasses, should he sit up, should he lean back. He'd adjust his seat to try to affect a position that didn't look sinister. If possible, he'd slide the BMW behind a truck as he came around the curve, attempting to block himself from view. When he knew troopers could see him, Randolph avoided eye contact, then worried it made him seem shifty.

Like clockwork, though, they would see Randolph pass and chase him down. It was always the same. The trooper walked up to his window and asked for his license, registration, and insurance, then asked if the car was his and if he had any drugs or weapons. Yes, no and no, Randolph would answer and hand over his paperwork. The trooper would go back to his car and sit for awhile, then come back on the passenger side. Randolph would roll down his window and, as the trooper handed him his papers, he'd lean into the car as far as he could stretch, scanning the console, passenger side foot well, and back seat. Sometimes he would ask to search his trunk. Randolph usually said okay. One day a trooper asked if he could open the glove compartment. He complied. Then the trooper asked to search the trunk. Exasperated, Randolph stood up to him.

"No," he said. "I refuse that."

The trooper returned to his car and sat there for 20 minutes, then came back and told him he could go. After that, Randolph always gave troopers permission to search when they asked. It wasn't worth the hassle. Regardless, he was often interrogated.

"Where are you going?" the trooper would invariably ask.

"I'm going to work."

"What do you do?"

"I'm a dentist."

One trooper found dental books and magazines in his trunk.

"Oh, you really are a dentist," he said.

Randolph was outraged. He firmly believed he was being stopped because he was a black man driving an expensive car. But he never complained, afraid if he did it would rile the State Police. Randolph finally traded in his flashy gold BMW for a conservative, black, four-door sedan. The stops diminished immediately, from two or three times a month to once every three months or so. He was almost never asked to open his trunk anymore. But, between 1984 and 1988, Randolph estimated he was stopped at least 100 times.

Darryl Beard's first experience at the fishing holes was his last. After the first stop, the white trooper drove to the 113-U and waited for another "good stop." Again, he interrogated the occupants, searched the car and let the driver go with a warning. Then he drove to the 111-U and did the same thing. The occupants of all three cars they stopped were black.

"What are you doing?" Beard finally said.

"This is how we do it out here. This is how we patrol."

"Why are we stopping only blacks?"

"Well, this is just how we do it. That's just the kind of night it is."

They didn't stop any more cars that night and Beard was never assigned to ride with the trooper again.

Chapter 16

A BLISTERING HEAT WAVE ENGULFED NEW JERSEY in August 1988. Thermometers rarely dipped below broil. In Trenton, lethargic state employees padded from one government building to another seeking air-conditioned sanctuary. Down the hill from the gold-domed Capitol sat the massive steel and glass Richard J. Hughes Justice Complex, home of the Attorney General. On the sidewalk outside, two figures remained unfazed by the scorching heat, one in vest and tie, one in a business suit, rapt in conversation, as visitors rushed past, oblivious that they were bronze sculptures, frozen in time. Inside, in a third floor office, six people sat at a long conference table. On one side were three women, on the other side three men. They were all lawyers and what transpired between them that day would—like the bronze figures outside—remain frozen in time for years to come.

Division of Criminal Justice Director Donald Belsole was second in rank only to the Attorney General. John Holl was his chief of staff. The three females were from the Appellate Bureau: Anne Paskow, Debra Stone, and Meredith Coté. Then there was Ronald Susswein.

If Jersey Justice had a drug guru, it was Susswein. He was a policy wonk, a brain in a jar, who some considered brilliant and others saw as arrogant, condescending, and not nearly as smart as he thought. At the height of the anti-drug frenzy, Susswein was singled out to author State Law 2-C:35, New Jersey's historic declaration of war against narcotics. He was apparently so proud of writing the momentous law

65

he had license plates made for his car: "2C35." A year later Susswein's supernova burst higher into the Trentonian stratosphere when he was picked to write SNAP, the drug war blueprint.

But now Susswein's magnum opus was under fire. Not by crack dealers or defense lawyers, but by the three women across the table. The conflict revolved around Directive 6.4 of SNAP, which called for creation of "offender profiles." For the female lawyers, the term "profiles" set off alarm bells. They claimed it was unconstitutional. Susswein was having none of that. Banning profiles, he argued, would gut his plan. Until now the battle had been a paper duel. Shots were fired by memoranda hurled from office to office, floor to floor, up the ladder, back down, then up again, on and on and on. Questions were asked, answers given, more questions, subtly different, but the answers always the same.

The opening volley came on February 18, 1988 when the Director of Criminal Justice posed a question to Anne Paskow: *"Is the use of a drug courier profile by police to stop and search a suspect constitutional?"*

Paskow was head mistress of the Appellate Bureau and, as such, rectored over 30 lawyers and more than 2,000 appeals a year. She worked her people hard and was stingy with her thank you's, but was a fine attorney and a strict constitutionalist. Paskow handed the profile interrogatory to her number two, Debra Stone, a slim, smallish woman with short dark hair, sharp, intelligent eyes, and a direct manner. Stone suspected the question was tied to Clinton Pagano's Highway Drug Interdiction Program. A fast worker, she answered the same day.

"It is clear under current United States Supreme Court opinions and New Jersey case law that a stop and/or search of a suspect based solely on the person fitting a 'drug courier profile' is unconstitutional," wrote Stone.

That was the start of a family feud in Criminal Justice that stretched through the winter, spring and into the long hot summer of '88. Drug courier profiles had been around a long time. The U.S. Drug Enforcement Administration and U.S. Customs Service used them at airports, train stations, bus terminals and border crossings. They consisted of a laundry list of tip-offs that allegedly helped agents identify drug *mules*. Critics claimed they had all the credibility of a psychic hotline and that the elements of the profiles were contradictory:

- Arrived late at night
- Arrived early in morning
- One of first to deplane
- One of last to deplane
- Bought coach ticket
- Bought first-class ticket
- Traveled from New York to Los Angeles
- Traveled from Ft. Lauderdale to Atlanta
- Carried no luggage
- Carried brand-new luggage
- Went to restroom after deplaning
- Walked quickly through airport
- Suspect was Hispanic
- Suspect was black female

Courts historically rejected the use of race or ethnicity by police as a factor in law enforcement. As far back as 1886—in *Yick Ho v. Hopkins*—the City of San Francisco was found guilty of "selective prosecution" of Chinese laundry owners for operating in wooden firetrap buildings, while ignoring non-Chinese guilty of the same offense. In *State v. Kuhn*, New Jersey courts ruled it illegal for police to consider skin color or ethnic origin as grounds to stop someone.

On February 22, 1988, four days after Deb Stone gave thumbs down to offender profiles, Paskow got another memo from upstairs, a slightly more detailed variation of the same question: *"Drug courier profile—expanded discussion of cases—when can a profile be used, if ever?"* Paskow funneled this inquiry to another lawyer, one of her bright young lights, Deputy Attorney General Meredith Coté.

Coté had been at Justice barely three years but had already developed a conservative attitude toward the law. If she was going to err it was better to err on the side of caution. Paskow agreed.

"Use of the profile only muddies the water and may taint the stop and seizure if improper – like race," Paskow wrote in a cover letter.

Coté restated Stone's position: *"Review of recent court opinions reveals no instance where the use of the profile—not in conjunction with other objective criteria—was held a valid justification for a stop and/or search of an individual."*

But the lords of Justice refused to give up. On May 19, yet another memo asked a more pointed question, which was underlined.

"The Director has questioned as to whether it would pose a Constitutional problem if the police chose to stop only speeders who fit the drug courier profile."

Race wasn't mentioned, but it was lurking—unstated—between the lines. Paskow shuffled the query to Coté, who made a more exhaustive search of court precedents.

"The decision to prosecute may not be deliberately based upon an unjustifiable standard such as race," she responded. *"Such a policy would be construed by the courts as a form of selective prosecution."*

Coté left no wiggle room. Profiles—especially involving race—were unconstitutional. But the Director's office refused to take no for an answer. Two weeks later, the brain trust requested still more research. Coté's third opinion was identical to her second, except for a postscript that slammed the door on profiling.

"Any policy decision which culminates in the singling out of individuals for different treatment based upon profile characteristics will, ultimately, be deemed impermissible."

Coté could not have been more absolute. But it still didn't satisfy the eighth floor. So on that torrid August day she, Stone and Paskow were summoned to the Director's office for a face-to-face with Belsole, Holl and Ron Susswein, the profile man, who was hostile at the women across the table for threatening his *tour de force.*

"You're wrong," he said. The case law was clear. Profiles were legitimate and a valuable law enforcement tool—as long as they were race-neutral. Deb Stone jumped on that. She told the men she'd been driving the Turnpike a lot in recent months and was seeing what seemed to her to be an inordinate percentage of blacks and Hispanics being pulled over and searched by troopers, a stark sign of a race-based profile in action. Susswein's response was something Stone wouldn't forget.

"I've confronted the State Police," he said, "and they say they are not using a profile based on race. We have to take them at their word."

"You're being incredibly naïve, Ron," Stone said. "Do you really think the State Police will use a profile that doesn't consider the driver's race or ethnicity?"

"We must assume good faith," Susswein said.

That was it. A few weeks later an edict came down from the Director. Susswein prevailed. Profiles would remain part of the State Narcotics Action Plan. The alarm sounded by Paskow, Stone, and Coté was ignored. More than a decade would pass before the three females were again consulted on racial profiling. But by then it was too late.

Chapter 17

ALBERT EINSTEIN CALLED THEM "thought experiments." He took widely accepted theories about energy and space, gravity and time, and juggled them, flipped them upside down, inside out, investigating them every which way. "There are things hidden in plain sight waiting to be discovered," the great physicist was fond of saying. In 1905 he asked himself: *What would I see if I were to travel alongside a light beam?* The answer was: *Time standing still,* the basis of his Special Theory of Relativity. Einstein died in Princeton, New Jersey, in 1955, only a few miles from the brand new Jersey Turnpike.

Thirty-three years later, just up the road, Walter Marvin also believed things hidden in plain sight were waiting to be discovered. Marvin—an Einstein devotee—was an M.I.T. trained chemical engineer who owned a linoleum adhesives business near the Jersey Shore until his life took a dramatic turn in the 1960s.

Marvin and several members of his Unitarian Church congregation came under police investigation after they protested the Vietnam War. Outraged that he had been made an object of suspicion simply for exercising his right to dissent, Marvin began to study the Constitution and, in 1970 at the age of 44, decided to get out of glue and into law. He enrolled at Rutgers University Law School and, three years later, became a Deputy Public Defender in Middlesex County.

By 1988, Marvin—now a gray-haired, veteran defense lawyer—was facing a conundrum stickier than any epoxy he'd ever encountered. The Jersey Turnpike cut through the heart of Middlesex County and

Marvin was witnessing a steady increase in drug cases coming off the highway. The vast majority of defendants were black. Some claimed they'd been physically assaulted by troopers. Many told strange stories of how they'd been arrested.

"The police car shined lights across the road and then came after me."

"What are you talking about—a police car shining lights across the road?" Marvin said.

"They were parked down by Exit 9 in a little area off on the shoulder and when we went by they shined their light at us and then followed us and stopped us."

Marvin suspected the State Police were intentionally targeting black motorists. He began making that argument in court, but judges refused to buy it. Bitterly disillusioned, Marvin decided to take a page from his hero, Einstein, and began conducting his own "thought experiment."

Marvin reasoned that the State Police were singling out black motorists because they *believed* blacks were more likely than whites to be carrying contraband. But did that give them "probable cause" to disproportionately stop and search black people? To Marvin the "probable" in "probable cause" was a mathematical concept. If a million people traveled the highway daily and 10% were black, that meant 100,000 blacks and 900,000 non-blacks, who were primarily white. If, for arguments sake, 30% of black travelers were carrying drugs, that was 30,000 narcotics violators. If only 10% of white motorists had drugs, that meant 90,000 white violators, triple the number of blacks. Ergo, troopers did not have probable cause, yet seemed to have eyes only for black travelers.

But Marvin needed hard proof to convince dubious judges that something was hidden right before their eyes. Einstein demonstrated gravity bends light beams in deep space. Marvin had to demonstrate troopers were bending the Constitution on the Jersey Turnpike. It wasn't as momentous as Einstein's work—unless you happened to be black. Then it was relative.

In November 1988, Marvin launched his own private test and began spying on the New Jersey State Police. The defense lawyer lived alone in an apartment just across the Raritan River from the East

Brunswick State Police Station. He bought a police radio scanner and a tape recorder, set them up on his dining room table and began secretly recording trooper radio transmissions. Nobody at the Public Defender's Office knew what he was doing. Every night he came home and eagerly listened to the tapes, logging each stop, night after night, week after week. After months of listening, Marvin finally had corroboration to back up his "thought experiment." Even Einstein might have been impressed.

Chapter 18

JANUARY 22, 1989 WAS GOING TO BE the proudest day of Geno Henry Barber's life. His son, Chris, was a professional football player, a safety for the Cincinnati Bengals, and on Sunday he was going to play against the San Francisco 49ers in Super Bowl XXIII in Miami. Geno Barber was a big man, six feet one inch tall and 215 pounds, a gregarious, fun-loving soul with a magnetic personality. But, regrettably, he had not been a model parent. Due to a penchant for robbing banks, Barber had spent most of the past 20 years in prison. But he was not going to miss his boy taking on Joe Montana and Jerry Rice in The Big Game.

At 46, Barber was on parole and working as a cook in Teaneck, New Jersey. The Tuesday before the Super Bowl, Barber left North Jersey with two friends—Bernard Hicks and Curtis Ingram—and headed toward Miami. They were in Hicks' Lincoln Continental, which had North Carolina license plates. Three black men driving on the Jersey Turnpike. They didn't get far.

Less than an hour later Trooper Robert Henig spotted their car. Henig was the Turnpike's premier anti-drug gladiator. He had 158 arrests and was the overwhelming favorite to be named New Jersey State Police Trooper of the Year. There seemed to be little concern among his superiors that an alarming spate of brutality complaints had been lodged against him. His personnel jacket contained more red flags than a hurricane warning.

- September 1988: Kenneth Lowengrub nearly died from internal bleeding that witnesses claimed resulted when Henig punched him the same night another prisoner, Stacy Brown, said Henig lifted him over his head and body-slammed him to the floor.

- October 1988: a motorist alleged Henig stole $160 cash from his car.

- November 1988: a Brooklyn man says Henig battered him with a nightstick.

- December 1988: Middlesex County jail refused to accept a severely injured drug suspect who claimed Henig punched and beat him while he was handcuffed.

- January 1989: a man arrested on drug charges alleged Henig handcuffed him, struck him with a blackjack and made him *"crawl like a worm"* along the side of the Jersey Turnpike.

Despite the string of allegations, no disciplinary action had been taken against him. When Henig spotted the black Lincoln Continental on January 17th, he stopped it for allegedly doing 70 mph in a 55 mph zone. Henig later reported Hicks' hands *"were shaking and his voice was trembling."* The trooper ordered him out of the car, patted him down, but found nothing. Then he ordered Barber out. Henig had a technique for detecting nervousness. He placed a hand on the guy's chest and felt his heartbeat; if it was pounding hard it was a signal he had something to hide. Barber was anxious. Henig asked for identification.

"He reached into his right jacket pocket and pulled out a hand full of papers," Henig reported. *"With his right hand he handed me a North Carolina driver's license and with his left hand discreetly threw a bag of marijuana onto the roadway. I covered the marijuana with my left foot. He knew that I knew it was marijuana. You could see he was getting more nervous and I told him to just relax, there was no problem."*

Henig said he patted down Barber and felt a hard object under his clothing that he guessed was drugs. Barber's eyes got big and he swung his right arm, knocking Henig off balance, and then took off running. Henig said he pulled out his gun and fired two warning rounds into the grass, but Barber didn't stop. Henig said he took chase and tackled him at the top of a hill.

"I jumped on top of him, straddling him. He wrapped both of his hands around my hand and gun. Some rounds went off…I forced the gun

around towards him and the next round that went off went into him," Henig reported. *"He let go of the gun and sat straight up and didn't say a word. I rolled him over and handcuffed him. I left him face down in the weeds and ran down the hill and handcuffed the driver who was still standing in front of his car. He was crying."*

Curtis Ingram, the third man in the car, had escaped. Later, after his arrest in North Carolina, Ingram told a completely different story. He said Henig shot Barber in the leg as he was running away. Then, as Barber was trying to push himself up the hill on his back, Henig walked up and shot him in the chest. Ingram said there was no struggle for the gun. Whatever happened, Barber died face down in the weeds. Five ounces of cocaine were found in his trousers. The State Police announced the shooting was justified.

"Trooper Henig was struggling for his own life," a spokesman said.

But behind the scenes not all State Police officials were certain. Late that night, a major from headquarters, Gary Boriello, confronted Henig near the radio desk at East Brunswick station.

"Just tell me one thing," Major Boriello said. "Did you shoot him before or after you put the cuffs on him?"

Henig lunged over the counter and grabbed Boriello by the lapels before being subdued by other troopers. Later he bragged: "I would have dropped him."

Turnpike Commander Thomas Carr was also becoming suspicious. Three days after the Barber killing, Carr sent a memorandum to Clinton Pagano about the allegation that Henig had stolen $160 from a motorist's car. The stop—if it occurred—had never been reported and Carr was skeptical of his star trooper.

"I personally feel the stop was made and never called in. What do the complainants have to gain and why have they gone out of their way to pursue the issue? (However) without further proof or an admission by the trooper it is the recommendation of this Command that no further action be taken."

Thus, Henig remained on track to be Trooper of the Year.

Chapter 19

ON JANUARY 27, 1989, FRANK SINATRA was crooning on the radio, something about vagabond shoes and the city that never sleeps, when Joe Collum got his first glimpse of racial profiling.

He was driving south on Interstate 95. Out of the window of his maroon Honda Accord, he could see the Empire State Building towering over the rocky palisade running along the Jersey side of the Hudson River. To the south, the World Trade Towers gleamed in the morning sun.

One of those perfect moments, like the previous night, when Collum and his colleagues had received the Alfred I. duPont-Columbia University Award at the stately Low Memorial Library on Columbia's Manhattan campus. They'd been honored along with TV legends Bill Moyers, Ted Koppel and Mike Wallace, among others. It had been heady stuff.

Now, as he drove to work with the duPont Silver Baton on the seat beside him, Collum was still buzzing from the adrenalin rush of the night before—and a whole new appreciation for Sinatra's song about making it in *New York, New York*.

Collum was an investigative reporter for WWOR, a television station based in Secaucus, New Jersey, about three miles from the Lincoln Tunnel and midtown Manhattan. He was the on-air reporter for the station's I-Team. The "I" stood for Investigative. They'd received the duPont for a series of reports the previous year on education, particularly a story titled *Flunk City*, about a politically corrupt public school system. Now, as Collum drove down the Turnpike, he wondered what he and his colleagues would do for an encore. Finding a story as powerful as *Flunk City* would not be easy. At the moment, they were in the midst of another investigation about a multi-million dollar welfare swindle, which was scheduled for broadcast in a couple of months. But after that, what?

Then he saw it, though he didn't know it at the time. On the opposite side of the Turnpike, in the northbound lane, a car was pulled over on the side of the road, a police car parked behind with lights flashing. Collum recognized the distinctive blue and yellow triangular markings of a New Jersey State Police cruiser. The doors and trunk of the civilian vehicle were open and two state troopers were leaning inside, apparently searching for something. He saw people sitting on the hood. They were black. The scene lasted only a few seconds before he sped past, but it struck a chord.

So that's what they're talking about, Collum thought. Almost daily for months now he had been hearing about this kind of thing.

"I saw it again today," Kevin Schwab would say. Schwab was an assistant assignment editor at WWOR who bore a striking resemblance to Radar O'Reilly of the TV show M*A*S*H. At age 26, Schwab wore thick glasses and had a hyperkinetic personality not uncommon among TV news assignment people. Every day, like clockwork, Kevin would walk into Collum's office and report what he'd seen driving to work on the Turnpike.

"Troopers had another car pulled over today. The people were sitting on the guard rail while they searched the car."

Schwab's next line was always the same.

"They were black. Something's going on. You guys should check this out."

"Okay, Kevin," was Collum's rote response. "It's on our list."

Schwab wasn't the only one. Collum lived in Ridgewood, a leafy North Jersey suburb. One of his neighbors was an attorney named Joel Reinfeld, who had also been bending his ear about something reprehensible happening on the Turnpike.

"I'm telling you," Reinfeld would say over the fence between their yards, "there's a huge Constitutional violation going on. It's outrageous."

"I'll look into it, Joel," Collum would say.

The reporter rarely drove the Turnpike to work, but after that first sighting he began taking the highway regularly. And almost every day he saw the same thing. Somewhere along the route troopers would have a car pulled over with the occupants sitting on the hood or guardrail while they searched the vehicle. And they were *always* dark-skinned. It went on for weeks.

What's going on here? Collum wondered.

He vowed to find out—as soon as he got a chance.

Chapter 20

Newark Station was starting to remind Kenny Ruff of a slave auction. The place always seemed to be packed with black people in shackles. They were manacled to benches, locked in the holding cell, strip searched in the interrogation room. To Ruff it was now crystal clear that some of his white colleagues were hunting black folks.

A cartoon on the *Ha-Ha Board* said it all. Seven figures dressed in Ku Klux Klan robes surrounded a black man tied to a tree. The caption said: *"Do the white thing."* Hostility permeated the barracks and there was no longer much in the way of small talk or camaraderie between Ruff and his friends and white troopers. The race issue had become too big to get around.

"Step into my office," Ruff would say to Greg Sanders, Darryl Beard and other black troopers and they'd file into the locker room to hold a kangaroo court, openly complaining about the racial targeting.

"We've got a double standard here," Ruff would say, loud enough for white troopers to hear.

"There's no difference between blacks in the lock-up and blacks in the locker room," Sanders was fond of repeating.

"How come they don't lock up white people?" a black trooper named John Perry added.

Whites were being arrested, but the percentage was small, and they were often picked up as part of a *salt and pepper team.* Sanders and Glenn Johnson were frequently assigned to drive prisoners to jail and sometimes the inmates came clean to them.

"Look, I had some drugs in the car, but why do they have to treat me like that? The guy hit me…The guy called me a nigger…The guy said 'I'll kill you if you run.'"

Ruff began to see his fellow troopers as slightly more sophisticated versions of racist cops in places like Alabama and Mississippi 25 years before.

"The only people being processed here are black people," Ruff complained to his sergeant, Walter Zukowsky. "The guys being promoted are the guys doing the dirty work. Do you see the paradox? Someday this is going to bring down the State Police."

Ruff didn't think Zukowsky condoned racial profiling. He believed the sergeant, like a lot of white troopers, was simply indifferent to it. He wasn't going to make waves. But some black troopers were ready to make big waves. Anthony Reed came to the Turnpike a few months after Beard, Sanders, and Ruff. Reed loved to ruffle feathers. Before long he was persona non grata at Newark Station.

"Why are we stopping this car?" he'd say to white troopers when they were chasing a black motorist. He'd point to a car with white passengers. "That car is speeding. Why aren't we stopping it?"

Reed showed up at Newark Station wearing *Malcolm X* T-shirts and carrying books about Joanne Chesimard.

Chesimard was the most hated fugitive in State Police history. A member of the Black Liberation Army, she was convicted in the 1973 murder of New Jersey State Trooper Werner Foerster. Sentenced to life in prison, Chesimard escaped in 1979 and fled to Cuba where she'd been living in exile ever since.

For Reed to imply he sympathized with Chesimard was like spitting on the Blue and Gold. White troopers called him *Malcolm X. Reed* and refused to work with him. One night Reed and Greg Sanders stopped to back up two white troopers who were searching a car. The black occupants were sitting on the side of the road. The white troopers waved them off.

"Let's go," Sanders said. "If they don't want me here I'm not going to stay here."

"No," Reed said. "Forget that. We're going to stay here anyway."

They got out of their cruiser and stood talking to the black motorists while the white troopers searched. Eventually the travelers were sent on their way. But the white troopers were angry and reported back to their supervisor that Reed and Sanders had been advising the motorists to file a harassment complaint. When the black troopers returned to the station the sergeant confronted them.

"Your job is to back these guys up, not tell people to file complaints."

"No one wants you on this job," one of the white troopers said to Reed. "You need to quit and get out."

"I'm not leaving," Reed said. "These guys are targeting blacks."

Newark Station was a powder keg and the fuse was burning.

Chapter 21

CHRIS STUBBS WANTED TO make something out of her life. For the 27-year-old, the only way to do that was to start her own business. The thing she did best was cook and friends and family all told her to open a restaurant. So she decided to go for it.

Stubbs was a round-faced woman with dark brown skin, an amiable smile, and a lazy southern drawl that camouflaged her ambition. She lived in Lumberton, North Carolina, a sleepy town near the South Carolina border where she would lie in bed at night fantasizing about a restaurant crammed with ravenous hoards clamoring for her ribs, chicken, beans, corn bread and sweet tea. She found a little place on Highway 41 at the corner of Deer Stand Road across from the Hi-Lo Gas Station. It had a roomy kitchen, a smoker, and a big sign outside. The place would seat 30 people at a time and the lease was affordable.

All Stubbs needed to make it happen was the money. She found a benefactor in her girlfriend's brother, who had tasted her cooking and was willing to take a gamble on her culinary gifts. The only thing she had to do was drive to Newburgh, New York, about 60 miles north of the Big City, where he owned a car dealership, to pick up the seed money. So Stubbs, her fiancé, her 2-year-old son, and two young nieces piled into her 1983 Thunderbird and drove north. When they got there, her friend's brother gave her $10,000 in cash.

Stubbs put the money in a bag, locked it in the glove compartment, and began the long ride back to North Carolina. They drove south into New Jersey and onto the Turnpike, past the New York City skyline, past the refineries, and into the open spaces of central and southern Jersey. Two miles before the Delaware Memorial Bridge they reached the toll plaza at the end of the Turnpike. As they paid the toll, Stubbs noticed a state trooper staring at her. She was in the far left lane, but wanted to get off at the exit for gas and food and to use the bathroom. The policeman watched as she put on her right-turn signal and waited for an 18-wheeler to pass. Then he switched on his overhead lights and signaled her to pull off the highway.

Trooper Anthony Disalvatore walked up to the car and asked Stubbs for her license and registration, then ordered her to get out of the car. When Stubbs asked why she'd been stopped, Disalvatore told her it was because her front wheel was wobbling.

"That's no problem," Stubbs said. "There's a spare tire in the trunk."

"Yeah, okay," Disalvatore said. "You haven't been drinking, have you?"

"No," said Stubbs.

"Okay," he said. "Do you mind if I search your car?"

Stubbs was surprised by the request, but she was scared and didn't want to make the trooper angry. Crazy things happened out on the road and she didn't want to be one of those people who get shot and left on the side of the highway.

"No problem," Stubbs said. "Just don't plant nothin'."

Stubbs unlocked her glove compartment. Disalvatore looked inside and saw the brown paper bag. He asked her what was inside the bag and she said money. He took it out and walked back to his car. After awhile he returned.

"Any cash of more than $5,000 has to be investigated," he said. "Could you all please get out of the car?"

Stubbs' passengers climbed out and they stood at the back of the car while the trooper went through her pocket book, looked under the seats, then asked for the key to the trunk. He searched the entire car but found nothing illegal. Then he said something that scared Stubbs even more than she was already.

"You know, you're going to go to jail for this."

"For what?" she said.

"For having all this money," he said.

Disalvatore ordered Stubbs to follow him in her car. They drove to the State Police barracks at Moorestown. When they arrived a trooper took her car and drove it around back to a carport where it was "ripped and stripped." Door panels were removed, carpet pulled up, and every nook and cranny searched. Stubbs was frisked, her mug shot and fingerprints taken, and she was interrogated about her friend's relatives in Newburgh. She suspected the troopers were deliberately trying to frighten her—and they were doing a good job. Then they locked her in a holding cell where she waited for an hour. When the troopers returned they said police in Newburgh told them her friend's brother was a drug dealer.

"He is not a drug dealer," Stubbs said, explaining that he owned two businesses, had never been arrested, and never been to jail. "He's a legitimate person."

The troopers went away again. A little while later they returned with the bag of cash.

"This money is contaminated," they said. "A dog sniffed it and it's got drugs on it."

Stubbs argued that the money was to open a restaurant, but the troopers weren't impressed. They dumped the $10,000 on the table and counted it.

"This is drug money," a trooper said. "We're keeping it. Here's a receipt. You can go now."

And that was it. Stubbs wasn't charged with a crime and wasn't issued a traffic ticket. The troopers just took her money. If she wanted it back, they said, she'd have to hire a lawyer and go to court and prove it wasn't drug money. Stubbs had no way of knowing, but she was far from an isolated case.

Chapter 22

DELBERT BLAIR NAVIGATED HIS RENTED Plymouth Sundance onto the Verrazano Narrows Bridge at about 7 p.m. on April 9, 1989. Sunday traffic was heavy and the spring air cool. Out his right side window, the sun was just setting behind Manhattan's enormous skyscrapers. Blair was a long way from Trelawny, the rural Jamaican parish where he grew up on his family's farm harvesting bananas and yams. In Jamaica, he had been a police constable before moving to the States four years ago. Now he and his wife, Dalton, were chasing the American Dream. Delbert had a good job in Maryland as a building engineer. Dalton was a nursing assistant. Six months ago they'd scraped together $5,000 for the down payment on a modest home in Germantown, Maryland.

Blair was returning to Maryland with Burton Wright, a police officer and an old friend who was visiting from Kingston, Jamaica. They'd spent the weekend in the Big Apple shopping, sightseeing, and drinking Red Stripe beer. On Sunday they drove to Queens and picked up Veronica Morris, Jennifer Kelly and her 3-year-old son, Jamaican friends they'd promised to drive to Maryland. The sky was black by the time they crossed Staten Island, entered New Jersey, and drove onto the Turnpike. It wasn't long before Blair noticed red flashing lights behind him.

"Why is that cop going to pull me over?" Blair said.

"What's happening?" Veronica Morris said. She turned and saw an officer walking toward them. He was a big man.

"Good night, officer," Blair said in fractured English.

"May I have your driver's license and registration?" said Trooper Robert Henig.

"Why do you need my documents?" Blair asked.

"Give me your license and registration," Henig said.

"What have I done wrong? I wasn't speeding."

"Shut up!" Henig said.

It had been three months since Henig shot and killed Geno Henry Barber. The shooting had been ruled justifiable and no action was taken against the trooper. If anything, the incident had galvanized Bob Henig's growing legend as no one to trifle with. Since then his arrest total continued to soar and he remained the odds-on favorite to be Trooper of the Year.

"Why did you stop me?" Blair said, looking up at Henig.

"Don't say anything," Henig said with an annoyed voice. "Give me your paperwork,"

Burton Wright was alarmed by the tone of the exchange. He reached into the glove compartment and pulled out an envelope containing the automobile rental agreement and handed it to Blair, who gave it to Henig, who shoved it back at Blair.

"Don't give me a hard time. Give me your license and registration," Henig said.

He opened the door, pulled Blair out of the car, and walked him back between the State Police cruiser and the Plymouth and stood in the glare of flashing lights.

"I used to be a policeman," Blair said. "This is not the way to deal with people."

"You were a policeman? Where?" Henig said.

"Jamaica."

"Do you have a green card?"

Blair fished out his permanent residence card from his wallet and handed it to Henig, who said, "Delbert, you are under arrest."

"For what?"

"I'm going to have you deported," Henig said.

"What do you mean, have me deported?"

"Do you know that if you get arrested in this country you will be deported?"

"Ridiculous," Blair said. "This is the first time I'm hearing about this."

"You might know your Jamaican law, but you don't know American law."

Henig handcuffed Blair and placed him in the back seat. Then he returned to the other passengers and asked Burton Wright if he had a driver's license. He didn't.

"I'll have to tow the car," Henig said.

"Why are you going to tow the car?" Wright asked.

"Your friend has been arrested."

"Arrested! For what?"

"It's none of your business," Henig said.

"I'm a cop from Jamaica," Wright said. "If my friend has been arrested I think I have the right to know what he's being arrested for."

"Keep on talking," Henig said, "and I'll have to arrest you, like your friend."

"What are you going to arrest me for?" Wright said.

"For being a pain in the ass!"

Wright could see the big trooper was angry so he returned to the car. Another State Police cruiser pulled up with lights flashing.

"What do you have?" Trooper Alvin Jennings said, walking up.

"Do you believe this guy is a cop?" Henig said, pointing to Burton Wright, then to Delbert Blair. "And this guy had an ounce of coke on him."

At about the same moment, Sgt. Lawrence Schiereck was arriving for the night shift at East Brunswick Station. He walked to the kitchen, put a submarine sandwich in the refrigerator, then dropped by the Detective Bureau. Wayne Burke was sitting at his desk with a blue can in front of him.

"How's it going, Wayne?" Schiereck asked.

"Something's wrong," Burke said. He was holding a blue Planter's Pretzel canister. A clear plastic bag containing white powder lay on the desk. "The file says there are two bags of cocaine. But there's only one here."

East Brunswick was a busy station with a lot of drug arrests. Detective Burke's job on Sunday night was to log evidence seized over the weekend. The night before, Trooper Peter Bruncati had arrested three men from Virginia. His evidence list said he found two bags of cocaine weighing 55 grams hidden in the false bottom of the Planter's Pretzel can. But Burke found only one bag weighing half what the evidence list stated. He went to the radio room and sent Bruncati a Signal 30: "Report to barracks."

"Did you have two bags of cocaine in that arrest?" Burke asked Bruncati when he arrived.

"Yes, there were two bags."

"Did you consolidate two bags into one?"

"No."

"Well, the second bag is missing," Burke said.

When Robert Henig arrived with Delbert Blair in handcuffs, troopers were searching for the missing cocaine, looking under desks, behind filing cabinets, and in garbage cans.

"Take off your shirt, undershirt, and underpants," Henig ordered Blair. The trooper examined Blair's rectum looking for hidden contraband, then rifled through Blair's possessions, pulling papers from his wallet, including a paycheck.

"You really do have a job," he said. Blair asked to go to the bathroom. Henig pointed him to the holding cell. "Wait a minute," Henig said, handing him a plastic cup. "Pee in this and bring it back to me."

The hunt for the missing cocaine was still in progress. Henig joined in, sifting through garbage cans, but the coke was nowhere to be found. Henig finished processing Blair's paperwork and drove him to the Woodbridge municipal jail. A uniformed patrolman greeted them.

"What's the charge?" he said.

"Possession C.D.S. and obstruction," Henig said.

"What's possession C.D.S.?" Blair asked.

"Don't worry about it," Henig said. "The judge will tell you in the morning."

The exchange struck the Woodbridge policeman as odd. Blair was taken to a cell. A white man was locked up across from him.

"What are you in for?" he said.

"C.D.S.," Blair said.

"Oh."

"What is C.D.S.?" Blair asked.

"C.D.S. means controlled dangerous substance."

"What controlled dangerous substance? Like what?"

"Like drugs."

"Drugs? What drugs? There's no drugs."

"Well," the inmate said, "you're in here for drugs."

Chapter 23

TWO DAYS AFTER DELBERT BLAIR'S ARREST, Joe Collum drove down a pleasant tree-lined street in Leonia, New Jersey, to a three-story red brick building with tall white columns. A Community Chest thermometer was posted next to the front door and a Little League baseball banner was stretched over Broad Avenue, the main street through town.

"Hi," the reporter said to a woman at the front desk. "I'm with WWOR-TV. I spoke to someone on the telephone about looking at your arrest books."

"That would be on the second floor," she said.

The municipal building housed everything from the Leonia mayor's office to the town's court clerk. Collum walked up a creaky flight of stairs where a pleasant white-haired woman handed him a heavy black hardcover book with *1988-1989* written on the spine.

"The log is in chronological order," she said. "Can I help you find something?"

"I'm looking for arrests made by the State Police," he said.

Collum was on a fishing expedition. In the more than two months since he first saw troopers searching black motorists on the Turnpike, he'd been driving the highway to and from work and seeing similar scenes repeated day after day. He knew they were looking for narcotics, especially after the recent spate of newspaper articles touting the spectacular success of the State Police with their Highway Drug Interdiction Program.

90

He'd discussed the situation with his producers on the investigative team—Gary Scurka, a tall fair-haired Rhode Island native, and Barbara Gardner, an African-American who looked far too young to be the grandmother she was. Collum and Scurka regularly debated Gardner's age, but couldn't pin it down, and she refused to say. They often threatened to rifle her pocketbook to get a look at her driver's license, but never carried out their plot.

They'd been working for months on a welfare fraud investigation that was about to go to air. In the meantime, Gardner and Collum had been doing some preliminary snooping into the State Police. Collum had been a journalist 15 years, mainly an investigative reporter, first in newspapers, the last decade in television. Over time, he'd developed an internal sensor, like a Geiger-counter, that told him when he was getting close to a story with some radioactivity. He hadn't dug too deeply into the State Police yet, but his Geiger-counter was clicking.

"There could be a good story here," he told Scurka and Gardner.

"Cops targeting black drivers for drugs?" Scurka said. "It could be a great story."

"Yeah, fellas, but how do we prove it?" said Barbara, the I-Team's mother hen and resident realist.

"I have no idea," Collum said. "But we need to check it out."

While they finished the welfare fraud story, they began laying groundwork for a possible investigation of the State Police. When they had spare time, Collum and Gardner made telephone calls, trying to understand how the system worked and what records were available. To their chagrin, they discovered there was no central repository for State Police Turnpike arrest information. Each arrest was recorded in the town where it occurred, and there were dozens along the Turnpike-Interstate 95 corridor. Leonia was near the George Washington Bridge, not far from WWOR, and Collum decided to take the morning of Tuesday, April 11, 1989, to look at the arrest records there, just to see what he'd find. Strictly a reconnaissance mission.

"Any arrest made on I-95 will be a State Police case," the friendly white-haired lady clerk said. "If the entry says 'NJSP' it will be off the interstate."

She left him sitting alone at an empty desk to study the book. It took awhile to decipher. Entries were handwritten and listed the date of each arrest, the defendant's name, home state, charge, and the arresting officer. He was pleased to see it also listed the defendant's race. He reached into his scuffed beige leather briefcase, pulled out a yellow legal pad and a red felt-tipped pen, and constructed a rudimentary chart.

<u>Leonia</u>

<u>Race</u>	<u>Name</u>	<u>Date</u>	<u>State</u>	<u>Charge</u>

Collum began with the most recent arrests and worked back in time. The day before—April 10—a trooper arrested two North Carolina men for possession of marijuana, heroin, and cocaine. In the column identifying race, there was a letter "B" next to each man's name, meaning both were black. He leafed through page after page, picking out every trooper arrest, filling his chart line by line. It took more than an hour to fill one page. Eager to see what he had, he pushed the logbook aside and tabulated the data.

Between September 4, 1988 and April 10, 1989, troopers had arrested 28 people on I-95 in Leonia. Two were gun cases, 26 drugs, and 75% from out of state. Then he counted the left column. Of the 28 arrests, 27 of the defendants were identified as "B," black. The 28th was "H," Hispanic. In the previous seven months, troopers had not arrested one white person.

Wow! thought Collum. His Geiger-counter was ticking faster now. It took another hour to examine all cases back to the beginning of 1988. During the 15-month period, troopers made 55 arrests: 43 blacks, six Hispanics, and six whites.

That meant 89% of the arrests were of minorities.

He closed the book, returned it to the clerk, thanked her, and walked outside into the parking lot. The spring day was blue and warm and the forsythias were in full bloom, their bright yellow flowers the first sign that winter was finally releasing its clutches on the northeast. He basked in the noonday sun, pondering what he'd found.

Could the numbers be accurate? Was he missing something?

Collum did some quick calculations. The United States population was roughly 25% black and Hispanic. Yet, in Leonia, they made up nearly 90% of State Police arrests.

Could that be happening along the entire Turnpike? he wondered, relishing the moment. For a reporter, there was a certain kind of thrill at a time like this. Not arm-waving jubilation. More subdued. A quiet elation, a realization he might have just stumbled across a hidden treasure. He'd plunged a single shovel into the ground and unearthed a tantalizing nugget.

Chapter 24

By the late 1980s the Blue and Gold was a dysfunctional family. African-American troopers were scornfully referred to by their white colleagues as "federal troops" foisted upon the organization by the courts. Kenny Ruff, Darryl Beard, Greg Sanders, Anthony Reed, and Glenn Johnson were branded the "Black Radicals" by white troopers, who were now refusing to ride with them. But it wasn't only Newark Station.

A black trooper named James Smith, who worked at a barracks in South Jersey, was attending a workshop on Affirmative Action when someone walked up to him. Smith looked up, shocked to see a white sergeant wearing a cone-shaped headpiece and a white sheet inscribed with "KKK," who pointed a tinfoil cross at him while a second trooper snapped a photograph. Smith was appalled. He reported the incident to his captain, who brushed it off as a joke.

Vincent Belleran—a dark-skinned Filipino/Puerto Rican —was assigned to a traffic task force headquartered in Bloomfield Barracks that consisted of him, two black troopers and a white female trooper. Belleran's sergeant dubbed the squad *"Gladys White and the Pips from Coonfield Barracks."* When Belleran called the sergeant "a racist bastard," he was suspended and ordered to turn over his gun, badge and uniforms and was forced to walk out of the station wearing only socks and jockey shorts.

Racial targeting was at the root of the tension, typified by programs like Operation Coflame, conducted on July 20, 1989. Coflame

94

stood for Cooperative (*Co*) from Florida (*Fla*) to Maine (*Me*). It was a 24-hour highway drug interdiction marathon by police agencies patrolling Interstate 95 up and down the eastern seaboard. New Jersey cancelled vacations and put 343 troopers on the Turnpike. A memorandum from Clinton Pagano's office instructed State Police press officers how to describe Coflame.

"The releases should focus on traffic enforcement and highway safety issues so as not to unnecessarily generate complaints from ACLU members and other such groups who oppose drug interdiction per se."

Ruff and Sanders patrolled together that night. One of their first stops was of a black man on the Turnpike near Newark Airport. When they walked up to his window they found the man in tears. He said he'd driven across the George Washington Bridge from New York into New Jersey and this was the fourth time he'd been stopped in 16 miles. He had three warnings in his hand and still had more than 100 miles to get out of New Jersey.

Most young troopers walked on eggshells because they could be fired without cause until they had five years of service. But the Black Radicals didn't care. What was happening around them was bigger than the job. They became more brazen, which inflamed white troopers.

Reed's tires were slashed and his car door locks glued. Ruff found three sets of uniforms in his locker covered with talcum powder. Someone spit on Glenn Johnson's uniforms. Then the written reports of black troopers began disappearing, creating enormous headaches.

"Nothing for nothing," Johnson said in a locker room kangaroo court session, "but this behavior is not going to stop until some of their reports start missing."

Soon reports written by white troopers were vanishing, too. Relations went from bad to worse. Confrontations bordered on violence. Rumors abounded that white troopers were planning a "blanket party," throwing a blanket over a black trooper's head and beating the hell out of him. Ruff and his friends took the threat seriously. Some of the white troopers had arms so big they looked like they'd have trouble combing their hair.

One night Sgt. Zukowsky called his squad into the station for a midnight meeting. As troopers sat down at the roll call table, Ruff sensed trouble. The meeting felt like a set up.

"You know," Zukowsky said, "there's been grumbling about some guys not doing what they're supposed to. I decided to have a meeting. Bill, you wanted to say something?"

Bill McDonough was a senior trooper. Everyone called him "Big Bill." He was taller even than Darryl Beard, who was sitting next to him.

"You guys aren't doing what you're supposed to do," Big Bill said in an angry tone, looking at Beard. "You write too many tickets. You are not holding your end up in arrests. You're out there thinking summonses are more important than making PRA's."

McDonough went on for several minutes, getting louder, until he was yelling at Beard.

"Why are you so angry?" Beard said finally.

"Because you guys are not meeting the standards," McDonough said.

"Who are you talking to?" Beard asked.

"I'm talking to you," said Big Bill, jumping up and slamming his chair against the wall. Beard jumped up, too, ready to rumble, certain McDonough was about to swing at him. Then everyone was up. As the two men squared off, Ruff pulled chairs out of the way, expecting Beard to drop Big Bill any second.

"Whoa! Whoa! Whoa! " Sgt. Zukowsky bellowed. "Hold on! Sit down! Everybody sit down! Listen, they have some good points and you have some good points. Either way, we can't be doing this. We can't be having a war in this station."

But his admonishment had come too late. Civil war had already broken out at Newark Station.

Chapter 25

THERE WAS NO DENYING New York and New Jersey had a horrific drug problem. With the murder rate soaring, drive-by shootings were daily events, and innocent people were being cut down by stray bullets. The one law enforcement agency that seemed to be combating the epidemic was Clinton Pagano's New Jersey State Police. Highway interdiction was a smashing success. Drug traffickers drove through New Jersey at their own peril. And law abiding citizens appreciated it. Thank God *someone* was doing *something!*

Against that backdrop, Joe Collum and the WWOR-TV I-Team began investigating the State Police.

Collum was no anti-cop reporter. Far from it. He had a healthy respect for police officers and good relationships with many local, state, and federal law enforcement officers, including the FBI and DEA. Collum knew a critical story about troopers would not sit well with a lot of viewers. Clinton Pagano was an icon and his troops were standing tall against a wave of lawlessness that threatened to overwhelm civilized society. But something was wrong on the Turnpike. He'd seen it with his own eyes, and his first foray into the public records reinforced his suspicion that troopers, in their fervor to stop drugs, were targeting minority travelers.

Collum knew he'd need powerful proof to go on television and accuse Pagano and the State Police of breaking the law. He and his producers, Gary Scurka and Barbara Gardner, decided they were not going to do a story about troopers violating the rights of people caught with narcotics. In the midst of a genuine drug plague no one would sympathize with drug traffickers moving kilos of cocaine having their civil liberties impinged upon, or even users caught with a joint in their ashtray. It may have been true, but the lawyers and judges could sort that out. The crucial question was whether the rights of *innocent* travelers were being trampled. If that was happening they had a story. If not, no story.

The I-Team had just completed an investigative report on welfare fraud called *Money For Nothing*. Reaction had been swift. The New Jersey Attorney General's Office had seized control of the welfare department and eventually arrested more than 40 people, including the department's top officials, who were ripping off millions of dollars a year.

Now Collum and his colleagues were free to devote their full energy to the State Police. Putting an investigative report together is like building a house. The bricks and mortar were the facts. But facts came in different forms. Cold, hard statistics were the foundation. But, for television, visual facts were imperative. If minorities were being stopped, interrogated and searched on the Turnpike, they had to show it. That meant they'd have to conduct covert surveillance of the State Police. A dicey prospect, particularly since taking pictures on the Turnpike was banned. Beyond that, the road was the troopers' domain. They knew everything going on out there and to spy on them without being detected was a tall order.

The investigative unit also needed to talk to people who'd been stopped and searched. And there were statistics to gather. Collum and Gardner came from newspaper backgrounds and were partial to public records and documents that gave credibility to an investigative report. Arrest records were available, but there were no public records identifying motorists stopped and searched by troopers and let go. They decided to go to traffic courts in towns along the Turnpike, gather names of drivers who'd been ticketed and send them letters.

"WWOR-TV is seeking important information you may have," the letters said. *"A record check indicates you were issued a traffic citation on the Turnpike sometime during 1988 or 1989. We would like to speak with you by telephone about what happened when you were stopped by the New Jersey State Police."*

They mailed more than a thousand letters, giving a toll-free telephone number to respond. Calls began pouring in from around the country. It wasn't a scientific survey but it did give them anecdotal data.

Some people lauded the State Police, like the 58-year-old Caucasian man from New Castle, Delaware who said the trooper who stopped him for speeding was "courteous." Then there were black motorists like Valerie Taylor, who called from Washington, D.C. about her nightmarish experiences.

Criminal defense lawyers became another source of information. William Kunstler worked out of a cramped office on a narrow side street in Greenwich Village. Collum had interviewed the renowned civil rights attorney on other stories and called to see if he knew anything about the Jersey Turnpike. Kunstler said he did. It turned out his partner—a bright, young, pony-tailed lawyer named Ronald Kuby—had an African-American assistant who had recently been stopped and searched by a New Jersey trooper. Ironically, Jelayne Miles was returning from an anti-racism rally in Washington, D.C. with two friends—one white, one Hispanic—when they were detained on Cocaine Alley.

"[The trooper] said: 'You don't have any drugs in the car, do you?'" Miles told Collum. "I said: 'No we don't have any drugs in the car. That's ridiculous.' He said: 'Well, you know there are a lot of people who bring drugs in and we're very concerned about it and I think there could be drugs in this car. You wouldn't mind if I searched the car would you?' And he searched us. I think we were stopped because we were a Rainbow Coalition and he found that suspicious. What else could we be doing other than dealing drugs?"

Collum called the Public Defender's Office in Salem County, N. J., where Cocaine Alley was located. Public Defender Ken Rubin said it was plain to him the State Police were targeting drivers based on skin color.

"I can't see how else to explain troopers sitting at the bottom of the Delaware Memorial Bridge at night shining spotlights at eye level," Rubin said. "Blacks and Hispanics in cars with Florida or Virginia or D.C. rental tags don't get far."

The American Civil Liberties Union in New Jersey said it was being deluged by complaints from minority motorists, so many that the organization was sending out instruction forms on how to file grievances with State Police Internal Affairs.

"We've had many cases where people were stopped," ACLU legal director Eric Neisser said. "They're told the reason is their windshield, their blinker, license or whatever. Then they go through all the questions, they're searched. Troopers find out they're really innocent and they don't even give them a ticket."

"What's the problem with that?" Collum asked.

"The police are supposed to protect and help the citizens. You help the citizens by arresting criminals. You don't help citizens by investigating innocent people."

"But how do they know the innocent from the criminals unless they investigate?"

"The theory of a democratic society as compared to a police state is that you don't have to account to the police for your movements," Neisser said.

The ACLU referred Collum to a Deputy Public Defender in South Jersey named William Buckman. An athletic looking man in his mid-30s with bushy brown hair, Buckman worked in Gloucester County about 20 miles north of Cocaine Alley. He said he was neck deep in State Police drug cases.

"Of the cases I carry from the Turnpike, all of them are minorities," Buckman said. "It's become alarming. White people wearing ties and jackets are not being pulled over. It's young black people. It is a campaign being waged against minorities."

Collum was struck by Buckman's passion. He said he was about to leave the Public Defender's Office to go into private practice, in large part to mount a challenge against the State Police.

"I for one do not want to give up my freedoms for the sake of getting the five or ten percent of the people who use drugs. Thomas Jefferson said it 200 years ago: 'If I give up my rights in favor of law and order, I'll end up with neither.'"

The I-Team began a daily surveillance routine. Every day one of them drove up and down the Turnpike in an unmarked car with a photographer looking for troopers searching cars. When they saw one they'd pull over some distance away and videotape the scene, hoping they weren't spotted.

One hot afternoon in May, Collum came upon a State Police cruiser and a navy blue Lincoln Continental on the side of the Turnpike. Two troopers were rummaging through the car while three black men sat on the hood. He pulled off the road a couple of hundred yards away and his photographer, Jim Cavanaugh, began videotaping as the troopers combed the car. It was 45 minutes before they released the men. Collum and Cavanaugh chased the Lincoln and caught up with it three miles down the Turnpike. Collum rolled down his window and held out a microphone with a WWOR-TV logo, waving at them to pull over. The men seemed startled, but complied.

"That trooper just pulled me over," said Mark Watts, the driver, a Newark resident in his early 20s. "He said I changed lanes without using the blinker, but I don't believe that."

"Why do you think he pulled you over?" Collum asked.

"I think he saw three people in a nice car and thought we was transporting something."

"Why do you think he thought that?"

Watts pointed to his arm. "Skin color, see, skin color."

"He pulled us over because we was black," said Wilbert Hall, one of the passengers. "I understand they got to do their job, but when it's unnecessary, I'm telling you straight up from me, it's a bunch of bullshit, man."

Chapter 26

THE DAY AFTER DELBERT BLAIR'S ARREST, a sealed, clear plastic cup containing Blair's urine sample and initialed "RH" for Trooper Robert Henig was delivered to the State Crime Laboratory in West Trenton.

A clerk assigned it Case No. 182585C and forwarded the sample to Maureen Low-Beer, a senior forensic scientist, who performed an EMIT—Enzyme Multiplied Immunization Test—which screened the urine for marijuana, barbiturates, amphetamines, opiates, and cocaine. The tests were negative for everything except cocaine.

Then another chemist, Nirmal Sawhney, performed a gas chromatogram to determine the level of drugs in the urine. Sawhney took 14 milliliters, about half of the specimen, dried it, and ran his analysis. He'd conducted the same test hundreds of times but the result this time was anything but routine. The cocaine level was almost off the charts. Sawhney knew something was terribly wrong. Anyone who ingested that much cocaine would surely be dead. But Delbert Blair was alive.

Sawhney went straight to laboratory supervisor Dr. Thomas Brettell, who ordered a High Performance Liquid Chromatography test and a Gas Chromatography Mass Spectrometry exam to measure Blair's benzolylecgonine.

Cocaine disappears from urine almost completely in 8-to-12 hours. More than 80% of the drug is absorbed into the blood where it breaks down into metabolites, primarily benzolylecgonine, which takes 10-to-12 days to be excreted. Due to the extraordinary amount of cocaine in Blair's urine specimen, Brettell expected his benzolylecgonine to be sky high. But the urine was clean. Brettell knew immediately that meant one thing—Blair's sample had been spiked.

As those tests were being performed, Blair was posting a $5,000 bond and was released from jail. He immediately filed a false arrest complaint against Trooper Henig. Several days later, on Friday April 14th, two investigators from the State Police Internal Affairs Bureau drove from New Jersey to Germantown, Maryland. Capt. John Leck and Sgt. Clement Mezzanotte took Blair's taped statement.

Three weeks later, on May 4th, Robert Henig reported for duty to East Brunswick Station. The odds-on favorite to be the next Trooper of the Year was met by Lt. Bill Davidson.

"Somebody is here to see you," Davidson said.

Henig had been through this drill before. He knew "somebody" was the Internal Affairs Bureau. He also knew dealing with IAB was about as much fun as a root canal. Henig was led to a room where Capt. Leck and Sgt. Mezzanotte were waiting. They immediately ordered him to turn over his service weapon. It was standard procedure. No one wanted to be trapped in a room with an armed cop when he was being told his career was over. Henig handed them his pistol.

"Have a seat Trooper Henig."

"I'd rather take this standing up," he said.

Leck told Henig he was the target of an Internal Affairs inquiry for suspicion of stealing an ounce of cocaine from a State Police evidence locker, planting it on Delbert Blair, and doctoring Blair's urine specimen.

"I can see where this is going," Henig said. "My career is finished."

"Trooper Henig," Sgt. Mezzanotte said, "it is my duty to inform you that you have the right to remain silent..."

Henig exploded. "I want a union representative before I say anything," he shouted.

A tense silence filled the room, the IAB investigators staring up at the massive trooper for several minutes, nobody saying a word until, finally, Henig broke the hush.

"I love my job," he said, his voice more controlled now. "I do the best I can. My record speaks for itself. There is no way I did this. I've got nothing to hide. I'm clean, so I'm going to talk to you."

"I want you to remember," Mezzanotte said, "you don't have to say anything to us without an attorney present."

"Do you want me to talk or don't you want me to talk?" Henig said testily. "Stop telling me my Miranda rights. I know them!"

So they talked—for three hours, Henig repeatedly denying stealing the drugs, planting cocaine, or spiking Blair's urine.

"Could somebody else have doctored the urine?" Mezzanotte said.

"Nobody fucks with my evidence," Henig said.

"Could Blair have added the cocaine to his own urine?"

"No, he couldn't because I already strip searched him."

Finally, Mezzanotte ended the interrogation.

"Trooper Henig," he said, "Captain Gunnell is here. He wants to see you."

For a trooper, a visit from Edward Gunnell was like an appointment with the Grim Reaper. He was the chief of Internal Affairs and Henig knew he hadn't come to pin a medal on his chest.

"Trooper," Captain Gunnell said, "could you please state your name and your badge number."

"You know my name and you've got my badge number," Henig snapped. "I'm not going to take this shit anymore. I'm tired of these wild accusations. I'm out of here."

Henig jumped up to leave, but was restrained by other officers.

"Trooper Henig, I regret to inform you that you are now under suspension without pay," Gunnell said.

They took the uniform right off Henig's back and he had to borrow a sweat suit from another trooper. When he tried to make a telephone call a supervisor stopped him: "Sorry, that telephone is for troopers only."

A few weeks later Henig was indicted in the Blair matter. He arrived at the Middlesex County Courthouse for arraignment, teeth clenched and face red as he waded through a sea of press and cameras. His lawyer described him as *"a hero superior to most, if not all, of his contemporaries."*

After being released on his own recognizance, Henig left the courthouse surrounded by a cordon of six muscular, crewcut, off-duty troopers, each wearing light shirts and dark pants, shouting obscenities as they shoved through a phalanx of reporters. A television sound man was tackled and a photographer was thrown to the ground. One reporter reached Henig and asked him to comment. The suspended trooper raised his left arm as if to strike the reporter before another trooper grabbed him.

"Take it easy, Bobby," he said.

Chapter 27

It got to the point where Joe Collum was asking every African-American he met if they'd ever been stopped on the Jersey Turnpike. The Federal Express man who delivered packages to the TV station said he'd been stopped and searched, but was afraid to talk about it on television. A colleague at WWOR, Kim Lowe, told him about a friend who'd been detained.

"Six or seven cars surrounded us," Tyrone Best told Collum. "They had us sit on the front end of the car and they started taking things apart, the lights, under the tires, under the engine. I asked the officer 'What are we being harassed for?' He told us 'Just don't worry about it. We're just checking to see if you have any drugs.'"

"How did they treat you?" Collum asked.

Best laughed mirthlessly. "Like an average criminal. They had us on display for about half an hour, everybody just riding by, watching us like 'We caught some more criminals.'"

One day the telephone rang in the I-Team office. The caller identified himself to Collum as Ted Wells, a musician from Newark who had an R&B group called *Men At Last.* He was trying to book an appearance on WWOR's morning talk show, hosted at the time by Matt Lauer, who would go on to *Today Show* fame. Collum told Wells he had the wrong number and transferred him to Lauer's office. A few minutes later the phone rang again. It was Wells. He'd gotten cut off and was trying to get back to the talk show. *Why not?* the reporter thought, and asked him about being stopped on the Turnpike.

106

Wells chuckled. "Why don't you come on down to our studio Saturday night?" he said. "We're rehearsing. My brother and I have an interesting story to tell you."

Saturday night Ted Wells sat with a guitar on his lap, surrounded by his band, and talked about an evening two months before. He and his brother Tony had attended a *New Edition* concert at Madison Square Garden in Manhattan and were driving home to Newark at 2 o'clock in the morning when troopers pulled them over.

"They told Tony he was driving 80 miles per hour. They searched us and the car. Then they asked us what we did. We told them we had a singing group. So they told us to sing to prove we were telling the truth. So we sung."

Wells strummed his guitar and sang: *"We used to be so happy in love; we were never far apart...*And if they'd told me to dance I would have danced because I felt threatened. I felt humiliated."

"It was very frightening, you know, because I've never been arrested," Tony Wells said. "So then he says 'I'm going to give you a warning.' Now if I was really doing 80 miles an hour I think I would have gotten a ticket. I guess the guy liked our singing."

But it wasn't only blacks. Manuel Fabian was a Cuban-born lawyer who lived and worked in the Jamaica section of Queens, New York. He said he was driving home from a Florida vacation in his new BMW when he was stopped by troopers just after crossing the Delaware Memorial Bridge into New Jersey. It was dark and one trooper with a flashlight started looking inside the car.

"I said: 'Officer, why are you searching my car?' He said: 'Who's searching your car?' I said: 'Well you have a flashlight. Obviously you're looking for something.' He said: 'I'll show you what a search is.'

"He took the flashlight and put it against my neck, threw me against my car and lifted the flashlight like a chokehold. He proceeded to pat me down and kept asking me: 'Where is the stuff? Where is it? Tell me where it is.' I said: 'What are you talking about?'

"He put his hands in my pockets. He took my wallet and went back to his car. When he returned his attitude had changed. The wallet had my lawyer's identification card in it and he was a little mellower, nicer, like nothing happened. He didn't apologize, but at that point I was not looking for an apology. I was grateful to get out of there.

"My feeling is it's definitely something to do with me being Hispanic. I was petrified. I grew up in Cuba in the 1960s. The secret police would come to our house in the middle of the night, wake us up, search the house, and take my father away for interrogation. And that night brought me back to having to deal with police officers who were acting without reason. I have never again driven on the New Jersey Turnpike because I don't know if I'm going to run into another trooper."

Chapter 28

IF THE NEW JERSEY STATE POLICE HAD a poster boy in the late 1980s it was a charismatic young trooper named Brian Caffrey. At six feet three, with broad shoulders and movie star good looks, Caffrey bore a striking resemblance to the Marlboro Man. Still in his early 30s, Caffrey was a living legend, the only trooper with the full cluster of yellow, blue, and red bars on his chest, the department's three most exalted decorations.

The yellow Meritorious Award was for Caffrey's stellar arrest record; the Blue Max for valor for saving the lives of fellow troopers during a 1985 shoot-out with drug traffickers; the red bar for being named 1982 Trooper of the Year when he arrested 229 people and recovered $3 million in drugs and stolen goods. When Caffrey walked into a room, other troopers stepped aside. Young officers were in awe of him. He was a superstar.

Caffrey was a protégé of two-time Trooper of the Year Sgt. Andrew Mastella, the scourge of Cocaine Alley. When Clinton Pagano launched his Drug Interdiction Training Unit to teach younger troopers how to catch narcotics smugglers, he put Mastella and Caffrey in charge.

After weeks of covert investigation, Joe Collum and the I-Team were ready to confront the State Police. When they requested to interview a trooper about drug interdiction, Caffrey got the assignment. He was the prototype State Policeman Pagano wanted the public to see.

"Profiling is illegal," Caffrey told Collum as he drove his cruiser down the highway. "We as State Police officers are not allowed to profile. I'll honestly tell you that we lock up more whites than we do blacks. I know that for a fact. I've done the statistics."

Caffrey was cordial and unflappable, explaining that New Jersey troopers—under his tutelage—were well schooled on the constitutional parameters of drug stops and searches.

"Our troopers are aware of what they can do and what they can't do. It's a science. You'll hear people say 'Well, you're profiling. You're stopping people on a profile.' Wrong! We're stopping them for motor vehicle violations. When a trooper conducts a search he has a reason. The majority of time we come up with something."

Collum told Caffrey he'd spoken to dozens of people who said they were stopped and searched for no apparent reason. When no drugs were found they were often released without even a ticket for their alleged traffic infraction, left with nothing but a mortifying sense of violation.

"I've searched vehicles and come up with nothing," the trooper said. "Maybe it's there, and you weren't able to find it. Sometimes you get the bear, sometimes the bear gets you."

Then Caffrey said something that gave Collum a chill.

"The idea that this is America and if I'm driving someplace and haven't done anything wrong, why should I be stopped and searched? We wouldn't be doing our job if we were to let everyone drive down the roadway without stopping them and looking for things."

Chapter 29

A FEW DAYS LATER JOE COLLUM WITHDREW $1,000 in cash from his personal bank account and drove to a dark, primeval building in Newark that looked like something out of the Inquisition. The old Essex County jail had long since been replaced by a modern facility and was now a favorite of movie directors keen to film in its shadowy labyrinth of dungeon-like cells. It was also the domain of the Essex County Sheriff's narcotics squad and its drug-sniffing dogs.

Charles Knox, the Narcotics Squad director, was a trim, middle-aged African-American. He led Collum and his camera crew up a set of stairs to a large, dank room with scuffed gray floors, institutional beige walls, and barred windows.

Two officers from the K-9 squad were waiting. One held a clear plastic bag containing cocaine and U.S. currency. The other held a leash attached to Vinnie the Drug Dog, a big black-and-tan German shepherd.

"He is certified by the State Police in Trenton," Knox said.

"Perfect!" Collum said, without explanation.

He'd been hearing about enormous amounts of "drug money" being seized on the Turnpike. It seemed troopers weren't New Jersey's only *crime dogs*.

The State Police employed a litter of *narco pups*, dogs with a sense of smell 1,000 times more acute than humans that could detect the presence of drugs on money with a single whiff. Working for Alpo and Milk Bones, the K-9 crime fighters had transformed the Black

Dragon into a river of gold. In 1987, troopers seized $2 million in cash. In 1988, the amount exploded to $5,720,900.

"Justice in New Jersey has gone to the dogs," a lawyer told Collum, only half in jest.

Some of the seizures had narcotics trafficking written all over them. Trooper Kenneth Dangler stopped an Illinois car for swerving on the highway. The official report stated: *"The trooper found $1,501,232 in small bills in three duffle bags in the trunk. Three people in the vehicle disclaimed any knowledge of the money. 'Buddy,' a yellow Labrador Retriever, was brought in and, upon close olfactory examination, reacted positively to the money."* For the State Police it was like hitting the lottery. Trooper Dangler was photographed standing beside a smiling Clinton Pagano in front of stacks of cash.

But huge seizures were rare. State Police guidelines declared that if troopers found cash amounting to $5,000 or more during a vehicle search, the money was considered "suspicious" and subject to "investigation," which meant calling in the dogs. If a canine "reacted positively" the currency was confiscated as "drug money." To get it back, the owner was forced to go to court to prove the money was "legitimate." Newspaper headlines trumpeted new confiscations almost daily: *"Drug-Tainted Cash Seized by State Police;" "Police Seize $9,000 in Cash;" "Police Seize $17,797."*

To Collum, there was something alarming about the seizures. Money was being taken from people whose only "crime" was carrying a wad of cash. And it wasn't white guys in business suits whose money was being sniffed and snatched. I-Team producer Barbara Gardner had tracked down several people whose cash had been expropriated. They were all black, all of them from out of state, and none had been charged criminally. But each had lost large sums of money because a dog barked at it.

The problem was that in America circa 1989 the odds were nearly 100% that a roll of cash—large or small—would have at least some narcotics contamination. Dade County's chief toxicologist, Dr. William Hearn, ran a test by collecting 135 dollar bills from banks in 12 cities and found traces of cocaine on 131 of them. A DEA analysis in 1987 found one-third of the cash in Chicago's Federal Reserve was contaminated by cocaine.

"The probability that every single person in the United States is carrying drug-tainted money is almost certain," said Dr. James Woodford, an Atlanta forensic chemist.

Collum had gone to the old jail to see if a dog trained by the State Police would detect drugs on his bank cash. First an officer spread the Sheriff Department's currency—which had been marinating in cocaine—across the floor. Vinnie the Drug Dog was released and raced right past the bills, running from one officer to the other, more interested in playing than detecting drugs. The antics went on like that for several minutes until a deputy led Vinnie to the bills. He finally took notice and barked.

"Dirty money!" an officer yelled with a hint of embarrassment.

Great! Collum thought with a sinking feeling that his experiment was about to flop. Vinnie could barely detect drugs on money bathed in cocaine! What were the odds a dog would smell anything on his $1,000? He handed the cash to a deputy, who spread it on the floor. An officer brought in a different dog, a beautiful black-and-white German shepherd named Sable. Seconds later, Sable ran across the room and started barking and pawing at a $100 bill, grabbing it between her teeth and ripping it in half.

"Dirty money!" another officer cried out. "I guess you can tape it back together."

"Does that surprise you?" Collum asked Knox. "I withdrew that from a bank today."

"It doesn't surprise me at all," Knox said. "Given the presence of narcotics in our society today it's very possible a person can go into a bank and get tainted money."

A few days later, Collum flew to North Carolina, rented a car, and drove to Lumberton. Chris Stubbs' restaurant was past a trailer park and fairgrounds just across from the Hi-Lo Gas Station. The sign said: "Open August 1st." Inside everything was white and stainless steel. Stubbs was cleaning the counter. A little boy sat writing at a table. Another woman was in the kitchen. A sign over the counter said: *"Tough times never last, but tough people do."*

Stubbs showed the reporter her Thunderbird and demonstrated how she'd locked $10,000 in her glove box a month before. She described how the New Jersey troopers searched the car, frisked and fingerprinted her, then locked her in a cell before finally setting her free, minus her ten grand. Stubbs insisted the cash was for her dream restaurant, not drugs.

"They seen black folks and decided what are they doing with all that money," Stubbs said in a slow drawl. "The impression I got, the way they was talking, they just wanted the money. Now I have to borrow more money. I don't like it. How can they just take people's money like that? We hadn't done anything wrong. Nothing! I'll never drive through New Jersey again. It's not personally New Jersey, it's just those troopers."

Chapter 30

"THE REAL SECRET TO THE SUCCESS OF COCAINE ALLEY is one word: Numbers!" Frank Hoerst III was standing at the foot of the Delaware Memorial Bridge looking more like a silk-stocking lawyer than a civil servant. The Hoerst name was well known in these parts thanks to his father Frank, who had once been a star pitcher for the Philadelphia Phillies.

But Frank III was carving a niche of his own as the dashing young prosecutor of Salem County, New Jersey. He was also the State Police's biggest cheerleader on highway drug interdiction. And why not? Cocaine Alley had become a profit center.

"I estimate we've picked up well over $1 billion worth of cocaine."

New Jersey's least populous county with 65,000 residents was the site of more major narcotics seizures than anyplace in the United States. Not that drug kingpins were being arrested and sent off to long prison terms. Typically, men and women caught at the bridge were lowly mules who Hoerst had turned into cash cows, thanks to his penchant for plea bargains. The prosecutor's standard deal for mules was one year in jail and an $18,000 fine. That was adding up to a $1 million-a-year bonanza for the county. In addition, enormous quantities of cash and vehicles were being seized and Hoerst and his investigators drove some of the flashiest cars in South Jersey.

As he stood at the bottom of the bridge shouting to Joe Collum over the blare of non-stop traffic whizzing past, the handsome, mustachioed prosecutor was effusive in his praise of the State Police.

"With 22 million cars a year going over this bridge and the troopers out here working 8-hour shifts, stopping 25-30 cars a shift, the probability of finding something is great," Hoerst said.

"The question is who are they stopping?" Collum said.

"I don't have a radar gun, but I would have to say just about every car that's passed us since we started this interview is probably exceeding the speed limit."

"Then it's up to the discretion of the trooper which car he wants to pull over?"

"Exactly!" said Hoerst. "If 12 cars went by at the same time, all going at identically the same speed, and that speed was 56 miles per hour, he could pick one of those 12 cars and it would be a legitimate stop."

"So under those guidelines 99% of cars traveling the Turnpike—?"

"Probably 99.5%."

"Are?"

"Are susceptible to stopping."

"And interrogation?"

"Yes, interrogation. 'Where are you coming from?' And they say Washington. If you look in the back seat and see a copy of *The Miami Herald,* or you see a crate of oranges, you have reasonable cause to be suspicious."

"But why should a driver have to be subjected to an interrogation just for doing what every other driver on the highway is doing?" Collum asked.

"I see nothing legally or morally wrong if someone is violating the law, illegal lane change, speed limit, that you can't also go out with an idea of let's see what we can find."

"Why are minorities being arrested so much more often than whites?"

"Not knowing what the exact statistics are, I would have to say that more than 50% of the people charged and successfully prosecuted are blacks or Hispanics."

"Would 86% minority arrests surprise you?" the reporter said.

"It would surprise me but it wouldn't shock me, no."

"Doesn't that indicate troopers are profiling minorities?"

"Prove your case. It's easy to throw spitballs. It is the policy of the Salem County Prosecutor's Office that there is no profile. Nothing has ever been proved."

"That doesn't mean it's not happening," Collum said. "The numbers are blatant."

"What are we missing here? Is our system of justice missing the cue? It's been alleged, but never proven. The courts are open. If we were doing it I'd like to believe the system works and we'd be caught, we'd be punished for something like that."

Months later, Hoerst's words would prove eerily prophetic.

Chapter 31

JOE COLLUM FIRST HEARD OF PAUL MCLEMORE from Nate Jones, the black school principal from Trenton arrested by troopers after being stopped in his Mercedes Benz. Jones referred the reporter to his lawyer, McLemore.

"By the way," Jones said, "Did you know Paul was the first black Jersey trooper?"

McLemore, now 51, was noticeably thicker at the waist than the lean young trooper in the photograph on his wall receiving his State Police badge 28 years before. He ran a law practice out of a spartan office near Trenton and his clientele included several black state troopers. It was immediately evident the emotional wounds McLemore had suffered during his years with the Outfit were not healed.

"The 15 years I served in the State Police there was pervasive racism," he said. "Judging from the kinds of materials I've received from minority troopers and from the kinds of complaints I've heard, there's still a lot of discrimination in the State Police."

McLemore pulled out a file of documents he said he'd been given by troopers and handed Collum a poster entitled *"Runnin' Nigger Target."* The image was a caricature of a black man running with a bull's-eye superimposed over him. Points were awarded for hitting various parts of the black body. *"Caution: Head Shots May Rik-O-Shay."*

"This was found recently posted on a bulletin board in one barracks," he said, handing Collum another poster that declared: *"Open season on porch monkeys—regionally known as jigaboos, boneheads, groids, saucer lips, jungle bunnies, coons, spooks, and spades."*

McLemore passed the reporter several more posters of the same ilk. "If white troopers treat brother troopers like this just because they're black, what's their attitude toward non-troopers?"

"You mean people like Nate Jones?" Collum said.

"Look, I have no problem with the concept of aggressive enforcement of the law. The problem I have is when it focuses only on one part of our society. We just can't have law enforcement officers arbitrarily stopping people. You've got to have a reason."

"Do you think these are pretext stops?"

"It's not just me that thinks it. You need to talk to some black troopers."

"I want to," Collum said, jumping at the opening. "Can you help me?"

"I can't promise anything," McLemore said. "But I can make some calls."

Weeks went by as Collum, Gary Scurka and Barbara Gardner continued digging up statistics and interviewing victims and experts, building what was becoming a credible case that New Jersey troopers were illegally targeting minority motorists. But they still had a hole in their data. They didn't have an insider. They needed a trooper to authenticate their findings.

The problem was troopers didn't snitch on the Blue and Gold. Telling family secrets was high treason. A trooper would have to be insane, or incredibly brave, to blow the whistle, especially on television. Collum and Gardner spent weeks networking, cajoling, pleading, trying to find a trooper. Finally, Collum called McLemore again. The lawyer gave him a name and telephone number. The person at that number supplied the names and phone numbers of two black troopers. Collum called each of them and, to his immense relief, both agreed to meet with him.

One morning in July, Collum and a photographer drove to the home of one of the troopers. He'd been with the State Police more than 10 years and seemed loose, relaxed, and eager to speak.

"I've felt very uncomfortable with the searches," he said. "Minorities are being stopped on a regular basis and searched without probable cause."

That was exactly what Collum had been hoping to hear. The trooper was going to verify everything. And he didn't seem crazy! If anything, he was defiant. But he had one caveat. He would do an interview, on camera, if the reporter vowed to keep his identity confidential. He didn't want his name used, his face shown, and he wanted his voice disguised. Guaranteeing anonymity to an interview subject was a solemn responsibility. Speaking out could cost a whistleblower his job, his reputation, or perhaps his life. A reporter who promised to protect someone's identity had to be prepared to do anything, even go to jail if necessary, to shield a source. Collum had made such pacts with mobsters, bureaucrats, FBI agents and rape victims. He agreed to protect the trooper.

There were several ways to videotape an interview to ensure confidentiality. The subject could be disguised with a wig, beard, glasses, or hat. The interview could be shot from behind the interviewee or lighted from one side, casting a shadow onto a wall so viewers would see only the person's silhouette. They finally decided to set up a light directly behind the trooper's head so that when he looked straight into the camera his facial features would be obscured beyond recognition. For good measure, Collum had him put on a ball cap. They would alter his voice electronically back in the studio.

Collum began the interview: "Are you aware of racial targeting of motorists by New Jersey state troopers?"

"Look, Joe, there's a lot of good guys in the Outfit, white guys, and I've worked with a lot of them. But nonetheless these incidents occur. Minorities are being stopped on a regular basis and, without hesitation, they are being taken out of their cars and searched."

"For just cause?"

"No. These cars are being stopped on the basis of people meeting certain profiles."

"What do you mean? What kind of profiles?"

"There's an overwhelming amount of blacks being stopped on the Turnpike. Illegal searches are being conducted."

"Why? For what reason?"

"With the new drug laws, the zero tolerance that's in effect, they're out there looking for everything and anything they can get," the trooper said.

"What's wrong with that if people are transporting drugs?"

"True, there is a problem with drugs and we have to make a stand and do something about it. But when it comes to the point where you're violating the United States Constitution, it's time to step back and regroup, I think."

The trooper attributed the problem to a heavy influx of young troopers onto the Black Dragon, some with as little as one year's experience.

"They're transferring to make a name for themselves. That's where the action is."

"I don't understand something," Collum said. "If what these troopers are doing is unconstitutional, how are they getting away with it?"

"The posture, as far as the division and the policy of zero tolerance, is anything goes."

The trooper didn't waffle or hedge and he verified everything. A couple of days later, Collum drove to the home of the second trooper. He was cordial, but extremely edgy. Collum could tell by his body language he had cold feet. The reporter was afraid he was going to bail out of the interview so he decided not to rush things and give the man time to get comfortable. The trooper poured coffee and they stood in his kitchen talking about his family, his second job, anything to relax him. Gradually Collum guided the conversation to the State Police, explaining what he'd found, the victims, the numbers, and the video they'd shot of troopers searching black travelers. He told him he'd interviewed another trooper whose name he couldn't reveal and vowed to keep his identity secret as well. The trooper's anxiety finally abated.

Taking advantage of the bright summer day, they opened the kitchen door and the trooper stood with his back to the doorway. The contrast of his dark skin against the outside light made it impossible to discern his facial features.

"Blacks have been stopped for no legitimate reason and searched illegally," he said once the camera was rolling.

"Why?"

"The attitude is that blacks are the bad guys. They all have drugs, they all carry weapons, they all rob, rape. That's the attitude throughout the whole State Police."

"Do you really think it's that widespread?"

"It's pervasive. I don't believe all the white troopers are bigoted. But clearly there is a problem with white troopers illegally stopping and searching black motorists. Racial slurs are common. To hear 'nigger' or 'black bastard' on the radio, or to hear 'Charlie Bravo,' 'I'll be stopping two Charlie Bravo's.'"

"Charlie Bravo?"

"'Charlie Bravo' is code for C.B., Colored Boy."

"What is the relationship between black troopers and white troopers?"

"They call us 'federal troops,'" he said, referring to the federal court mandate to hire minority officers. "We're not treated as equal. We're just perceived as second class flunkies."

"I can't believe it's that bad," Collum said. "It sounds like the Deep South in the 60s."

"To me the New Jersey State Police is the most bigoted and racist law enforcement agency in the country, bar none."

Chapter 32

CREWCUT STATE TROOPERS IN T-SHIRTS and gym shorts jogged on a sun-dappled trail along the Delaware River as Joe Collum turned into the sprawling headquarters of the New Jersey State Police shortly before 10:30 a.m. Monday, July 24th. He felt like he'd just entered enemy territory. Collum and his colleagues had been investigating the State Police for months now, examining thousands of files, interviewing dozens of victims, secretly videotaping troopers, building a damning case against a proud organization not used to being placed under a microscope.

Collum had never met Colonel Clinton Pagano, but was well aware of his reputation as "the J. Edgar Hoover of New Jersey." The reporter and his cameraman were escorted into Pagano's office and shook hands with the Superintendent.

Pagano, dressed in a light-blue civilian suit, was trim and fit, but shorter than Collum expected. The colonel knew he was not there to do a puff piece and would be asking hard questions about racial targeting, but he was cordial and pleasant and there was none of the chill in the air Collum had anticipated. Pagano had the self-assurance of a man who knew he wasn't going to be rattled by a reporter. Not that Collum was the second coming of Mike Wallace. He had a low key interview style: Ask the questions and let people respond. They could be honest, deceptive, courteous, or hostile. Some had even been violent. He reported what they said. If the evidence showed they were lying, that was their problem.

Pagano sat behind his desk facing Collum and Fred Sengstacke, his photographer, set up the tripod and camera directly behind the reporter's shoulder. Collum began with a few softball questions about drugs.

"Drug enforcement is our first priority," Pagano said. "The criminal element uses the highway. Crime is mobile, especially when you look at drug movement. We train our people to interdict this kind of activity. I think it's been a success. We have sent our troopers to 41 states to teach our techniques to other law enforcement agencies."

Pagano spoke in a clipped staccato that reminded Collum of Walter Winchell, the old-time radio man he'd heard as a kid narrating the 1960s TV cop show "The Untouchables," and wondered if the Colonel saw himself as some kind of latter day Elliot Ness. After a few stress-free interrogatories, he zeroed in on the crux of the matter.

"There are claims by some people that troopers are targeting or profiling minority motorists, especially blacks," Collum said.

"Let me say very clearly that we don't condone, nor do we train our people to use a profile," Pagano said, obviously expecting the question. "Profiling is a common plea of many people who have no other defense."

"How do you explain, then, that the vast majority of drug and weapon arrests on the Turnpike are of blacks?"

"The New Jersey State Police, as a matter of our own record, does not have a majority of black arrests. We have a majority of white arrests," Pagano said.

"Colonel," said Collum, "we examined 1,300 arrests by your people on the Turnpike last year. Blacks accounted for 76% of those arrests. Down south around Cocaine Alley, 86% of State Police arrests were of blacks and Hispanics. Up north near the George Washington Bridge it was 89%. Nine out of ten arrests were of minorities."

Collum detected a flicker of alarm in Pagano's eyes. He couldn't have known how deeply the TV people had been digging and the numbers had caught him off guard. Pagano's eyes hardened, his mouth compressed, and the mood suddenly became tense. The interview took an adversarial turn.

"Mr. Collum, I challenge the figures you have," Pagano said. "Be careful of the figures you're going to use. I think I'll rely on my own statistics. The bottom line is these stops weren't made on the basis of race alone. That would be foolishness."

Collum told Pagano he'd interviewed a number of people who told stories about being stopped by troopers and searched, sometimes verbally and physically abused, then released, often without a traffic ticket.

"Do you have any idea how many people are stopped and searched who have nothing illegal on them?" he asked.

"No idea. No idea. I would say in most cases where you have the probable cause for a search you usually come up with something and you have an arrest."

Collum knew if Pagano was going to blow his cork, his next question would be the trigger.

"Colonel, I've interviewed some black troopers who agreed to speak to us if we promised not to identify them. They told me racial targeting of black drivers by troopers is widespread."

Pagano looked like he'd just been stabbed in the chest. It was one thing for civilians to criticize the Outfit, but for troopers to tell stories outside the family was blasphemy. But the Superintendent kept his cool.

"You may very well find somebody who would say that. I could probably find people who would tell me today is Wednesday and I know its Monday. The kind of people who say things like that really should have the courage of their convictions and come forward and say them publicly. Our troopers are out there doing a good job and I don't take a back seat to anyone for the kind of drug interdiction we've been engaged in. The public right now is saying 'Do something about this drug scourge. How are you protecting us?'"

From Collum's perspective, the issue wasn't about combating crime, but whether a police agency was engaged in the legally and morally irreconcilable practice of knowingly breaking the law in the name of enforcing the law.

"People do feel as though they've had their rights violated," he said. "Is that something that should be of serious concern?"

"It is of serious concern," Pagano said, "but nowhere near the concern I think we have got to look to in trying to correct some of the problems found with the criminal element in this state."

Collum let Pagano's words sink in, wondering if he'd heard the Superintendent correctly. It sounded like New Jersey's highest ranking police officer had just said catching criminals took precedence over the U.S. Constitution. He was a journalist and not a lawyer, but it seemed like a startling statement. Maybe he was being naïve, but Collum had always believed the Constitution was sacrosanct. If he'd heard Pagano right, though, in New Jersey the supreme law of the land had now been superseded by the war on drugs.

Chapter 33

Two DAYS LATER, WALTER MARVIN, the mild-mannered glue maker-turned-public defender, walked into the Middlesex County Courthouse and filed papers accusing troopers of racial targeting. Warren County Public Defender Sheri Woliver had filed similar charges 18 months earlier, but for Clinton Pagano that had been a minor brushfire. This promised to be a major conflagration.

The new charge was the culmination of Marvin's spy campaign, so secret he didn't tell his boss about it for months. Marvin was a most improbable candidate for such an audacious enterprise. He was a bit of an odd duck in the Public Defender's Office, twice the age of most of the firebrands drawn to the heavy workload and low pay of public defense. But, although gentlemanly and kind, in his donnish way Marvin was as fierce and diligent as the youngsters.

After months of surveillance of State Police radio transmissions and long forays up and down the Turnpike, Marvin believed he could now prove that minorities were being stopped and searched in overwhelmingly disproportionate numbers. He took his tapes and records to Brad Ferencz, chief of the Middlesex Public Defender's Office, who was stunned to learn of Marvin's rogue adventure.

To other defense lawyers in the office, Marvin's findings were like a jolt of adrenalin. Finally, they had ammunition to attack the State Police.

Ferencz promptly marshaled his resources and began what for the PD was an unprecedented investigation. They hired a Rutgers University professor to design a statistically sound study. Secretaries were recruited to pull drug arrest files and compile data for the analysis. Investigators began shadowing troopers, racing to Turnpike stops, recording occupant races, the state registrations of vehicles, and whether cars were being searched.

By the dog days of late July, Marvin and his colleagues had what they believed was a prima facie case of selective enforcement against the State Police. On Wednesday, July 26, 1989, Marvin filed papers claiming black and minority drivers accounted for 90% of trooper stops in Middlesex County. The numbers, he wrote, *"represent a clear pattern and practice by New Jersey state troopers of violating defendants constitutionally protected rights to freedom from racial discrimination and freedom to travel."*

Marvin called for the dismissal of hundreds of arrests stemming from "racially motivated" stops. But Clinton Pagano was having none of it.

"This is nothing but artistic creation devised to avoid a criminal trial," he said, barely containing his rage at a hastily called press conference at HQ. "If I were a professor teaching statistics I would fail anyone who provided documentation of that type."

Chapter 34

DESPITE THE HOT AUGUST NIGHT, a glacial chill permeated the air as Darryl Beard and Greg Sanders watched a throng of stern-faced troopers file into the kitchen at Newark Station. Thankfully, at least on this night, the hostility was not directed at them. Tonight the villain was a television reporter.

For the past several weeks, word had been spreading through the rank and file that the State Police were being investigated by a news team from WWOR-TV. Colonel Pagano and Sgt. Brian Caffrey had been interviewed about racial targeting and a camera crew was spotted filming on the Turnpike. The television in the kitchen was tuned to Channel 9 when the news came on at 10 o'clock. Anchorman Rolland Smith and Joe Collum appeared beside each other. After a brief introduction, the title *Without Just Cause* scrolled across the screen followed by video of a New Jersey State Police cruiser pulling onto the highway and racing off with its lights flashing.

"Interstate 95 in northern New Jersey," Collum narrated. "A state trooper parked near the mouth of the George Washington Bridge takes off in pursuit. A mile down the road he stops a car containing three black men from North Carolina. Their offense: an improper lane change. But that minor infraction has provided the trooper with an opportunity to search their car and inside he finds 15 grams of cocaine. It's another bulls-eye for the New Jersey State Police in its war on drugs."

Then Clinton Pagano's face filled the screen.

"We're in the public safety business and we're in the business to serve the citizen and keep that citizen free, free from the harmful effects of drugs," Pagano said.

The story talked about the drug war and how violence surrounding illegal narcotics was killing people every day, from police officers to the victims of drive-by shootings. Then Collum appeared, standing on a bridge overlooking the Turnpike. Beard and Sanders felt the frost in the room thicken.

"On at least one front in that war on drugs, something has gone terribly wrong. A Channel 9 I-Team investigation has found that right here on the New Jersey Turnpike state troopers are routinely fighting the drug war along racial lines. We've found case after case in which blacks and other minorities have been stopped, searched, sometimes even bullied and abused, for no apparent reason other than the color of their skin."

"This is bullshit," a trooper blurted out.

The story continued with more surveillance video of troopers searching a Lincoln Continental as three young black men from Newark sat on the hood. "Another day, another state trooper, another car carrying three black men is stopped for making an improper lane change. For nearly an hour troopers comb their car from end to end looking for drugs. It's a common sight. This time, though, they come up empty and the men are let go—without a traffic ticket."

The scene shifted to the men standing beside the highway, Collum saying they were angry because they believed they were stopped for one reason.

"Skin color, see," Mark Watts said, pointing to his arm.

"I think he pulled us over because we was black," said Wilbert Hall. "I understand they got to do their job, but when it's unnecessary I'm telling you straight up from me, it's a bunch of (bleep) man."

Beard and Sanders couldn't believe what they were seeing. Someone was saying publicly what they'd been fighting behind the scenes for more than a year. As the story continued, Nate Jones, the black school principal, claimed he was racially targeted by troopers who stopped and searched his Mercedes and arrested him for questioning them.

"That was my personal feeling," Jones said, "that I was stopped because I was a minority driving a certain type car."

Pagano appeared again saying the State Police did not condone or train troopers to use a profile and that the State Police arrested far more whites than blacks for drug offenses.

Collum countered Pagano. The I-Team, he said, had examined more than 1,300 court cases and found 76% of Turnpike drug arrests were of blacks. At the major gateways to New Jersey—the George Washington Bridge and Delaware Memorial Bridge—the arrest rate was almost 90% minority. He cited statistics from the American Council for Drug Education that showed 75% of illicit drug users in the United States were white.

For Greg Sanders the story seemed to go on forever. Exhilaration was coursing through him. He and his friends weren't alone. Finally something was going to be done. Then his heart sank. A silhouette came on the screen of a man wearing a baseball cap. His voice was electronically altered and Collum introduced him as a black state trooper.

"There is an overwhelming amount of blacks being stopped in selected areas of the Turnpike," the shadow said. "Cars are being stopped and searched without probable cause. Making that arrest is tantamount to anything else. There is obviously a pervasive problem today with illegal searches and it's going on every day."

Sanders elation instantly turned to dread. He could feel every eye in the room on him and Beard. He knew they would be prime suspects among fellow troopers for being the shadow talking on the television. When the story finally ended the reviews at Newark Station were pretty uniform.

"That motherfucker!" one trooper said.

"What a bunch of lies."

"Don't let me catch him on the Turnpike. I'll kick his ass."

Kenny Ruff watched the report at home before coming in to work the midnight shift. He was ecstatic. This was just what the Outfit needed—someone to shine a spotlight on what had been happening. It would be a cold slap in the face to the *crime dogs*. And now that the whole world knew, the big shots at HQ would have to put their foot down and force an end to racial profiling.

But if Ruff expected to find his fellow troopers contrite and remorseful he was woefully mistaken. When he got to Newark Station the place was stirring like a hornet's nest. Troopers were livid. At roll call the news report was the main topic of conversation. Ruff was asked his opinion.

"I believe it. I've seen guys doing that. I've seen some of *you* guys doing that."

That night Ruff and Beard went on patrol together. They understood the magnitude of what had just happened, but had no idea where it would lead.

"Yo, man," said Beard. "The shit just hit the fan."

Chapter 35

THE DAY AFTER THE FIRST INSTALLMENT of *Without Just Cause,* the mood inside the State Police was ugly. Troopers were angry and frustrated. The blistering August weather only made it worse. When Anthony Disalvatore arrived for the afternoon shift at Moorestown Station he noticed the shirts of troopers coming off duty were grimy and sweat stained. It was so hot, as John Starks wrote in *Troopers Behind the Badge,* that Disalvatore toyed with the idea of not wearing his bulletproof vest. On days like this troopers often opted for comfort over safety. But then he remembered a trooper who left his vest home one day to be cleaned and was shot to death. He wore the vest.

Disalvatore was 25 years old and two years out of the State Police Academy. He patrolled the Turnpike near Cocaine Alley and had been on the road only a short time that day when he saw a maroon Pontiac Bonneville with New York rental plates driving south with three black men inside. Disalvatore followed the car and pulled it over for speeding. When he walked to the window and asked the driver for his license and rental papers, James Arrington couldn't find them and seemed nervous. The trooper examined a man in the back seat with his eyes closed and suspected he was only pretending to sleep. Disalvatore sensed the men were dirty.

"You stopped me for speeding?" said Arrington.

"Yes."

"How fast did you get me?"

"Seventy."

"That's about right. You can give me a ticket."

It was an odd comment for a driver to make and Disalvatore asked Arrington to step out of the car. He wore blue sweat pants, a blue shirt, and blue cap. Disalvatore took his keys, patted him down, and asked who rented the car. Arrington said he didn't know. The trooper had a hunch the vehicle might be stolen and ordered him to sit on the hood. Then the right front door opened.

"Hey, man, what's going on?" the passenger said.

"He just wants to search the car," said Arrington, who suddenly took off running, the passenger at his heels. Then the backseat sleeper jumped out. He had a machine gun in his hands.

"Look man," he said, "just give me the keys and I'll let you out of here."

Disalvatore told author Starks that he reached for his service weapon, but too late. He saw a flash and felt white-hot pain as blood gushed from his hand. Four more shots came rapidfire, two striking the vest, one hitting his left shoulder, another penetrating his lower back. The trooper hit the ground and lay there, wondering if the shooter was going to finish him off. He struggled to his feet and took a step toward the car when another shot hit him in the left leg and he went down again. The gunman walked toward Disalvatore. His cohorts had returned and the trooper figured they were moving in for the kill.

He forced himself off the ground and shouted, "I'm gonna kick your asses!" Then he tumbled back to the dirt.

"Shit, the motherfucker's still alive!" one of them yelled.

"Shoot him! Kill him! Kill the motherfucker," another hollered.

Disalvatore raised his 9-mm pistol and began firing. His first shot hit the back of their car and the gunman fired back. Puffs of dirt exploded around the trooper and Disalvatore kept returning fire until his gun was empty. He tried to reload a fresh clip, but collapsed and lay riddled with bullets in the grassy ditch, bleeding profusely, feeling like he was about to die.

At about the same moment, Joe Collum was standing beneath a shady grove of sycamores on the banks of the Delaware River shooting the last video for *Without Just Cause*. The first segment had aired the night before. Part two was ready for broadcast that night. The third story was being edited and Collum was shooting a stand-up for the final installment. He wanted to put racial profiling in historical context and explain why the practice was contrary to what America was supposed to be all about. Washington's Crossing on the Delaware River seemed a uniquely symbolic place to do that.

"Americans have always fought against unreasonable searches," he said into the camera as the river sparkled gently behind. "On Christmas night 213 years ago, George Washington and his troops crossed the Delaware River right here on this spot to do battle. It was a turning point in the American Revolution, a war fought in great part because the British were conducting unreasonable searches against Americans. Ironically, Washington crossed the river to fight in New Jersey."

The stand-up was to be followed by an interview with Bert Neuborne, a renowned legal scholar from New York University, who explained the role unwarranted searches played in the birth of the nation.

"It precipitated the revolution," Neuborne said. "I think today we look back and like to think it was political freedom that made people want to have a revolution. But in fact what was driving people really crazy in those days was the fact they could not keep British officers out of their houses, out of their businesses, out of their lives."

The script called for the Bill of Rights to appear over Collum's narration. "After the Revolution came the Constitution. The Fourth Amendment to the United States Constitution prohibits unreasonable searches and seizures."

At that point Collum would tell the story of Chris Stubbs having her $10,000 confiscated on the Turnpike. He would not, however, mention the name of the trooper who had stopped her: Anthony Disalvatore.

After the stand-up was shot, Collum and his photographer, Micki Sellers, headed back toward North Jersey. The reporter could feel the pressure ebbing. They'd been on the story five months and had amassed a mountain of data and 40 hours of videotape they'd had to distill to 40 minutes of air time, extraordinarily lengthy for a single TV story, but it had been like trying to stuff an elephant into a bikini. For the last month Collum, Scurka, and Gardner had been pulling 18 hour days, seven days a week and they were running on empty.

The strain had been exacerbated by reaction to the previous night's first installment. Viewers were in a purple rage that the TV station was castigating the one police agency cracking down on narcotics and WWOR's switchboard was swamped:

"Slanted...Biased...Yellow journalism...Shame on you!...Morons!...The worst report I've ever seen...Blacks are being pulled over because it's blacks that are guilty of drug abuse...I will not watch your news again."

At least now the videotaping, writing, editing, and legal reviews were almost over. A couple more days and nights and they could rest. Then, as they drove away from Washington's Crossing, the car telephone rang. It was Gary Scurka.

"Are you sitting down?" he said.

"Of course I'm sitting down. I'm driving," Collum said, accustomed to his producer's dramatics.

"You're not going to believe this."

"What now?" he said, trying to imagine what could have happened.

"A trooper was just shot by three black guys with a trunk full of crack."

Collum felt like he'd been punched in the stomach.

"Get outa here," he said, hoping it was some kind of twisted joke.

"I'm not kidding," Scurka said. "It just came over the wires. The trooper's in critical condition. It sounds like he's shot up pretty bad."

"I can't believe this," Collum said in disbelief.

"You better get back here. We're already getting phone calls from people blaming us."

"My God!"

"The bosses are talking about stopping the series, not running the rest of the stories."

"They can't do that."

"That's what I say too. Get back here."

An hour later, Collum walked into the office of his boss, Tom Petner, the WWOR News Director, who was meeting with his news department managers, some of whom wanted to kill the story. Petner was a tall, mustachioed Pennsylvania Dutchman, a tough, mercurial boss with a reputation for having a short fuse. Two years earlier, Petner had created the I-Team and hired Collum as his investigative reporter. Since then they'd bumped heads on occasion, but Collum liked and respected Petner. He was a serious journalist, a rare commodity in the ratings-driven business of TV news.

"You heard?" Petner said.

"Yes. Do we know how the trooper is?"

"It doesn't sound good."

The station had sent a reporter to South Jersey to cover the story and troopers on the scene were in a hostile mood with much of their anger directed at WWOR.

"We're getting a flood of calls from people blaming the shooting on us," Petner said. "Some people think we should hold the story, not run it tonight, and maybe continue it next week out of respect for the trooper and his family."

Collum was in shock, devastated by the possibility his story might have led to a cop killing. Was it possible the drug runners had seen last night's story and decided to shoot it out with the trooper? He prayed that wasn't the case, but the fact remained that a trooper was lying near death and he was being blamed.

"Look, Joe, I've decided to go with the story tonight," Petner said.

"Okay," Collum said, dazed but relieved the report wasn't being spiked.

"There's no evidence this shooting was caused by our story."

"I hope it wasn't."

"But you're going to have to deal with this thing on the air tonight. You are going to have to talk about what happened and explain why we're running the story. And you've got to respond to the callers blaming us."

"Okay," he said, feeling like a piece of raw meat about to be thrown to the lions.

Collum went to his office thinking the story was dead, buried beneath an avalanche of vitriolic recrimination. Telephones were ringing off the hooks, the vast majority of calls coming from people spewing venom at WWOR and him. He'd never been the target of so much hate. It was the second worst day of his life. The worst had come 11 years earlier when the second of his four sons was born prematurely. Doctors had told him and his wife, Donna, not to expect the child to survive. They waited days, grief-stricken, as the baby's life hung by a thread, before he finally pulled through and survived. They named him Simon and called him their "miracle baby." Now Collum prayed for another miracle.

At 10 o'clock, WWOR led its newscast with the Disalvatore shooting. The trooper had been flown by helicopter to a South Jersey trauma center and was in critical condition. His assailants were apprehended in the vicinity of the shooting. Colonel Clinton Pagano, standing in front of a bank of microphones, described them as violent offenders with long criminal records who controlled the drug trade in Annapolis, Maryland.

"What you have here is a typical drug dealer group, as best we can determine, heading south from New York, heavily armed, en route to Baltimore to sell drugs," Pagano said.

The Superintendent didn't blame the shooting on WWOR, but he made it clear that it demonstrated why the Highway Drug Interdiction Program was important.

Minutes before Collum went on the air word came that Trooper Disalvatore was expected to survive. As he waited to be introduced, he felt like he'd gotten a reprieve just before stepping in front of a firing squad.

"A few minutes ago we told you about a New Jersey State Trooper shot on the Turnpike," anchorman Rolland Smith began. "All law-abiding citizens are appreciative of the great risks law enforcement men and women take each day. That's a given. We'll talk more about that in a few minutes. But this brings us to the story we started telling you about last night."

Then Smith introduced Collum. In his mind, this was the most important moment of his career. His credibility as a journalist and the credibility of his investigation was riding on what he'd say in the next few seconds.

"Rolland, today's shooting of the trooper on the turnpike was indeed a tragedy," he said. "But as we discussed last night the battle over drugs has become a full blown war. We can only hope that the trooper who was shot today survives. But I think the shooting, in light of what we've been reporting, makes something clear. Society is sending police two different sets of signals. One is that they must stop drugs at all costs. At the same time we tell them they must do so legally without violating our most precious rights. New Jersey State Police pride themselves on being part of an aggressive police agency and drug enforcement is their number one priority. It is recognized as one of the most successful police agencies in the nation when it comes to intercepting drugs on the highway. But at the same time there are those who claim that at least part of the troopers' success is due to selective enforcement."

The story began with Ted and Tony Wells playing with their band, then describing how they were stopped and searched by state troopers who made them sing on the side of the highway. The State Police had recorded a 122% increase in drug arrests on the Turnpike the prior year and Pagano came on and said the majority of those arrested were whites. Then Collum presented his statistics that blacks comprised 76% of Turnpike drug arrests, even though a survey by the investigative unit found blacks represented only 7% of Turnpike traffic.

"This is a great disparity," said Dr. Joseph Naus, a Rutgers University statistics professor the TV station had hired to analyze its numbers. Naus said troopers were jailing blacks at a rate 30 times higher than non-blacks. "It's such a big difference. It's not like blacks are 40% of the arrestees and 20% of the traffic. That would be a big difference too. Here you're talking about 70% and 7%. That's a very big difference."

"Profiling is illegal. We as State Police officers are not allowed to profile," Sgt. Brian Caffrey said from behind the wheel of his State Police cruiser. He insisted trooper searches were conducted after legitimate stops and almost always bore fruit. "I don't feel a trooper searches a car without coming up with something."

But a procession of minority motorists followed saying they *had* been stopped and searched and no drugs were found. When the story ended, Collum appeared again live.

"Racism is probably one of the most emotional issues we have to deal with in society today," he said. "Response to last night's story is a good indication of just how emotional it is. We've gotten hundreds of calls; many from people who say the same thing we're reporting has happened to them. On the other hand, we've gotten a lot of calls from people who say what we're reporting is not good, that it makes the police job much harder and more dangerous, which is a good topic today."

"I guess that is the question we have to ask ourselves," anchorman Smith said. "How do you answer those who are saying our report was in some way responsible for the shooting of the trooper today?"

It was the moment of truth. Collum had to deal head-on with the Disalvatore shooting. He felt too strongly about his story to let it be overwhelmed, even by such a terrible tragedy. Knowing the trooper would survive was an enormous relief, but he knew a lot of viewers were blaming him for the shooting. He took a deep breath and stated his case.

"It's a horrible fact of life, but there have been many police officers who've been shot before today and, although we hope it doesn't come to this, there will almost certainly be policemen shot in the future. The press was not responsible before and I don't think we were responsible today. I think our job as journalists is that when we become aware of a problem, a significant social problem, it's our job to go out and find out if it's true and, if it is, to lay it out on the table and expose it to the light of day so it can be dealt with. What we're dealing with here is a significant segment of our society claiming they are the victims of racism. They are not drug dealers, they're decent law-abiding citizens, but they are being made to feel like criminals. It's a very tough problem. It's a complex problem. But it's a problem that has to be dealt with. It's not going to go away, no matter what happened today."

By the end of the week the flood of hate calls had slowed to a trickle. Most callers were people reporting that they, too, had been victims of racial targeting. Collum believed the weight of evidence had convinced all but the most hardcore skeptics that the allegations had substance. The final segment ended with Pagano's response to Collum's question about whether he had a serious concern about minorities feeling their rights were being violated.

"It is of serious concern," Pagano said, "but nowhere near the concern I think we have got to look to in trying to correct some of the problems found with the criminal element in this state."

Chapter 36

THE NEW JERSEY STATE POLICE had been humiliated on national television (WWOR was a superstation carried by 1,800 cable TV outlets across the country and as far away as Guam), one of their brethren had been shot and nearly killed, and the Outfit had been betrayed by two black Judas Iscariots. But anyone who expected troopers to crawl off like whipped dogs to lick their wounds didn't know the State Police. There would be no sudden spasm of soul searching, no admissions of guilt, not even promises of investigation. Instead, they lashed out.

Troopers had the license numbers of WWOR's news vehicles and, in the days following the airing of *Without Just Cause,* several station employees were ticketed and told they could blame Joe Collum. The reporter had become a regular topic of roll call scuttlebutt. There was talk about where he lived and what kind of car he drove and a printout of his driving record was taped to the Newark Station squad room door.

"If you see that scumbag, write him a ticket," one sergeant told his squad.

Inside the barracks, the ill wind that had been blowing became a full-scale squall.

As Greg Sanders feared, a manhunt began to identify the anonymous black troopers in silhouette. The organization became obsessed with finding the turncoats. Vocabulary became a key clue. Who among the *federal troops* was smart enough to use a multi-syllabic word like *tantamount?*

White troopers asked black troopers to put on baseball caps and say *pervasive*. The Black Radicals were the primary suspects. Their academic credentials were better than most of the white troopers and the culprits were narrowed down to Sanders and Anthony Reed.

"I heard Sanders say 'pervasive'," a trooper told Glenn Johnson.

"Was Tony Reed one of them guys?" a lieutenant asked Darryl Beard.

"What do you mean, sir?" Beard said.

"We know its not you because the guy wasn't as big as you."

Reed's picture and badge number were superimposed onto a wanted poster and pinned to the walls at Newark Station with the caption: *"Last seen on Channel 9 I-Team Report."* But the black troopers refused to be cowed.

"How can you say that's profiling? It's a technique," a white trooper argued.

"Eighty to ninety percent of the Turnpike is used by whites," Sanders said, "but 75-80% of the people arrested are black. Something's wrong with that."

"Shut up. You don't know what you're talking about."

At HQ, Clinton Pagano went on the offensive, too. He believed *Without Just Cause* had been wildly inaccurate and ordered the State Police Analytical Unit to dig up numbers to refute it. At the same time, racial tension in the organization had reached a tipping point. He was inundated by white troopers demanding he launch an investigation to identify the anonymous black troopers. Pagano had to act quickly to sustain order.

Within days of the broadcast, the Superintendent ordered every trooper to watch *Without Just Cause* followed by a videotaped statement from Pagano. The tape opened with a shot of a big blue and gold "State Police NJ" sign and dissolved to the Colonel sitting on the front edge of his desk with arms folded, dressed in his blue State Police blouse with a gold triangle on the shoulder.

"What you have just seen is, I guess, a television exposé of the operations of our Division on the New Jersey Turnpike. The thrust of this presentation is that we seem to be discriminating, we are targeting black motorists, we are harping on minorities. And that really is not the case in my judgment. Joe Collum said in the last segment that I don't seem to understand the problem or that I won't recognize the problem. What I say to you is he really doesn't understand the problem. He doesn't understand what law enforcement is about," Pagano said as the camera slowly zoomed in.

"Drugs are a tremendous menace in our society, the number one priority for enforcement in this Division. And we've done amazing things in this area and we're going to continue doing them. I don't want and you don't want discriminatory enforcement. I said a long time ago when you put this uniform on you leave your biases, you leave your prejudices behind. That does not mean when we put the heat on and we begin arresting the kind of offenders that we have been arresting, that we're not going to get some reverse flow coming in our direction. It unfortunately, for Trooper Anthony Disalvatore, came in a very violent confrontation last week."

Pagano talked about some of the allegations. He said Nate Jones had assaulted the troopers who'd stopped him in "his fancy new Mercedes." Paul McLemore, he said, should be the last person to call anyone racist. "I don't know exactly what to call him, but if nothing else I'd call him an ingrate.

"I don't want every white trooper looking at every black trooper thinking he was the guy who appeared in these segments. I think that's something we've got to get beyond very quickly. What we've accomplished is absolutely super. Get out there and keep the heat on drug abusers," Pagano said, speaking more rapidly. "Here at Division headquarters we'll make sure that when the wheels start to squeak we'll do whatever we can to make sure that you are supported out in the field. Don't you be discouraged, don't you be suspicious of the people around you. You just do the job and we'll see these problems through and I appreciate the work you've done. Thanks a lot, fellas and girls."

But despite the confident assurances, Pagano was under fierce attack from the outside. The influential *New Jersey Law Journal* called for an investigation of the State Police.

"In our judgment, the Channel 9 investigation, if as represented, makes a prima facie case of impropriety not rebutted by Col. Pagano's self-serving declaration. The charges made by the Channel 9 investigative reporters are among the most grave that can be made against a state entity and its director. If true, they would mean that our premier law enforcement agency is engaged in unconstitutional conduct."

The *Law Journal* carried a letter from a private attorney, Philip De Vencentes, calling for Pagano's ouster.

"Col. Pagano's position seemed to be the all too familiar but nonetheless chilling one that if it is necessary to impinge upon fundamental rights in order to win the 'war' on drugs, it is an acceptable price to pay. It is not an acceptable price to pay, and anyone in Col. Pagano's position who suggests it is should either resign or be summarily fired."

But Pagano remained pugnacious as ever. He refused to concede there was a problem and, in a written response to the *Law Journal,* made it clear he was not about to be bullied by a TV station or defense lawyers.

"In the writings of Mr. De Vencentes, I find the same frustration that I have witnessed on the part of many other attorneys where, when the facts and the law are uncontroverted, they resort to any device to defend their clients. Claims of targeting, racism and profiling are common but it is up to the judge sitting in review of the facts that really counts."

Pagano's defiant response wasn't mere saber rattling. He was about to surpass the legendary Herbert Norman Schwarzkopf as the longest serving Superintendent in State Police history. Pagano was an icon, an institution, invulnerable, untouchable. And the possibility didn't seem to occur to him, or anyone else, that his reign of power might be doomed.

Chapter 37

THREE WEEKS AFTER *WITHOUT JUST CAUSE* was broadcast, Collum returned to State Police headquarters.

The sensation of crossing enemy lines was even more palpable this time. He was back for a follow-up interview with Clinton Pagano. He'd requested a meeting shortly after the report aired, but the State Police put him off saying they were investigating the validity—or lack thereof—of his allegations.

In the meantime, WWOR was being swamped by callers claiming to be victims of racial targeting by the State Police. One was David Charles, a 25-year-old African-American from New York, who said he'd been stopped and searched eight times but never ticketed. In January 1989—long before *Without Just Cause* had aired—Charles paid $207 to have a sign made for the top of his car. He still had the receipt. Collum's team filmed him driving down the Turnpike with the billboard strapped to his car roof.

"N.J. STATE POLICEMEN MUST STOP HARASSING BLACK MOTORISTS."

"If I'm not doing something wrong, I don't deserve to be hassled," Charles said. "I certainly don't deserve to be stopped and searched because some police officer feels black males are druggies."

Lynn and Nathan Carr, a black couple from Connecticut, thought what happened to them had been an isolated case, that they'd simply run into a malicious cop on their way home from Atlantic City. Now they realized they weren't alone.

"It's something I'll never forget," Lynn Carr said. "He searched the trunk, under the hood, our luggage, and our packages. He was very cruel and mean. He was talking down to my husband. He made my husband feel inhuman. When it was all over we had to sit in the car and just get ourselves together because we were actually in a state of shock."

The avalanche of calls led Collum to suspect racial profiling might be more widespread than he'd imagined. Nonetheless, when the State Police called to say Pagano was ready to talk, he was wary. He walked into the Superintendent's office with a vague sense of dread, half expecting Pagano to drop some kind of grenade in his lap that would blow *Without Just Cause* out of the water. Why else would he expose himself to another interview?

Collum knew Pagano believed he'd been a victim of yellow journalism and expected him to come out swinging. But, as before, Pagano was gentlemanly, if not as cordial as their first encounter. He also seemed a trace nervous, not as confident, which made the reporter wonder if he had that grenade, after all. There was one surprise. A State Police camera crew was waiting. Pagano said he didn't think he'd been fairly represented in the report and wanted his own record of this interview.

"We deny targeting," he began. "We deny orienting our people or that it's a general practice on the part of members of the State Police to stop people on the basis of race or ethnic origin. We don't want to offend the constitutional rights of any motorist. We're the keepers of the Constitution."

Pagano said the statistics Collum presented didn't prove anything, that he'd examined the wrong data. Instead of *arrests* the reporter should have looked at *searches*. Collum said he wasn't aware of any records on searches. Pagano said "Consent to Search" forms were filled out every time a trooper searched a car. They listed the driver's race and the *probable cause* that prompted the trooper to search.

"I'd like to see those forms," Collum said.

"You can't. The people involved are innocent parties. When you go splatter-board and release all these reports they are really impugning the constitutional rights of people who weren't convicted."

Pagano was playing a game of *Catch 22*, claiming Collum had looked at the wrong records, but refusing him access to the right ones, then invoking the Constitution to protect the same people whose rights were being violated.

"The last time we spoke you challenged my statistics," Collum said. "You said troopers arrested more whites than blacks on the turnpike. Do you stand by that?"

Pagano had been waiting for the question. He opened his desk drawer and pulled out a thin sheaf of papers. The cover page said: "Confidential: For Official Use Only." Collum held his breath. This had to be the bombshell he'd been dreading.

"We've done an analysis," Pagano said, passing a single page across the desk. "In one respect this particular report, in a statistical sense, takes us closer to the figures that you extrapolated."

Collum wasn't sure what Pagano meant and winced as he studied the paper. It was a breakdown of State Police arrests for 1988. The first thing that jumped out was that 70% of the Outfit's arrests statewide for all crimes were of whites. And nearly 60% of drug and weapons arrests across New Jersey were also of whites. That confirmed what Pagano said before. Then he read the fourth paragraph. He was flabbergasted.

"In 1988, blacks accounted for 76.3% of all drug and weapon arrests on the I-95/Turnpike corridor."

"When you narrow just to the Turnpike," Pagano said, his words not coming easy now, "you'll realize it validates in some respects the statistics you portrayed in your series."

Validates! 76% black arrests was *exactly* what Collum had reported, the same number that Pagano denied and warned him about using. It was a bombshell alright, but Pagano had dropped it on himself. Collum's dread suddenly turned to elation.

"How can you say troopers aren't racially profiling when your own analysis confirms blacks make up three-quarters of arrests?" he said.

"When you look at the corridor nature of the New Jersey Turnpike," Pagano said hesitantly, "that joining together of Washington, Philadelphia, and New York City, what you find really is probably that it's the demographic phenomenon that results in the otherwise illogical apprehension of black offenders on the Turnpike. I would say it's more of a phenomenon than it is a targeting. We disagree with your perspective."

It took Collum a few seconds to digest the Superintendent's words, but it sounded like Pagano was blaming the high rate of black arrests on the fact the Jersey Turnpike was a conduit between New York and other big cities with large minority populations.

"I think, if anything, we validated some of your statistics," Pagano said, almost as if trying to appease the reporter.

No kidding! Collum thought. The colonel let him scribble some notes from the analysis, but then took it back without allowing him to examine the rest of the report. Collum could only imagine what kind of juicy tidbits he was not seeing. But, at that point, he didn't care. A giant weight had been lifted from his shoulders. Then, out of the blue, Pagano volunteered one other piece of information.

"Maybe it's my ego speaking, but I think that some parts of the series had a binding effect on our people, bringing them closer together."

At the time, Collum had no way to know that the exact opposite was true.

Chapter 38

As 1989 CAME TO A CLOSE, THE WOES mounted for the highway drug interdiction gang. In October, flamboyant Salem County prosecutor Frank Hoerst III was abruptly yanked from office after state auditors uncovered evidence he had embezzled and misused large sums drug money seized on Cocaine Alley. More than $380,000 was unaccounted for and Hoerst had spent $15,000 taking friends and relatives—including his girlfriend—to Florida and California, supposedly for "training sessions." He spent $8,000 learning to fly an airplane and $5,000 to install a stereo system in his car. Hoerst saved himself from prison by doing what he'd done best as a prosecutor. He cut a deal and pleaded guilty to a lesser charge that kept him out of the slammer.

Another high profile prosecutor, Sam Asbell of Camden County, was also forced from office after he claimed Jamaican drug dealers tried to assassinate him during a high speed chase in retaliation for his aggressive war against narcotics. But it turned out Asbell had blown out his own car windows with a .12 gauge shotgun, in an apparent attempt to make himself look like a tough, law-and-order prosecutor. Asbell resigned and signed himself into a psychiatric treatment program and, like Hoerst, avoided prison.

While Hoerst and Asbell were flaming out, Clinton Pagano was trying to put out several fires that threatened to engulf him. A number of Turnpike troopers, including Robert Henig, were indicted on new charges. The Highway Drug Interdiction Program was showing signs of collapse with drug arrests dropping by more than half.

A hullabaloo erupted when it was disclosed troopers had been hanging out in men's bathrooms at the Vince Lombardi Turnpike Service Plaza in North Jersey trying to catch homosexuals. Scathing newspaper editorials accused Pagano of entrapping gay men.

Then Pagano got a telephone call from Attorney General Peter Perretti. He wanted a meeting with Alfred Slocum, New Jersey's first African-American Public Defender. Slocum had long believed state troopers were targeting blacks on the Turnpike and refused to even drive on the highway. Even so, Slocum was no zealot. Walter Marvin was chomping at the bit to go public with tape recordings and other evidence he'd accumulated during his months of undercover surveillance in Middlesex County. To Marvin's dismay, Slocum refused to allow it, saying he didn't want to destroy the State Police.

"I've got a wife, I've got children, and 95% of what the State Police are doing is in my best interest," Slocum argued. "Why because I'm upset about 5% of what they do would you have me dismantle the entire thing so we don't get the 95% benefit?"

The meeting with Pagano lasted about 45 minutes. Slocum produced Marvin's surveillance tapes and explained that his office had been spying on the State Police for months and identified a score of troopers they believed were targeting black motorists. All of them had black arrest rates of 70-to-100%. Slocum savored the look of shock on Pagano's face, but said he wasn't there to crucify the State Police. Instead, he wanted what was best for his clients. He wanted a deal.

"When I give you this stuff I'm done with it," Slocum said. "I told my people they were done with it."

Slocum got his deal. He turned over the tapes and the State eventually dismissed more than 600 criminal drug arrests by Turnpike troopers in Middlesex County. Slocum believed the problem simply would go away. First there had been the television investigation, and now this. Pagano and the State Police had no choice but to cease and desist targeting minority drivers. Slocum was convinced of it.

Chapter 39

ON AN ARCTIC SUNDAY NIGHT IN EARLY FEBRUARY 1990, Clinton Pagano sat facing two men in a dimly lit office on the eighth floor of the Hughes Justice Complex in Trenton. He had known both men for years, yet there was no exchange of pleasantries. One of them, Robert Del Tufo, was the new Attorney General of New Jersey. He got right to the point.

"The governor thinks a change is needed. We agree with him."

Pagano's eyes betrayed a glint of astonishment. *He did not expect this,* Del Tufo realized. A few days before, Pagano had a cordial face-to-face with new Governor Jim Florio and came away believing his job was secure. Elated, he returned to HQ and told his closest aides they were safe for four more years. Pagano would surpass the legend Schwarzkopf's unprecedented 15 years at the helm of the Outfit. But he'd misread Florio. The unthinkable had happened. Pagano was being fired.

"Who?" he asked. Del Tufo told him his successor's name. Pagano flinched.

He should have seen it coming. Too much had gone bad in recent months. All the nasty racial profiling business on television, troopers indicted, hundreds of drug cases thrown out of court. As all that played out, Florio watched with distaste. After the election he appointed Del Tufo Attorney General and told him to fix the State Police. He thought Pagano had become too high and mighty. Del Tufo did not disagree. He'd known Pagano since the 1970s when

Del Tufo was the number two man in the Attorney General's Office. Even then Pagano was a handful. Somewhere along the line he'd left the reservation and created his own empire built on a cult of personality. Del Tufo's predecessors, Cary Edwards and Peter Perretti, told him Pagano was a monumental headache. If he didn't get his way, he simply went over their heads to the Governor or Legislature. Edwards was tempted to fire Pagano but knew he lacked the political clout.

Getting rid of New Jersey's *J. Edgar Hoover* would be sticky business. Pagano had powerful friends. And no one knew if he had secret dossiers, or what might be in them. If his sacking wasn't handled delicately, things could get ugly. Del Tufo needed more information.

That led him to Justin Dintino, the former State Police sage of the underworld. After his retirement five years earlier, Dintino was offered several jobs, including chief of security for the Casino Association, a coalition of Atlantic City gambling houses. He'd have a car, office, secretary, staff, and a lucrative long term contract. For a man with three children in college it was an enticing proposal. But Dintino didn't feel right about it. He'd spent his career building a squeaky clean reputation. Working for the casinos might sully that. His kids told him to take the job. "You'll still be the same honest person," they said.

Dintino was tempted, but he'd also been offered another job as Chief of Intelligence for the State Commission of Investigations, a New Jersey watchdog agency created to root out government fraud and corruption. The State job paid only half what the casinos were offering, but Dintino took it, deciding he'd rather be able to sleep at night.

Del Tufo had known Dintino as long as he'd known Pagano and considered him intelligent, strong willed and a man of impeccable integrity. He told him he needed an unvarnished analysis of the State Police and asked Dintino to put together a confidential white paper for Florio. Dintino quickly said yes. After 33 years as a trooper he still cared deeply about the Outfit. The State Police had serious problems and it was an opportunity to get in his two cents worth and have some influence on the department's future.

Dintino got right to work. Racial profiling was the hot button issue and he highlighted it. He'd seen the practice grow from the early 1980s when the cowboys patrolling Cocaine Alley started generating gaudy drug arrest statistics chasing the Trooper of the Year award.

Dintino had warned Pagano there was a problem, but to no avail. It all came to a head when the TV report *Without Just Cause* put a face to the statistics. Dintino had watched, deeply affected by the accounts of people like Valerie Taylor, the young mother from Washington, D.C. who described her terror on the side of the Turnpike as troopers threatened to take her kids away if she didn't let them search her car. In his report, Dintino criticized highway drug interdiction as a product of small-time thinking designed to generate flashy statistics but making zero impact on the drug problem. While troopers were pre-occupied busting people with dime bags of marijuana, sophisticated organized criminal groups were going untouched. Worse, though, it was illegal. Citizen rights, he wrote, had to be the number one priority.

Dintino didn't know a decision had been made to replace Pagano and didn't criticize him by name, although he did refer to problems the "next Superintendent" needed to address. If there was a new leader, Dintino planned to push for Major Richard Jankowski, a former protégé. Jankowski was smart and a straight shooter who Dintino thought would make a good Superintendent. Dintino had no ambition to return to the State Police. He was collecting a nice pension and was happy at the State Commission of Investigations. But after he turned in his white paper he sensed Florio was considering him as the next Superintendent. He suddenly realized it would be a chance to go back and fix the State Police. It also occurred to him that de-throning Pagano would be extremely gratifying.

Dintino was asked to meet with Florio and, a few days after Christmas 1989, the two of them sat down alone to dinner at Matha's Farm, an out of the way Italian eatery in South Jersey. Their only contact previous to this had come when Dintino testified before one of Florio's committees during the governor-elect's term in the U.S. House of Representatives. Where Florio was a liberal Democrat, Dintino was apolitical. He was registered as an independent but, being philosophically conservative, usually voted Republican.

Florio was an intriguing character. He came across to many as a cold fish, but Dintino liked what he knew about him. He was a product of the rough-and-tumble Camden Democratic machine, and he looked it. The left side of his face was caved in, the result of his cheekbone being crushed as a young boxer. Unlike so many New Jersey pols, there was no outward evidence Florio had cashed in on the spoils of office. In 1980 the FBI tried to hook him in the ABSCAM bribery sting operation which snared New Jersey's U.S. Senator Harrison A. Williams, Jr. and several members of Congress. But the Feds never got to first base with Florio. If he was crooked he hid it well. While in Congress he lived in a one room apartment over a Washington, D.C. tailor shop. His New Jersey residence was a modest apartment. His financial statement was pathetic, showing a lower net worth than the average trooper. Florio drove up to Matha's Farm in a used black police car he'd bought at a state auction. To Dintino it was the mark of an honest man.

The Governor-elect didn't waste time on small talk. He wanted to replace Pagano and asked Dintino if he'd be interested. After Dintino said yes, Florio asked if there was anything embarrassing in his background. The worst thing Dintino could think of was that he sometimes bet on horse races at the track. That was good enough for Florio. He told him to keep the job secret until the change was announced. Dintino told no one but his wife, afraid if Pagano got wind he'd try to undermine his appointment. And Pagano and his people did have their tentacles out. Dintino suspected they'd even gotten to his barber.

"Could you come back as Superintendent?" the barber asked him.

"Yeah, I could, but I ain't interested in going back," Dintino said, even creating a cover story. "I'm going to buy a house in Florida and retire."

Florio was sworn in January 17, 1990. A few days later he met with Pagano. They had an amiable discussion and Florio gave no indication he planned to axe him. The dirty work was left to Del Tufo.

On that bitter wintry night, the Attorney General and Florio's chief counsel, Steve Perskie, broke the news to Pagano. He was out and his old rival Dintino was in.

Pagano protested that it wasn't fair. He'd given 38 years to the State Police and built it into one of the premier law enforcement agencies in America. Now, he was getting the boot? It was humiliating. Pagano said he deserved better. Wasn't there something they could do for him? Wasn't there another job in the administration, something that could be portrayed as a promotion? Del Tufo and Perskie looked at each other. They knew Pagano could cause problems if he was dragged out kicking and screaming. The Department of Motor Vehicles Director's job was open and would at least let him save face. He'd earn a $90,000 salary plus collect a handsome State Police pension, a total of $158,000 a year, enough ointment to salve his wounded pride.

Perskie left the room and made a telephone call. Dintino was home in bed asleep. He knew the boom was being lowered on Pagano that night, but turned in early anyway. Perskie explained what was happening and asked if he would object to Pagano being given the DMV job. Dintino was surprised by the question. Who was he to say no? Besides, he wouldn't have to work with Pagano at DMV. No, he said, he didn't object.

The next day Florio announced Dintino's appointment as State Police Superintendent. Pagano would take on a "new challenge" at DMV. The governor refused to criticize Pagano and said his new position was "mutually agreed to." But the spin control didn't fool anyone. Pagano's new assignment wasn't a promotion, lateral move, or even a step down. "It's a 12-story fall," one senator said. Even Pagano couldn't muster a happy face.

"I'm absolutely disappointed," he said. "I'm not sure if I got a pat on the back or a kick in the ass."

On the morning of February 15, 1990, the New Jersey Senate unanimously confirmed Dintino as Superintendent of the State Police. Two hours later he was sworn into office.

That afternoon Dintino drove to State Police headquarters for the first time in five years. When he walked into the Superintendent's office, Clinton Pagano was kneeling on the floor packing his belongings. Someone snapped a photograph of Dintino standing over Pagano, smiling down like an avenging angel. It was the happiest moment of Dintino's professional life.

In Pagano's quest to retain power, he had betrayed Dintino and dozens of senior troopers. Now he'd been unceremoniously shorn of that power and, adding to the indignity, it had been bestowed upon Dintino. Ironically, Pagano's duplicity had made Dintino's appointment possible. By selfishly cutting a deal for himself in making the Superintendent the only State Police post exempt from mandatory retirement at age 55, Pagano had set the table for Dintino to replace him at age 61.

But Dintino had no time to savor the poetic justice of it all. He faced a daunting task. The State Police's lustrous reputation had been badly tarnished and a proud organization had been branded as a gang of racist thugs. The day before Dintino's confirmation, two more troopers were indicted for beating and robbing motorists on the Turnpike.

"It's an embarrassment and a black eye to the organization," Dintino said his first day in office. "I promise you abuse of authority will not be tolerated."

A few days later Dintino held his first staff meeting, a three-and-a-half hour affair. The entire State Police hierarchy was present. Dintino came on strong. Pagano had been their supreme commander for 15 years and he wanted them all to know it was a new day. Particularly where minorities were concerned.

In the 15 years since a federal court ordered Pagano to boost minority representation among troopers to 14%, blacks still comprised less than 2% of the force. Dintino vowed to change that.

"What does that mean?" a major asked.

"It means that in hiring and making promotions, minorities will get preferential treatment," the new Superintendent said.

Dintino could see shock on their faces. Clinton Pagano had never said anything like that and it hit them right between the eyes. It was obvious a lot of them didn't like it, but Dintino didn't care.

Then he dropped another bomb—highway drug interdiction was no longer the number one State Police priority.

"I'd rather see a drop in drug statistics than have troopers violate the rights of the driving public. Let the word go forth there will be no activity that abridges the rights of any citizen. Take that message back to the troopers today."

Chapter 40

WILLIAM BUCKMAN'S FIRST ENCOUNTER with the New Jersey State Police occurred on a summer day in 1970. He was 17 at the time and he and a friend were hitch-hiking at an entrance ramp on the New Jersey Turnpike, wearing the uniform of the day: longish hair, T-shirt, and faded jeans. Two troopers drove up and did something that astonished and frightened Buckman. They eased the front bumper of their cruiser up to the teenagers' knees and slowly inched forward, smiling as they forced the boys backwards 10, 20, 30 feet. They finally stopped and got out. Buckman's friend was wearing a backpack which the troopers took and searched.

"You can't hitchhike on the Turnpike," one said. "Get the hell off this ramp."

The incident only reinforced Buckman's already negative attitude toward authority. He'd learned about the abuse of power early in life, his education coming inside a Philadelphia row house on a large corner lot at 6338 Summerdale Avenue.

Buckman was the third of Joseph and Betty Buckman's four children, born in 1953, raised in Oxford Circle, a white, middle-class, primarily Jewish enclave populated by World War II veterans and their families. "Dr." Buckman, as everyone called him, was an optometrist. The Buckman's weren't rich, but they had more than most families on the block, like the first power lawnmower and first color TV. By all outward signs they were a wholesome all-American family, a Jewish Norman Rockwell painting.

But, as far back as Buckman could remember, he lived in fear. Two or three times every week Joe or Betty Buckman, or sometimes both, would erupt in volcanic rage over some indiscretion committed by their son—real or imagined. Mom or Dad would grab the dog's chain leash and flog him, screaming: "You miserable, rotten kid! You're killing us!" Buckman would wail in agony and run to his bedroom for sanctuary, cowering in terror until the storm passed.

His life was dominated by the violence. Yet, almost miraculously, he was a bright, precocious kid who liked to work with his hands and had a mechanical mind, tinkering, building models, figuring out how things worked.

By the time Buckman was 8 or 9 he'd developed a vague perception that the beatings were unjustified. He began to see his mom and dad were not stable people and that he was a victim of irrational violence. The concept was still hazy, but it was his first awareness that the arbitrary use of power, unchecked, could lead to abuse, even destruction.

There were other lessons to be learned in Oxford Circle. There were no blacks or minorities in the neighborhood. Like many Jewish families, the Buckman's were slightly left of moderate. They were also racist. Racial jokes were often told around the dinner table. The word *nigger* was rarely uttered but *schvatza*—the Yiddish equivalent—was common. In their cloistered world, blacks were alien and even the children openly made fun of them.

Yet, one day Buckman and his brothers were watching *The Huntley-Brinkley Report* on NBC News. Rev. Martin Luther King was giving a speech and the children were mocking the *schvatza* when their father walked into the room. Despite his own prejudices, Dr. Buckman scolded his kids.

"I will not have you talk like that about this man who is doing great things," he said. "He is trying to free his people."

His father's words hit young Buckman harder than the dog's chain. He'd grown up in walled isolation, oblivious to the outside world, and it was the first time he realized the United States was not the same place he was being taught about in history class. The "land-of-the-free" was a segregated society where people were fighting for basic human rights like voting, going to the same schools as whites, eating at the same lunch counters, even using the same toilets. People were risking their lives standing up against hate and discrimination. Buckman began regarding the Negro protesters he saw on TV being beaten, sprayed with fire hoses, and attacked by police dogs in a new light, as flesh and blood human beings.

When Buckman was 16 his parents sent him away for the summer, mainly to get him out of the house. Friends recommended a place called Fellowship Farm, a Quaker facility just outside Philadelphia. His mother and father assumed it was some kind of summer camp, but it was actually a learning center for civil rights and anti-Vietnam war activists who flocked there from around the country to be trained in non-violent protest. Rosa Parks, Martin Luther King, and Malcolm X had lectured there. For the first time in his life, Buckman lived and ate and conversed with people of all faiths and colors.

Fellowship Farm had a big, pleasant dining hall with a fireplace and one night after dinner, during the nice quiet time after tables were cleaned and there was nothing pressing and people were going back for second desserts, a half dozen people sat around shooting the breeze. Buckman was the youngest of them. As they talked, attention eventually turned to him and Bill started telling them about his home life. As he spoke he realized everyone had grown quiet, their faces painted with shock. All his life the Buckman's had been an Ozzie and Harriet kind of family, at least to the outside world. Now he had told them the family *secret* and they were appalled.

"This should not be happening," someone said. "You are being abused." No one ever told him that before.

When Bill returned home the inevitable happened. Joe Buckman became enraged over some small incident and, as was his pattern, came out swinging. But over the summer his son had grown into a man. When his father attacked, Buckman knocked him to the ground. As the father lay stunned, his son screamed at him.

"Win, lose, or draw, you try to touch me again and you're going to be in a fight and as I get stronger you're going to lose and, even if you don't, it'll be ugly."

"It's your fault!" Joe Buckman bellowed at his wife "You sent him to where all those free thinkers are!"

Joseph Buckman never apologized to his son, but he never raised a hand to him again. Bill always regretted using violence against his father, but it was a watershed moment in his life. He had learned that, one way or another, it was imperative for him to stand up to tyranny.

Buckman's first job out of law school was clerking for New Jersey Superior Court Judge Herman Belopolsky, a large, heavyset man with big jowls who looked like a fat Doberman pinscher and spoke like the actor Charles Laughton, minus the British accent. Belopolsky was a good judge who also had a salty streak. After sentencing a violent criminal to 15 years in prison the convict shouted: "Fuck you, Judge!" Belopolsky ordered his court stenographer to stop typing and turned to the defendant. "Fuck you, too!" he said, then nodded to his stenographer to begin typing again. "You have a right to appeal my sentence. Have a good day, sir."

Belopolsky handled a lot of State Police cases in South Jersey and Buckman noticed that defense lawyers routinely asked him to suppress or throw out evidence, claiming troopers had violated the rights of their clients. Unlike many judges who almost automatically disregarded such motions, Belopolsky frequently challenged State Police officers, refusing to accept their testimony as gospel. In one case involving a van stopped on the Turnpike, the people had a cat with them and a litter box. The trooper arrested them on drug charges after, he said, he smelled marijuana.

"Did you smell the cat piss too?" the judge asked him.

"No," the trooper said, "I'm only trained to smell marijuana."

Belopolsky threw out the case.

During that time, Buckman detected a disturbing pattern. The vast majority of drug cases coming off the Turnpike involved young long-haired white guys and he became convinced troopers were targeting hippie-types. One day while having lunch with a group of clerks, the conversation turned to a particular trooper whose arrest reports seemed identical, like carbon copies. A long-hair *"stopped for weaving between lanes prompted a search where drugs were found."* Most of the clerks suspected something was afoot, but didn't think it was illegal.

"The law says [state troopers] can stop them if they have a reasonable basis," they argued. "Weaving between lanes is a reasonable basis."

Buckman disagreed. There had to be a way, he said, to show that troopers were stopping long-hairs based on a pretext and that the law was being used cynically. It was a rudimentary argument, just a seed of an idea, but it was the first time Buckman articulated the legal premise that, a decade-and-a-half later, became the basis of a court action that would shake the New Jersey State Police to its core.

Chapter 41

ROBERT HENIG WAS FACING A WORLD of trouble. He was under indictment for the Delbert Blair case, for allegedly stealing $160 from a motorist, and for purportedly brutalizing Kenneth Lowengrub and Stacy Brown at East Brunswick Station. He needed a champion.

Francis Hartman was a burly, white-bearded barrister from South Jersey renowned for a homespun courtroom style he used to convince juries his clients were "on the side of the angels." Hartman had been an attorney for 30 years and the law was ingrained in his family's genetic code. His three daughters were lawyers, as were a couple of nephews and two brothers-in-law, plus his father-in-law was a judge.

"I've heard about you," Henig told him at their first meeting. "I'd like you to represent me, if I can afford you."

"First of all, don't worry too much about affording me," Hartman said. "When I represent good guys, I get the bad guys to pay a little more to even things out."

"If it makes any difference to you," Henig said, "I didn't do what I'm accused of."

"Well, it does make a little difference, but not a lot. I've never really been concerned whether my clients did the act they're accused of because there are other things besides the act that make it or don't make it a crime." Hartman could see his new client was stressed. "In these police brutality cases we have a pretty good edge," he said. "The people accusing you are criminals."

"Well," said Henig, "the main witness against me was Trooper of the Year."

"Oh!" said Hartman. "I guess we do have a problem."

William Sweeney had edged out Henig as the 1988 Trooper of the Year, the first black trooper to win the honor. Now he was going to testify that he'd seen Henig viciously beat a defenseless prisoner, Lowengrub. Hartman's working theory was that the State Police were making Henig a sacrificial lamb to appease critics of racial profiling. But five other troopers had also been indicted in the case for brutality and/or cover up. Their lawyers considered Henig a leper and were planning to let him take the fall to save their clients. Hartman was ready to go to war with them.

"Henig's defense will be proving the guilt of his co-defendants," he wrote in one of his first court motions, serving notice to his co-counsels that he would let the bad blood flow if they tried to make Henig their scapegoat.

The threat prompted a meeting between the defense lawyers. Sitting around a conference table munching pizza, the other attorneys told Hartman their clients intended to testify that Henig had in fact beaten the men. If that meant he was convicted, so be it. Hartman argued forcefully that they should stick together.

"Henig is the pivot of the case," he said. "If the jury doesn't believe my client did the things he's accused of, it's not going to believe your guys covered up for him."

By the time they finished Hartman had sold them. Saving Henig would save everyone. There was only one problem. No one but Hartman believed Henig could be saved.

Chapter 42

A FEW DAYS AFTER BEING SWORN IN AS New Jersey State Police Superintendent, Justin Dintino had a coming out party of sorts. The banquet room of the Mastoris Diner in Bordentown was packed with hundreds of troopers and their families who'd come to pay tribute to Anthony DiSalvatore, the trooper bushwhacked by drug smugglers six months earlier.

DiSalvatore had been one of the rising stars of Clinton Pagano's highway drug program when he attained the solitary distinction of surviving more gunshot wounds than any trooper in State Police history. On this night he was to receive one of the Outfit's highest honors—the Distinguished Service Award for courage under extreme pressure—to be presented by Governor Jim Florio.

The occasion was also Justin Dintino's first official appearance as Superintendent and, when he was introduced, the large crowd greeted him with polite but tepid applause. A few minutes later Pagano walked in and the room erupted in thunderous ovation. Dintino stood by, rock-jawed, surveying several tables of brawny young troopers near the front of the room heaping the most boisterous adulation on Pagano. Each wore his hair shaved so short that, to Dintino, they looked disturbingly like skin heads.

The contrasting receptions spoke volumes about the mood in the Outfit.

Dintino had wasted little time ruffling feathers. He didn't intend to be on the job long, certainly not 15 years like Pagano. He wanted to strike fast and with resolve and had promptly begun promoting, demoting, issuing edicts, and stepping on toes.

One of Dintino's first acts was to give a symbolic slap in the face to his predecessor. For years Pagano had hosted an annual State Police golf tournament to raise money for families of troopers killed in the line of duty. It had grown into a huge event with more than 700 guests, many from the trucking and casino industries, which were regulated by the State Police. Participants paid $400 for a day of golf, food, and libations. Patrons could also pay $1,000 to become members of *The Colonel's Club,* giving them entrée to an exclusive cocktail party, a photograph with Pagano, and a gold membership card. Pagano denied the cards were intended to inoculate holders from traffic tickets, but that's what they were used for. Dintino considered the tournament a shakedown and cancelled it.

"It may not be illegal, but it sure as hell is unethical," he said. "We're in the law enforcement business, not the fund-raising business."

Dintino had also been left with the odious task of taking an axe to the State Police. Pagano had enjoyed an embarrassment of riches as Superintendent, but the gravy train had left the station. Governor Florio inherited a billion dollar deficit from the Tom Kean administration and New Jersey's cupboards were bare. Dintino was forced to freeze salaries, cut overtime, chop more than 500 jobs and even bag the State Police Pipe & Drum Corps.

It didn't win him any popularity contests. He saw the angry faces as he toured the State, going from barracks to barracks, holding informal gatherings late into the night with 300 to 400 beer-drinking troopers, watching them steam as he laid down the law according to Dintino. Among them, minority troopers would get preferential treatment over whites for promotions when all other measures were equal.

"You're promoting them over us?" asked thunderstruck white troopers.

Dintino also announced he was de-emphasizing highway drug interdiction, which had been the career express elevator for young troopers. He instituted strict new rules. Troopers had to have "reasonable suspicion" a crime was being committed to search a car. And a sergeant had to be called to the scene and sign off on every search. Dintino knew nothing would change unless he put supervisors' asses on the line.

The rank-and-file didn't like their new world but Dintino knew they'd obey him. That was the thing about the State Police. The tail didn't wag the dog. The Superintendent was a dictator who could make or break careers at will. Troopers followed their leader, whether they liked it or not—even the young skin heads who still worshipped at the altar of Clinton Pagano.

Chapter 43

On March 4, 1990, Bill Buckman fired the first volley in a war that would last more than a decade. It was a campaign almost no one—including Buckman—believed he could win. But he was undaunted and decided to put on blinders and make a run at it. In his wildest dreams he never expected what was to come.

After several years as a Public Defender, Buckman was now a private attorney. He represented four clients who'd been arrested on the Turnpike for possession of small amounts of narcotics. He inherited the cases from a 70-year-old lawyer named Emerson Lippincott Darnell, a tall, skinny bag of bones who bore a striking resemblance to Abe Lincoln. Darnell had a long, gaunt face that was so ugly it was almost handsome and dressed in drab corduroy slacks and tweed jackets that often had holes in the elbows. They betrayed the fact that he was the scion of a wealthy Quaker family that traced its roots back to William Penn. In his youth he'd been partial to fast cars and pretty women. Now he was dying of pancreatic cancer.

Darnell was a respected civil rights attorney who'd moved to the Deep South in the 1960s to defend Freedom Riders. Buckman met him when he was a young law student working for the ACLU. Buckman was leaving the Public Defender's office just as Darnell's cancer was beginning to ravage his strength and the protégé took over a large part of his mentor's law practice. Among them were the Turnpike drug cases. All four defendants were black.

"Emerson, I think I'm going to move forward and consolidate these cases and challenge this thing," Buckman told him.

"That's an excellent idea," the old lawyer said. "It's long overdue."

They brainstormed about a plan of attack. Buckman would be sailing treacherous waters. The racial profiling challenges of Sheri Woliver in Warren County and Walter Marvin in Middlesex County had both foundered. They had navigated uncharted seas and chosen the wrong routes. But after analyzing both cases Buckman concluded they'd each been heroic in failure. They not only had shown him the path not to follow, they had also pointed him toward a course that might succeed.

It dawned on Buckman that the miscalculation Woliver and Marvin made had been basing their cases on the 4th Amendment to the U.S. Constitution. He couldn't fault their logic. The 4th Amendment descended from the English common law dictum: *"Every man's house is his castle."* British statesman William Pitt explained it best in 1763: *"It may be frail, its roof may shake, the wind may blow through it, the storm may enter, the rain may enter, but the King of England cannot enter."* Ironically, while Pitt was defining the tenet in England, the King's men were routinely ignoring it in America. James Madison introduced a Constitutional provision to protect citizens and their property *"from all unreasonable searches and seizures (which) shall not be violated by warrants issued without probable cause."*

The 4th Amendment was designed to safeguard the sanctity of the home, but the judiciary had never extended the same degree of protection to vehicles that it did residences. Police did not need a warrant to search a vehicle *if* they had *probable cause* to believe it contained contraband. But the courts did set limits. Random stops were condemned as too intrusive. Policemen needed some "articulable and reasonable suspicion" that a traffic violation or some other crime was taking place before they could legally stop a vehicle.

In 1979, the U.S. Supreme Court issued a landmark ruling in *Delaware v. Prouse.* The case involved a policeman who stopped a car because, he admitted in court, he had nothing else to do. He hadn't observed any traffic violation and arrested the driver only after walking up to the car and seeing a bag of marijuana on the floor. The Court threw out the evidence because the stop had been *"capricious and therefore violative of the Fourth Amendment. A random stop of a motorist in the absence of specific articulable facts which justify the stop is constitutionally impermissible."*

Prouse set an important precedent, but it also cut the legs out from under defense lawyers who tried to use the 4th Amendment to fight racial profiling because it defined exactly what police needed to justify a stop. In New Jersey it was called *Title 39*, the traffic code. Police simply had to observe a traffic violation—be it speeding, swerving, or any of a myriad of offenses—to constitute a valid stop. If the trooper subsequently searched the car and arrested the motorist for possession of contraband, a racial profiling claim under the 4th Amendment was doomed.

Buckman realized a new attack plan was needed. He'd been studying civil rights law and decided on a novel approach. He would launch his assault more like a class action lawsuit, examining stops through the prism of the 14th Amendment, the post-Civil War provision enacted in 1868 to assure emancipated slaves enjoyed the same rights as whites. *"No state shall deny to any person within its jurisdiction the equal protection of the laws."*

The 14th Amendment had led to a string of momentous court decisions on child labor, minimum wages, and collective bargaining. It was the basis for striking down racial bias in housing and laws that forbade fornication between blacks and whites. But its potency was most prominently demonstrated in *Brown v. Board of Education*, the 1954 U.S. Supreme Court ruling that declared segregated schools denied blacks an equal education. Buckman hoped the 14th Amendment would be the wrecking ball that finally razed the rampart protecting the State Police in court. He drafted a simple motion.

"The stopping and searching of out-of-state motor vehicles occupied by black patrons on the New Jersey Turnpike constitutes a clear pattern and practice by the New Jersey State Police in violation of defendant's constitutionally protected rights to freedom from racial discrimination and freedom to travel," Buckman wrote.

He knew it was a long shot. Even if he could prove his case, the chance of winning a favorable ruling were somewhere between zero and zilch. The political and institutional pressures that existed in New Jersey were enormous and he couldn't fathom a judge courageous enough to ignore them.

Chapter 44

IT WAS HARD TO SAY WHICH BLACK RADICAL at Newark Station was hated more. Anthony Reed had a genuine knack for getting under the skin of white troopers. But even at his most exasperating, Reed never came across as a wild-eyed fanatic. He was an agitator, yet possessed a subtlety and intelligence that blunted some of the edge. Kenny Ruff, on the other hand, wore his anger like a badge, ranting about racial profiling, hazing, the 20-20 rule, getting in the faces of white troopers. The angrier he got, the shriller his voice would become, until his tirades were so loud everyone could hear.

"Kenny is a hard line trooper," Darryl Beard tried to explain to people. "He believes in right and wrong. He doesn't have a gray area. That's how he lives. No excuses."

The Radicals looked up to Ruff. He was the boldest and smartest among them. But he'd become so militant it bordered on professional suicide. Older black troopers steered clear of him. Yearlings were supposed to fly below the radar. Ruff was a kamikaze pilot. In retrospect his crash was predictable, but that made it no less shocking.

At 3:45 on the morning of August 20, 1990 two officers from the City of Newark Police Department arrived at the State Police barracks. They asked to speak to the supervisor on duty. Sgt. Walter Zukowsky came out to meet them. They spoke for a few minutes and the sergeant thanked them. After they left Zukowsky picked up the telephone. Gossip spread faster inside the State Police than at a women's coffee klatch. It wasn't 7 a.m. yet when Beard was awakened by a knock on his front door. Thomas Lewis, a black trooper, was standing outside with the news. Beard was dumbfounded. He telephoned Greg Sanders. That afternoon, Sanders caught up with Ruff filling his car at a State Police gas pump in Sommerville. Ruff's wife, Dwanda, was in the front seat. Sanders pulled him off to the side.

"I've got to talk to you," he said. Ruff had never seen Sanders look so shaken, as if he'd just lost his best friend. The problem was Ruff *was* his best friend. They stood at the back of the car while Sanders spoke, closely watching his friend's reaction. Ruff's face registered disbelief. Then, after a few seconds, he laughed.

"You're kidding, right?" Ruff said. "This is a joke."

"No, no, no, Ken, you don't understand, I'm serious. This thing is all over the Outfit."

The New Jersey State Police was a testosterone-driven organization that oozed machismo. Being branded a *coward* was the worst insult a trooper could suffer—with one exception. That was to be called a *faggot*.

At 2:45 that morning, the two Newark police officers were patrolling one of the seediest parts of the city. Cops called it the "he-she turf" because it was the domain of male prostitutes wearing women's clothing. The officers claimed to see a woman run across the street and jump into a dark blue car. They said they pulled up next to the vehicle and ordered her out. As she exited the car she pulled off her wig to reveal *she* was actually a *he*, a six-feet-three-inch tall *he*, clean shaven, with short hair, a muscular build, wearing make-up, a black mini-skirt, stockings, high heels. And he was black.

"I'm a cop," the policemen quoted him as saying.

They said a leather billfold inside the car contained a badge and a New Jersey State Police identification card. The transvestite, they said, looked exactly like the photo on the I.D. that identified him as Trooper Kenneth L. Ruff, Badge Number 4485.

"What are you doing?" one of the patrolman asked.

"I'm working undercover," he said the man replied.

"If that's true you would have back-ups."

"The State Police don't know about the investigation," Ruff supposedly said. "A friend of mine contracted AIDS from a prostitute here and I'm looking for the hooker."

The Newark cops said they didn't believe him. But he was polite and there was no law against a man, even a cop, wearing women's clothing. He showed no signs of being on drugs or alcohol, so they copied his name and badge number and let him go. Their boss ordered them to report the encounter to the State Police in Newark.

The story erupted inside the State Police like a volcano, spewing a torrent of pus and bile that had been bubbling like hot lava. A lot of white troopers were ecstatic. The most belligerent black trooper in the Outfit was a *faggot!* The next day Sanders and Tony Reed walked into Newark Station. Posters of Joanne Chesimard, the trooper killer, wearing Kenny Ruff's hat and badge number were plastered everywhere. *"I'm Trooper Kenny Ruff,"* the inscription said. *"Don't blow my cover."*

Reed began ripping down the pictures.

"Why are you tearing them down?" a trooper barked at him. "I'm just going to put them back up."

"Because this shouldn't be up in the station," Reed said.

"You're a troublemaker, Reed. If you hate it so much, just get out."

Reed was quickly surrounded by white squad members that reminded Sanders of a lynch mob. Frightened, he pulled his friend away and they left the station. Reed returned later. Hundreds more Chesimard-Ruff posters were taped to the walls. Reed began tearing them down again. Sgt. Zukowsky was in the squad room preparing for roll call.

"Why are you bothering to do that again?" Zukowsky said. "The joke will be over in a couple of days."

But to Kenny Ruff's friends this was no joke.

Chapter 45

THE TROOPER INDICTMENTS WERE THE BIGGEST SCANDAL in State Police history with the potential to become a blood bath that would end with a lot of State Police officers in prison. When the first trial began, the courtroom was packed with press, spectators, lawyers, and judges who'd come to witness a drama that would feature two marquee players: Robert Henig and William Sweeney. One was a misunderstood Super Cop, the other New Jersey's most loathsome law enforcement officer. The jury's challenge was to decide which was which.

The prosecutor was a tall, lanky, graying Deputy Attorney General by the name of Charles E. Waldron, who kicked off the proceedings with the State's version of the night of September 23, 1988, when the overnight shift erupted in an orgy of violence.

"The evidence will have you reliving a nightmare," Waldron said. "The assaults never would have occurred if the troopers had not had an expectation that everything was going to be covered up."

The prosecutor detailed how Kenneth Lowengrub was beaten with a billy club by two troopers who arrested him then, later, by Henig, who punched him repeatedly with powerful "body shots" while other troopers stood by. Waldron said Henig—the former college All-American wrestler—also punched another prisoner, Stacy Brown, then lifted him over his head and slammed him to the floor.

"Unbelievably these injuries were caused by members of the New Jersey State Police, who had taken an oath to uphold and obey the laws of the state," the prosecutor said.

This would be the highest profile trial of Francis Hartman's long career and, as Henig's attorney, he would be at center stage. Hartman and the other defense lawyers were now in lockstep. They'd agreed to forego an internecine war and preach the same sermon: The charges were fiction: Henig didn't assault anyone; no one saw him beat anyone; nobody lied; nobody covered-up.

The State bolted from the starting gate with its first witness, black trooper Karlton Crawford who'd driven Lowengrub from the State Police barracks to the county jail.

"What did Mr. Lowengrub look like when you first saw him?" prosecutor Waldron asked.

"He was very pale and sort of slumped over," Crawford said.

"Did he say what happened to him?"

"He said: 'Two troopers beat the shit out of me.'"

Crawford testified Lowengrub was hurt so badly the jail refused to accept him. By the time Crawford got the prisoner to a hospital he was near death. Doctors had to perform emergency surgery to save his life. The testimony cast an immediate pall over the defense.

But Hartman was a masterful attorney and he immediately began punching holes in the prosecution's case. He got Crawford to admit he'd never mentioned anything to investigators about Lowengrub being "slumped over." The trooper finally conceded he'd made a mistake and that Lowengrub "walked upright" into the jail that night. Crawford also drove Stacy Brown and Christopher Moore to the jail the same evening.

"Did Stacy Brown say he'd been punched?" Hartman asked Crawford.

"No."

"Did he say a trooper had picked him up and slammed him to the ground?"

"No."

Lowengrub was the prosecution's second witness and Hartman twisted him like a pretzel. Short and doughy, Lowengrub was not an impressive-looking person. Hartman wanted the jury to see him as a drugged-out space cowboy who was injured not by Henig or the other troopers, but by ramming his car into another vehicle in a hit-and-run on the Turnpike while he was stoned on painkillers. Hartman had Henig stand up.

"Do you recall this man pressing you against a wall and pummeling you?"

"No, I don't remember that," Lowengrub said.

"Do you even remember being assaulted at the troop station?"

"No."

Stacy Brown didn't have a problem remembering Henig. He testified that he agreed to let the trooper search his car only after Henig punched and threatened him.

"He took his gun out of his holster and pointed it at my face and said, 'I should kill you now, nigger,'" Brown testified. When Henig discovered Brown had given him a phony name, Brown said the trooper "leaned me over the fingerprinting desk and bit me on the nose. He picked me up over his head and dropped me to the ground."

Brown glowered at Henig from the witness stand. At one point, while the lawyers and judge were immersed in a bench conference, he looked over at Henig and muttered: "Fuck you!"

On cross examination, Hartman attacked. He got Brown to admit he and Moore were caught with two ounces of cocaine in their car and that he was currently serving four years in prison on a drug conviction.

"By testifying against Trooper Henig do you hope it will help you fight the drug charges Trooper Henig filed against you?" Hartman asked.

"Yes," Brown admitted, "but nobody made no promises to me."

All of a sudden the prosecution's watertight case seemed leaky. As Hartman predicted, the prosecution was banking on the testimony of drug dealers to convict a half-dozen men who had dedicated their lives to upholding the law. As the wily old lawyer liked to say, he was standing on "the side of the angels."

Chapter 46

By 1990, New Jersey's criminal justice system was on the brink of a "catastrophic breakdown." The reason: the State's "Zero Tolerance for Drugs" policy. That wasn't ACLU alarmism, but the conclusion of a blue ribbon committee appointed by the Chief Justice of the New Jersey Supreme Court.

The Garden State was locking up drug offenders faster than any state in the nation. Courts and prisons had been overwhelmed by the landslide of humanity. The inmate population had tripled in less than a decade and there were 7,000 more prisoners than cells to hold them.

Not surprisingly, the prison census mirrored what was happening on the Turnpike. Blacks comprised 15% of Jersey's population, but more than 80% of its drug inmates. The committee begged lawmakers to revise severe mandatory sentences and recommended drug treatment programs rather than prison for non-violent offenders.

"If we are going to avoid a collapse of the criminal justice systems we must enhance our systems of intermediate sanctions and make them effective," the Supreme Court Task Force on Drugs and the Courts reported.

But politicians—terrified of being branded as soft on crime—turned a deaf ear. "You will have an outcry from the public," one senator said. "They will tell you: 'We will vote you out of office,'"

Justin Dintino was no politician. He agreed with the committee, and said so.

"We've got to get away from this concept of just arrest everybody and warehouse them and the problem will go away, because it doesn't,"

176

Dintino said shortly after taking over the State Police, announcing that he was tripling the number of troopers going into schools to educate children about drugs. "Our job is to reduce the drug problem. If we can do that by prevention that's the way we ought to go."

Such talk would have been sacrilege just a few months earlier, but Dintino was trying to trigger a cultural revolution in the State Police. He saw his mission as reshaping an organization gone astray under Clinton Pagano. Dintino became the anti-Pagano. He had forced out his predecessor's top aides and did away with some of his favorite institutions, like the golf tournament. But he was just warming up. He did things Pagano wouldn't have conjured up in his worst nightmare.

Dintino brought in the ACLU, NAACP, and Lambda Legal— the gay and lesbian civil rights organization—to conduct sensitivity training for every trooper *"to reinforce understanding and appreciation of different cultures, ethnicities, and sexual persuasions."* He promoted more blacks and Hispanics than the previous nine Superintendents combined and raised requirements for entrance to the State Police Academy from high school diploma to four-year college degrees. He cut staffing in Atlantic City casinos, saying he didn't want troopers being used as "bouncers." But Dintino's primary target was racial profiling, even though he publicly downplayed the problem.

"High-level staff may have sent the wrong signal to the troops," he said. "A few people got a little loose about what they were doing."

But Dintino knew it was more than just a few. A lot of troopers had been indoctrinated to believe it was more important to stop drugs than obey the Constitution. And who could blame them? Pagano had said virtually the same thing on television! That mindset was at the root of profiling. Dintino had to deprogram his people and send an explicit message that civil rights came first.

Three months after taking office, Dintino issued the first Standard Operating Procedure on highway stops and searches, designed *"to respect, first and foremost, the Constitutional rights of all citizens."* The 11-page manual—SOP F-55—explicitly forbade "profile" stops based on *"physical and personal characteristics such as race, age, sex, length of hair, style of dress."* It prohibited threats or intimidation to coerce drivers to allow searches and required troopers to file written reports justifying every search.

Drug arrests on the Turnpike—which had been doubling every year—plummeted from 3,013 in 1989 to about 1,000 in 1990. The road warriors who'd built careers on big Turnpike arrest numbers were livid. In their minds Dintino was handcuffing them and giving free rein to the drug runners. But the disenchantment was hushed. Dintino knew troopers might not like the new order, but they would obey. That's how the Outfit worked.

The flip side was that minority complaints all but evaporated.

"You have to ask yourself: 'At what price were we making all these arrests?'" Dintino said. "I feel much happier about what's occurring today."

Chapter 47

BILL BUCKMAN WAS FLYING BY THE SEAT OF HIS PANTS. He felt he'd made the right tactical decision by basing his racial profiling challenge on the 14th Amendment rather than the 4th Amendment. But proving his case was another matter.

A month after he filed his motion he was approached by an attorney named Justin Loughry. Buckman and Loughry had known each other for several years. Both men were in their mid-30s and seemed to be on the same philosophical wavelength.

Loughry worked at the 35-member South Jersey law firm of Tomar, Simonoff, Adourian & O'Brien. The local NAACP office had asked Loughry to take on the case of a young black man who'd been pulled over on the Turnpike for *"failure to keep right."* Troopers found cocaine on a passenger in the back seat. Loughry suspected the men had been stopped because of their skin color and he and Buckman decided to consolidate their cases.

Before long, Buckman got another call; this one from Fred Last, his former colleague at the Gloucester Public Defender's Office. The two men had been the PD's most outspoken State Police critics and Buckman's motion had whetted Last's appetite to join the fray. He began urging his boss, Jeff Wintner, to throw in with Buckman. Wintner was reluctant. The Public Defender's Office was supposed to represent clients, not causes. Besides, it would take tons of work that Wintner knew would come to naught. Everyone was aware the State Police were profiling, but no judge in New Jersey was ever going to call them on it.

"Well, I want to do it anyway," Last said.

"Okay," Wintner said finally, "go ahead and do it."

Buckman was happy to have his friends beside him. The Public Defender's Office had 17 cases that fit his motion. With his four clients and Loughry's one, they consolidated the 22 drug cases under a single motion to suppress the evidence. All the defendants were black or Hispanic and most had been arrested on nickel and dime drug charges. One was a Maryland man named Pedro Agaury Soto, who'd been arrested in 1988 with two ounces of cocaine. By luck of the draw, he was listed first among the defendants in *State of New Jersey v. Pedro Soto, et al.* His name would eventually be immortalized, although he and the other defendants would play almost no role in the case. *Soto* would not be about them; it would be about the State Police.

The defense had a steep mountain to climb. They needed to build an incontrovertible body of evidence, analyze years of State Police records, conduct studies, dig up corroborative evidence and locate travelers who'd been stopped and searched. Finally, they had to find troopers to step forward and bear witness against the Blue and Gold. Even then, the odds against them were astronomical.

To narrow the scope of their task, they decided to focus on the south end of the Turnpike, where the WWOR-TV investigation *Without Just Cause* had documented a minority arrest rate of 86%. But while arrests were a bona fide sign something was amok, Buckman knew the litmus test would be stops and searches.

First, they had to persuade a judge to give them State Police internal files. Unfortunately, the man who would oversee *Soto* was Superior Court Judge Joseph Lisa, the presiding criminal court judge in Gloucester County. Lisa was a respected jurist, but he ran his court like a drill sergeant, often more concerned with keeping his docket moving than giving attorneys time to make their cases. Buckman wanted a full-blown hearing where they could call witnesses, present facts and get as much evidence on record as possible. To get that, he knew, Lisa would make them walk through fire.

The lawyers scavenged for every shred of evidence. They asked Judge Lisa for reams of raw data; summonses, patrol charts, radio logs, "Consent to Search" forms, anything they could dredge up. State prosecutors resisted. They'd been through this twice and it was getting tiresome. They'd staved off the challenges in Warren and Middlesex Counties largely by plea bargaining hundreds of drug cases, but it was becoming morally repugnant to let so many druggies off the hook. Besides, things could snowball. New Jersey had 21 counties and defense lawyers could launch racial profiling litigation in all of them. Thousands of criminals might escape justice. After *Soto* was filed a crucial decision was made in the upper reaches of the Attorney General's Office. Enough was enough! No more plea bargains. The State would draw a line in the sand. The racial profiling battleground would be Gloucester County.

For what promised to be a Herculean clash, the *Soto* defense was operating on a shoestring. The PD's office didn't have a budget for a class action-type case, but at least its attorneys were collecting steady paychecks. Justin Loughry was on salary too. But the only name on Buckman's shingle was *William H. Buckman, Esq.* He generated every penny that came into his firm and money was tight. From the start, he devoted large chunks of time to *Soto*. His clients were indigent so he was paid by the court system, with its fee scale of $15 for every hour of work outside court and $22.50 for courtroom time. That didn't even cover Buckman's secretary and office rent, let alone put bread on the table for him, his wife and infant son. His money quickly began to dwindle.

Buckman and Fred Last did most of the work during the early stages of *Soto*. Like Buckman, Last had grown up in an insular, middle-class Jewish family in Westfield, New Jersey, 25 miles from New York City. His first awareness of racism came as a kid on family vacations to Miami Beach. Driving through the Deep South he was shocked to see colored people prohibited from eating in white restaurants or using white bathrooms and drinking fountains. Last was expected to follow in his father's footsteps and become an engineer. But when he was 12 he read a book about celebrated trial lawyer Clarence Darrow and, to his father's immense disappointment, from that point on his destiny was the law.

Last and Buckman had handled countless Turnpike drug cases and knew first-hand that judges almost always sided with the State Police. They were not optimistic Judge Lisa would be any more accommodating. But to their surprise—and the State's vexation—Lisa ordered prosecutors to turn over massive amounts of data.

The decision energized the defense team. Maybe Lisa wasn't as unsympathetic as they feared. But the judge hadn't changed his stripes. His ruling actually set the stage for *Soto's* demise. Lisa gave the State Police almost nine months to comply, but gave the defense only two months to analyze the material and report back to him. It was a harsh time limit—even without the mistake.

The defense team learned the hard truth behind the maxim: "Be careful what you wish for—you might get it!"

They'd asked for three years of Turnpike records and the apparatchiks at State Police headquarters had responded with uncharacteristic largesse, swamping them with a paper tsunami, more than 1,000 days of police reports, radio logs, tickets, and warnings—thrown into boxes in total disarray. The lot was disgorged onto Fred Last's desk in the spring of 1993, which started the clock ticking for the defense to perform its analyses. Last was supposed to make copies and deliver them to Buckman and Loughry. But—overwhelmed by the conglomeration of documents—he did nothing.

In late May, when Buckman walked into Judge Lisa's courtroom he should have been terrified. Instead, he had no clue of the dire straits they were in. He assumed the State Police missed its deadline and looked forward to pointing his finger at the prosecution and saying: "Judge, they haven't turned the records over. You've got to give us more time." Not until they were in court did Buckman discover Last had been sitting on the material.

Holy shit! he thought. *We're in trouble.*

Judge Lisa was an impatient man who expected everything done yesterday. Buckman suspected he wanted to blow them out of the water and they'd just lit the fuse for him. He could kill their case right there. Fred Last was standing between Buckman and Loughry trying to tap dance around a dismissal, but it wasn't going well. He was tentative and unsure and when the judge pressed him on what the defense had done so far, he faltered. The correct answer was: *"Nothing!"* But he couldn't say that. The prosecutor smelled blood and made a motion that Judge Lisa throw out *Soto.*

Buckman had a sick feeling in the pit of his stomach. The judge was about to chuck the case and, if that happened, it would be dead forever. *Soto* was the epitome of why he'd became a lawyer—to protect people from abuse of power. If he didn't do something quick, the case would be history.

Fred Last was an excellent lawyer, but he was blowing it and Buckman wasn't going down without a fight. He'd spent most of his career learning to milk judges for time and was an expert in *case procedure* and *discovery,* tedious legal disciplines that didn't raise goose bumps, but were invaluable courtroom tools. Buckman never needed them more.

The lawyer stood up, cut off Fred Last, and began doing his own sword dance, desperately lunging at whatever might score points. Yes, Judge, we may be late with our report, but the State took too long to turn over the information. They dumped an *avalanche* of raw data on us. We just got it! Thousands and thousands of pages! *This is outrageous! They* made it impossible for us to meet the deadline. *And* they left out critical records. *Incredible!* Besides, even if the defense studies are slightly delayed, it won't harm the State in the least.

Buckman bluffed and blustered and darted and dodged. And it worked. He'd boxed Lisa into a corner. Even if he wanted to zap *Soto* it would have looked transparently unfair. The judge reluctantly agreed to give them an extension. The lawyers left the courtroom knowing they'd just dodged a bullet. Buckman got Last off to the side. They were good friends and Buckman had great respect and affection for him, but he was furious.

"Fred, this guy is out to kill our case. We can't play games. You've got to share this stuff with everybody. Get these goddamn things copied and let's get going."

When Buckman saw the enormous load of paperwork, he could almost hear the pencil pushers at State Police HQ tittering: *"What are they going to do with all that shit?"* Yet, the most important documents were missing. They had specifically asked for State Police "Consent to Search" forms, but the State refused to turn them over.

"I must object to your request and will not be providing you with the materials you seek," prosecutor Brent Hopkins wrote. *"I fail to see the relevance of the materials…and also feel that the retrieval and production of such materials would truly be overbudensome to the State."*

Even without the search data, the heart of the defense case would still be statistics. Unfortunately, the legal team was statistically challenged, to the point of being clueless. Justin Loughry had taken one statistics class in college—and earned a "D." But that was more than the rest of them combined. He thus became the defense's statistical *expert*.

The lawyers' heads were soon spinning at the sheer mass of paper. They pleaded with the judge to pare down the focus of the case. It was agreed that 35 days between 1988 to 1991 would be selected randomly and those records would be used in the analyses. They began sifting through the boxes like archeologists trying to translate ancient Egyptian papyrus scrolls without the Rosetta Stone, burning precious time struggling to decipher trooper handwriting that was often as illegible as hieroglyphics. They made piles for arrest reports, radio logs, tickets, warnings, organized them into chronological order, then tried to connect the dots. Attempts to determine the race of motorists were short-circuited because troopers roundly ignored State Police rules to document skin color in its stops. Of 3,060 stops, only 1,200 had racial data. They were trying to put together a puzzle with two-thirds of the pieces missing.

Time was running out and they still had a mountain of State Police material to analyze. They needed a hi-tech solution, but it was 1993 and, while the Computer Age had begun, the techno revolution wasn't yet in orbit. E-mail and the Internet weren't widely used. America Online had 500,000 subscribers (versus 27 million a decade later). Computer spreadsheet programs were primitive. Microsoft's now ubiquitous *Excel* didn't even exist.

Justin Loughry was part of a large law firm and everyone—including Loughry—assumed it had the computer resources to collate the material. He recruited some paralegals and hired a college intern to begin loading information into an off-the-shelf database program. But, after several weeks work, the software crashed, a total failure. It looked like their entire statistical case had fallen apart.

"What the fuck are we going to do now?" Buckman said.

It was a critical moment. The snafu set them back so far they were in real danger of missing Judge Lisa's final deadline. Buckman came to a bitter realization: *"Attorneys don't do data."* They needed a knight in shining armor.

The closest John Lamberth came to being a white knight was the color of his hair. Lamberth was a psychology professor at Temple

University who had garnered some eminence as an authority on statistical analysis in racial discrimination cases. Desperate, the *Soto* team pleaded for his help.

"Let me check with a friend of mine first," Lamberth said, "before you guys spend any more time and effort trying to reinvent the wheel."

He went to a computer whiz at Temple, Dr. Charles Arbuckle, who agreed to build a data base. But they were still behind the 8-ball. They had what seemed to be an insurmountable amount of work to do. Nonetheless, they vowed to meet the deadline, by hook or by crook.

Chapter 48

GLENN JOHNSON AND THE OTHER Black Radicals could not fathom the notion of Kenny Ruff wearing a mini-skirt and padded bra.

"That woman must have been one ugly bitch," Johnson said, "because Kenny's got a mustache. You can't tell me he was clean shaven at three in the morning and he walks into work with a mustache at nine the same morning."

Johnson and the others believed there was a conspiracy to destroy the organization's most militant black trooper. The Radicals had become closer than brothers and if Ruff had been a homosexual or had aberrant tendencies the others would have seen signs. They'd never found lingerie or eye shadow in his car, never heard him humming show tunes and never noticed him checking out other men. He was married, had a baby, and wasn't a carouser. When they were out partying, Ruff was the guy who went home early. No way was he running around at three o'clock in the morning dressed in drag.

But some African-American troopers weren't so sure. Lines were drawn a couple of days after word got out about the Newark incident when 20 black troopers crammed into Darryl Beard's small apartment. Kenny Ruff stood before them and swore he was innocent.

"It wasn't me," he said over and over. He kept saying that he'd been home asleep in bed with his wife, that he wasn't homosexual, that he wasn't a cross-dresser and that it hadn't been him in Newark. The meeting was meant as a show of support, but Ruff had always made some black troopers nervous. State Police were programmed not to gripe and Ruff had violated that code. They didn't want to get caught in the line of fire. The gathering became an inquisition.

"Was it you?"

"Why would they make this up if it's not true?"

"This is what happens when you're too radical. They chop your head off."

"If you're smart you'd wait five years until you get tenure and then speak."

"What are *you* going to do?" a veteran trooper asked. The question resonated. It wasn't: "What are *we* going to do?"

Ruff was stunned. He faced a room packed with men he thought were his friends, but instead of standing with him they had turned their backs. The exception was the Radicals.

"We're sticking with Kenny," Beard announced.

His friends argued Ruff was victim of a smear. There were too many inconsistencies. Why did the cops describe Ruff as clean shaven? Why didn't they call someone from the State Police to come to the scene? Ruff was hated inside the State Police. It would have been easy for someone to slip his description and badge number to the Newark cops. If the case was legitimate, it would have been handled as a sensitive Internal Affairs investigation. Instead, copies of the Newark police report were posted on State Police bulletin boards.

Distraught, Ruff spent countless hours on the telephone with his friends, rehashing the facts, dissecting the inconsistencies, as if trying to convince even them that it was all a mistake.

"It just doesn't add up," he'd say. "Where are they headed? What do you think?"

"Listen, Kenny," Sanders said, "you've got to get an attorney and fight this thing."

But Ruff told his friends he didn't think he had to defend himself, that he was confident he'd be cleared by the State Police investigation. The other Radicals knew different. They understood the magnitude of Ruff's dilemma. He might as well have been accused of being a child molester. Even if he was innocent, there were certain things a cop could not survive. Ruff had been branded like a steer with a hot iron and the stigma could not be washed away. The Radicals knew he was finished as a New Jersey State Policeman—all of them, except Kenny Ruff.

Chapter 49

EVEN THOUGH FRANCIS HARTMAN was representing Robert Henig, the wily old lawyer had a jaundiced view of police officers. Early in his career he'd come to the conclusion that too many cops had no qualms about committing perjury. He'd watched officers on the witness stand lie through their teeth to make the *facts* fit the Constitution, even if the *facts* were *fiction*. He knew they rationalized perjury as serving the greater good. If that's what it took to get bad guys off the street, so be it.

Hartman believed William Sweeney was just such a policeman. Sweeney was the 1988 Trooper of the Year whose prodigious arrest record surpassed even Henig's. Unlike Henig, though, Sweeney did not enjoy widespread esteem among his peers. Many troopers believed Clinton Pagano had given him the Red Ribbon only because he was black. Sweeney became an object of scorn; fliers mocking him as a self-promoter and second-rate cop were pinned to bulletin boards at East Brunswick Station. When Sweeney committed the cardinal sin of bearing witness against his brother troopers the enmity toward him multiplied exponentially. He was a Benedict Arnold in blue and gold.

Hartman already knew Sweeney and considered him to be a liar. A year before taking Henig's case, he had represented a man Sweeney arrested on a Turnpike drug possession charge. Sweeney claimed he stopped the man for speeding, but Hartman's client claimed he was actually at a service plaza gassing up his car when the trooper pulled up and, without permission, started looking inside his vehicle, where he found a small amount of drugs. Sweeney stuck to his story at trial and the lawyer couldn't trip him up. Hartman left the courtroom infuriated. He sent an investigator to the service plaza, who quickly found witnesses who corroborated his client's story and the man was acquitted. But the case stuck in Hartman's craw. Now he was going head-to-head with Sweeney again and the lawyer was worried. The jury would be impressed by the trooper's impeccable record. And he knew from experience that Sweeney didn't rattle on the witness stand.

Sweeney strode into the courtroom erect and proud in his State Police uniform. Under direct examination by Prosecutor Waldron, he gave a chilling account of coming into the barracks the night of September 23, 1988 and hearing "punching sounds."

Sweeney stood in front of the jury shadowboxing, his head bowed, throwing punch after punch. "Trooper Henig had Mr. Lowengrub standing against the rear wall and he was throwing punches to his body," Sweeney testified. He said he walked away, but "I could still hear the punching. It started to get louder. The walls were shaking. I could hear Mr. Lowengrub saying 'Why are you doing this to me? Why are you doing this to me?' Then the sound of punches would start again. Then he ran from the room, and he was bending over, holding his stomach."

Sweeney said he subdued Lowengrub and locked him in a holding cell. Then he heard Henig tell the radio operator to call the troopers who'd arrested Lowengrub and have them return to the station to charge their prisoner with resisting arrest. The implication was Henig had orchestrated a cover-up to explain Lowengrub's injuries. Sweeney said he reported the beating to his supervisor, Lt. Phillip Pelligra, but that Pelligra told him "next time, turn your head."

It was devastating testimony. Refuting the word of junkies and drug dealers was one thing, but now a celebrated trooper had given them credence. A big finger was pointing at Henig, but when Sweeney took the witness stand he, too, became a target, and you didn't want to be a target of the Outfit.

Before his cross-examination, Francis Hartman got a telephone call from a State Police major he'd known for years who said he had information about Sweeney. The lawyer was all ears. The major said that a couple of years earlier, Sweeney had falsified evidence about a Turnpike arrest he'd made. He'd transported the prisoner to the Burlington County jail, where guards discovered cocaine on the man. But in his report Sweeney claimed he found the drugs and didn't mention the jailers. Internal Affairs got wind of the incident and confirmed Sweeney had lied. He was suspended for 10 days.

Hartman was ecstatic. On cross-examination he forced Sweeney to confess he had falsified his report. Sweeney tried to defend himself by saying he'd done it to simplify his paperwork, but yes, he admitted, he lied.

"In fact, isn't it true, Trooper Sweeney," Hartman thundered, "that you would have lied three times if you'd been given the chance? You lied once in your arrest report. And you would have lied again to a grand jury if you had been called, wouldn't you?"

"Yes, I would have."

"And, had the case gone to trial, you would have repeated the lie again, right?"

"Yes."

"In fact, isn't it true that you are guilty of the same crimes which you have accused your brother officers of—falsifying a report?"

"No," said Sweeney. But the damage was done.

"You'd walk over anybody, including Robert Henig's body, to get ahead, wouldn't you?"

"That's not true," Sweeney replied.

Desperate to save its case, the prosecution called the State Police Turnpike Commander Captain Thomas Carr. But Hartman also turned him into a witness for the defense.

"Trooper Sweeney is one of the most hated troopers patrolling the New Jersey Turnpike," Carr testified, saying he had Sweeney transferred because "he has no credibility. How could he raise his hand under oath in Burlington County?"

"But you were really very proud of Trooper Henig?" Hartman asked.

"Yes, I was," Carr replied.

Hartman had ripped the heart out of the State case. The one prosecution witness with credence suddenly had none at all.

Chapter 50

KENNY RUFF REFUSED TO BUDGE from his story that he'd been home in bed with his wife the night two Newark cops claimed they'd caught him dressed in drag.

"Why would anyone fabricate these allegations?" a State Police Internal Affairs detective asked him.

"Maybe because I've been outspoken. It didn't make me a lot of friends," Ruff said, but he could offer no evidence to prove anyone had set him up.

"When did you begin wearing a mustache?" the investigator asked.

"I usually wear one," he said.

After the interview, Ruff began to have reservations about the IAB investigation. He finally took the advice of his friends and hired Paul McLemore to represent him. McLemore filed a *"Defamation of Character"* complaint against the Newark policemen, accusing them of lodging *"a false and malicious report"* against Ruff and claiming the allegations were part of a conspiracy to destroy the trooper's career because of his outspoken criticism of racial profiling. The State Police ordered Ruff to submit to a psychological evaluation conducted on the department's behalf by psychologist Dr. Alvin Krass, PhD.

"Is it true?" asked Krass.

"It is not true, absolutely not true," Ruff said.

"What if it is true?"

"There is absolutely no truth to it," said Ruff, with more than a trace of indignation. "I was at home with my wife."

"Who made the complaint?"

"Two Newark police officers."

"Why?"

"Come on, I can't read other people's minds. I don't know what motives are behind it."

Based on the statements of the Newark cops, his interview with Ruff, and a battery of psychological tests, Dr. Krass' diagnosis was that Ruff was not victim of some sinister conspiracy, but of a seriously troubled psyche.

"The diagnostic impression is transvestic fetishism. Mr. Ruff appeared to be a sexually maladjusted individual and definitely is a candidate for ongoing psychotherapy. Mr. Ruff, from a psychiatric point of view, should not be employed as a police officer."

McLemore hired another psychologist who found Ruff to be perfectly normal. But it was too late. A short time later Ruff got a letter from State Police headquarters informing him he was terminated. No reason was given. The leader of the Black Radicals was no longer a New Jersey State Policeman.

Chapter 51

DURING THE TROOPER TRIAL A RUMOR circulated that Bob Henig had become a professional wrestler and was competing in body building contests. It was a tantalizing morsel for reporters covering the trial and they tried to get Henig to confirm it. But Henig hated the press, which he felt had portrayed him as a brutal caveman. One persistent reporter kept asking him about his wrestling and body building.

"Take a picture of this," Henig said finally, turning to the cameras and going into a classic body-builder's pose, flexing his massive biceps. Henig did need a new career. Like Kenny Ruff, his days as a New Jersey state trooper were finished, even if he was acquitted. Henig was also still a probationary trooper and Superintendent Justin Dintino had the power to fire him without giving a reason. Dintino looked at the litany of brutality complaints against Henig and decided that, convicted or not, he wasn't the kind of trooper he wanted working for him. He fired Henig.

Francis Hartman didn't call Dintino as a character witness, but Clinton Pagano was another matter. Hartman knew Pagano liked Henig. He was the kind of tough, aggressive trooper the former Superintendent treasured. The other defense lawyers objected.

"What if he says Henig was a bad guy," one warned. "It's going to carry a lot of weight."

"Well, I've got to run that risk," Hartman argued.

With Pagano on the witness stand, Hartman read excerpts from a thick stack of commendations the former Superintendent had written, including one where he described Henig as *"the best among the best."* Pagano didn't disappoint the lawyer, testifying that Henig was an "impressive" and "outstanding" trooper.

Finally, it was Henig's turn to take the witness stand. Despite his reputation, he came across as low key, controlled, even charming, more gentle giant than ogre.

"I'm not guilty," he declared, denying he'd assaulted Stacy Brown, Christopher Moore or Kenneth Lowengrub. "I really don't recall having any contact with [Lowengrub]."

"Did you bite Stacy Brown on the nose?" Hartman asked.

"That's absolutely ridiculous," Henig scoffed. "One of the biggest fears we have is coming into contact with the blood of drug abusers who may be infected with AIDS. I would never risk spreading a disease like that to my wife or three young children."

Momentum had shifted decidedly to the defense. In closing arguments lawyers for the troopers attacked the State case as "a shotgun conspiracy" orchestrated by "a parade of liars." The alleged victims were "drug pushers" trying to "turn the tables" on the troopers who'd arrested them. William Sweeney was "a certified liar."

Prosecutor Charles Waldron tried to mount a counter-attack, arguing that Sweeney "had nothing to gain by testifying against fellow troopers" and was likely to be "ostracized by the State Police community." Henig and the other troopers had taken the law into their own hands, Waldron said, then tried to hide behind "a blue wall."

"They do not have the right to break the law just because they're police officers. If you condone such conduct by acquitting these men then we might as well just be barbarians."

But Hartman had the final word and, in his folksy, homespun manner, he invoked the principle of law that says "false in one, false in all."

"If I prove this man lied about Fact A, you can disregard everything," Hartman said of Sweeney. He asked the jury if it was going to believe an admitted liar or a "super trooper" like Robert Henig. "You have the last word. In fact, you have the last two words: Not guilty."

After six hours deliberation, the jury acquitted the troopers of all charges. The courtroom erupted with cheers and applause. Robert Henig left the courthouse angrily pushing his way through a sea of media. He shoved one television cameraman and slammed a door on his camera.

"You are all miserable people," he said. "Go to hell."

Over the next year, Henig endured two more trials—the Delbert Blair case and the charge he stole $160 from a Turnpike motorist. Francis Hartman represented Henig and won acquittals in both cases.

Chapter 52

THE *SOTO* DEFENSE TEAM HAD THE HEEBIE-JEEBIES. It was Sunday, four days before their racial profiling report was due to be delivered to Judge Joseph Lisa. Bill Buckman, Fred Last, Dr. John Lamberth and Justin Loughry were sitting in the library of Loughry's law office. They'd been working days, nights, and weekends for more than a month and were exhausted. Their hard work had paid dividends. They'd analyzed thousands of State Police records and believed they had plenty enough evidence to force Lisa to give them the full hearing they desperately wanted. Yet, as the last grains of sand ran from the hourglass, a sense of foreboding permeated the library. Something seemed to be missing, some crucial element that would allow Lisa to pull the plug on *Soto.*

"What do we need?" Buckman asked. "What are we not seeing?"

For the umpteenth time they scoured their Bible, the Appellate Court decision in Sheri Woliver's Warren County case, *New Jersey v. Kennedy,* looking for flaws in their evidence. Then something caught Justin Loughry's eye. Just one sentence, but as soon as he saw it he knew that was it. He read the Appellate Court's words to Lamberth.

"We would have been more comfortable had the Public Defender been precise in estimating the racial composition of those who exceed the speed limit."

Woliver had based her 1988 attack on the disproportionate number of black out-of-state drivers *arrested.* The Appellate Court wanted a racial breakdown of *traffic violators.*

"John, doesn't this mean that we need some kind of a violator survey?" Loughry said.

Lamberth studied the ruling for several minutes. "It sure does mean that," he said finally.

"What?" Buckman said, suddenly queasy.

"What this says to me is that the population study and the stop analysis aren't enough," Lamberth said. "They don't tell us the races of the people *violating* traffic laws."

"Shit!" someone moaned. The final report was due on the judge's desk by the close of business Thursday. After three years in court, facing a do-or-die hearing before an unfriendly judge, they could feel the ground crumbling beneath them.

Buckman felt panic, then just plain sick. It brought back a terrifying memory. When he was 16 he drove to the mountains and went rock climbing with no equipment and no clue what he was doing. He got into a ludicrously dangerous situation, stuck high in the rocks, unable to move up or down, paralyzed by fear, and wanting to vomit. Then he realized he must act or die. The memory stuck with him; the sheer panic, followed by an instinct to survive.

"Well, let's do a violator study," he said.

There was just one catch. No such study had ever been performed—anywhere. The Appellate Court was asking for something without precedent.

"How do we do a violator study?" someone asked.

It was 12:15 p.m. and for the next half hour they sat around Loughry's table, like mad scientists concocting formulas on cocktail napkins, until they came up with a plan.

"We'll do speeders and anyone else we can identify," Lamberth said.

"How do you do speeders?"

"The speed limit is 55. Add an extra five miles an hour and anybody doing over 60 miles an hour is a speeder."

They'd already performed a gargantuan Turnpike Census, counting more than 42,000 vehicles and determining that 13.5% of travelers on the highway were black. The plan was for Fred Last to drive the Turnpike, set his cruise control at 60 miles per hour, and record the races of everyone who passed him. By comparing those numbers with their census they would get a ratio of black violators versus non-black violators.

"Can you defend this?" Buckman asked Lamberth. "Can you testify this is statistically reliable?"

"Yes, I can do that," said the professor.

Last left Loughry's office, bought batteries for his tape recorder, gassed up his old blue Honda Accord, and was on the Black Dragon by 2:30. He calibrated his speedometer using an electronic stopwatch that gave read-outs to 100th of a second. The Turnpike had markers every one-tenth of a mile. He brought his speedometer to 60, engaged the cruise control and timed his vehicle against the mileposts until it timed out between 60 and 60.2 miles an hour. Then he began driving laps between Exits 1 and 3, looping back and forth. Every time a car passed him he'd click on his tape recorder and recite the race of its occupants and the car model.

"Black Lexus…white Buick…white Volvo."

When Last finished he went home and made tick marks on a rudimentary chart and called them in to Dr. Lamberth, repeating the same drill for the next three days. He made his last ride Wednesday afternoon and had the final batch of numbers to Lamberth by nightfall.

In four days they had devised and performed a study unlike anything before. On Thursday they were in court armed with the State Police stop analysis, the Turnpike Population Census, *and* the Turnpike Violator's Survey. The crisis had passed. They were home free. They would get their day in court.

Chapter 53

AFTER KENNY RUFF'S TERMINATION, ANTHONY REED was also *"not re-enlisted,"* which was the way probationary troopers were fired without explanation. The two most vociferous Black Radicals were gone. Glenn Johnson, another Radical, was about to be dismissed when his Air Force Reserve Unit was sent to Kuwait for Operation Desert Storm. His friends joked he should thank President George Herbert Walker Bush for saving his job—if only temporarily.

In April 1993, six black troopers—including the three remaining Radicals, Johnson, Greg Sanders and Darryl Beard—filed a federal complaint accusing the State Police of discrimination. Minority troopers had never gone outside the Outfit to air their grievances. It was a bold step, and maybe foolhardy.

The complaint was filed with the U.S. Equal Employment Opportunity Commission and alleged that black troopers who spoke out against racism had been *"arbitrarily"* terminated. They claimed other minority troopers were subjected to racially antagonistic work conditions, evidenced by leaflets posted in barracks, like the *"Runnin' Nigger Target"* and *"Mr. Watermelon Head."*

"This is old-fashioned racism," said their attorney, Renee Steinhagen.

The lawsuit was big news, garnering extensive coverage in newspapers and on TV. A short time later, Sanders found watermelon crammed through the vents of his locker, the rotting fruit staining his uniforms. The word "RAT" was written next to his name on the squad work schedule. Beard, who had always received *"good"* job assessments from supervisors, was suddenly getting *"poor"* evaluations.

On July 27, 1993, Sanders, Beard and Johnson traveled to Washington, D.C. They'd been invited to testify before a Congressional committee investigating retaliation against workers who filed EEOC complaints. Sanders knew testifying could kill his career, but he was angry. He hoped speaking out would prompt someone from outside to step in. He testified about the watermelon in his locker and how other troopers had been harassed and retaliated against.

"To me it was very offensive and had racial intent. The administration has told troopers not to associate or meet with us," he said. "I've lost friends who feel the livelihood of their families could be at risk."

Congressman Donald Payne, a black Democrat from Newark, said he had long viewed the State Police as "an institution that is racist and in need of serious reform. I hope this is the first stage of bringing the State Police into the 21st century."

The day after the Congressional appearance, Glenn Johnson was suspended. His suspension lingered for three years before he was finally terminated, the third of five Radicals eliminated.

Chapter 54

As the *Soto* hearing approached, Bill Buckman was confident they'd accumulated the most extensive body of evidence ever assembled about police activity on the Jersey Turnpike—or any highway in America. It was a formidable arsenal, but they still lacked one critical ingredient—an insider.

They needed a trooper to testify. But the chances of that were slim. It would be career *hara-kiri,* at best, and possibly life imperiling. There was one long shot. Buckman called Renee Steinhagen, the attorney representing the black troopers. Thirteen troopers had now joined in the complaint and Buckman thought he might be able to convince them to testify. Steinhagen agreed to arrange a meeting and, in the fall of 1994, she and 10 troopers sat down with Buckman at Darryl Beard's home.

The lawyer made his case. The *Soto* team had powerful statistics that showed 20 to 30 innocent motorists were being stopped and illegally searched for every one arrest. The vast majority were black. Buckman said he needed to put a human face to the numbers and asked them to testify against the State Police.

The troopers were caught off-guard. They thought Buckman just wanted background information about how the system worked, how to break down codes, interpret the lingo, where the bodies were buried. They had no problem with that. They'd be glad to help. But they didn't expect to be asked to testify. The problem was Buckman's clients—they were criminals and parasites who'd been caught with drugs. Regardless of color, the troopers would not testify on their behalf.

"It might be different if you were representing the other 20 people that were stopped to get one of your clients," Greg Sanders said. "But my theory is that the innocent people are getting dealt the bad hand because of the people you're representing."

Buckman was taken aback. He'd expected a more sympathetic reception and used all his persuasive powers to change their minds, reasoning, debating, cajoling, even trying to lay a guilt trip on them, but the troopers wouldn't bend.

"Your clients should not only be in jail," Beard said. "From where I stand, from the hardships they cause our community, they should be under the jail."

"It has nothing to do with us being cops," Sanders said. "It has everything to do with us being from the black community."

Buckman was out of luck. Then, shortly before the *Soto* hearing began, two insiders agreed to testify. Neither had pristine résumés. Both were black former troopers who'd been fired and who prosecutors would certainly portray as disgruntled.

Once upon a time, Kenneth Wilson had been a gung-ho profiler. He'd bought into the drug interdiction program early in his career. Narcotics arrests were the bullet train up the State Police pecking order, even if it meant targeting people his own color. In 1989 Wilson and two other troopers were charged with stealing $200 in cash from motorists. Wilson pleaded guilty and turned State's evidence against the other troopers, who were white. They were acquitted. Wilson got probation and never again wore a badge. Now a bus driver, he agreed to tell what he knew.

The other was Kenny Ruff. Newark Station's former Black Radical was now a high school mathematics teacher. Buckman found Ruff to be sincere, intelligent, and credible. Ruff said he'd been taught to racially profile his third night on the Turnpike. He talked about *spotlighting, fishing holes,* the *20/20 rule,* and how troopers called blacks *mutts* and *johnnies.*

The night before Thanksgiving 1994, the *Soto* team gathered at Buckman's office in Mount Holly to prepare Ruff for his testimony. The hearing was set to start the following Monday and the lawyers had been working non-stop for weeks. They were fatigued, but also giddy with anticipation. After four long years they were finally getting their shot.

Ruff would be a crucial witness. Even though it was Thanksgiving eve, they spent hours going over his testimony, peppering him with questions, critiquing his responses, helping him mold his answers, advising him when to talk and when to shut up. They anticipated trick questions from the prosecution and pitfalls to avoid. By 10 o'clock the lawyers were satisfied Ruff was prepared and they could finally go home. Everyone was drained. They had their coats on and were walking out when Buckman remembered he'd forgotten to ask a question he always posed to witnesses.

"By the way Kenny, what's the worst thing the State Police could say about you?"

"Well," Ruff said matter-of-factly, "they might say I was in a State Police cruiser in Newark at two in the morning dressed as a female prostitute."

There was a moment of stunned silence. Buckman stifled an impulse to burst out laughing. He looked at the other lawyers and they looked at him and then they all looked down at their shoes. Nobody knew what to say. Buckman finally found his tongue.

"Oh, don't worry about that, Kenny. We'll be able to deal with that. No problem."

It was too late to get into it and they were too shocked to try. Ruff said the charge was bogus and he was set up for being a rabble rouser. The lawyers asked a couple of perfunctory questions, bid Ruff a Happy Thanksgiving, and left as quickly as possible, knowing if they didn't they'd erupt in front of him. They adjourned to Dunleavy's, a nearby watering hole, where they promptly lost it.

"What the hell was that?" Buckman said, laughing hysterically.

"This is absurd," one of the lawyers said.

"I can't believe this is happening," said another.

"This is nothing!" Buckman kept repeating between guffaws. "Our witness was a trooper in a dress? Not to worry!"

They were laughing so hard they couldn't eat. Instead, they drank and wondered if their case was falling apart before they even got into court.

Chapter 55

SHORTLY BEFORE THE *SOTO* HEARING commenced, the Attorney General's Office filed a motion to disqualify Fred Last as an attorney in the case. Last was intimately involved in developing the defense evidence and would be a primary witness and the State argued he could not sit at the counsel table. They won their point and Last was disqualified, but the maneuver backfired. His exclusion proved to be providential, allowing him to spend the bulk of his time outside the courtroom developing what became an astonishing cascade of new evidence after the hearing began. It also meant Jeff Wintner would take Last's seat.

Wintner was a roundish, balding man with a ruddy complexion that made him appear perpetually sunburned. A career Public Defender who ran the PD's Gloucester County office, he became the defense's frontline inquisitor. Wintner wasn't flamboyant or overtly aggressive, but he was a dogged interrogator with a knack for picking apart witnesses—if given time.

Time was the dilemma. The *Soto* team was drooling to confront troopers with its evidence and grill them at length. But Judge Lisa was prone to keep lawyers on a tight leash and, without time, their razor thin prospects were doomed. That's where Last's elimination paid its biggest dividend. His primary job at the Public Defender's Office was representing clients in Judge Lisa's courtroom. Last had appeared before Lisa hundreds of times and the two men interacted daily. That raised legitimate questions about whether Lisa could objectively judge Last's credibility as a witness. Lisa agreed and disqualified himself.

Thus, in early October 1994, *Soto* was assigned to Judge Robert E. Francis. At age 51, Francis was a 16-year veteran of the Superior Court bench. He was also South Jersey's Chancery Judge, handling the most complex and challenging cases in the three county judicial district. Chancery Court was a plum assignment, the most prestigious job for a Superior Court judge and often a stepping stone to the Appellate Court.

Francis was regarded as a fair and thoughtful jurist who took an almost academic approach to his cases. But Bill Buckman was not thrilled. Francis was a Republican and a former prosecutor, not the résumé of someone likely to stand up against the State Police. On the positive side, though, Francis was polite and gentlemanly and had a reputation for giving lawyers a great deal of latitude—if it meant getting to the truth. He didn't run his court with a stop watch and Buckman consoled himself that at least Francis might permit them the time to build their case.

The *Soto* hearing was held in the graceful Gloucester County Courthouse in the center of Woodbury. The brownstone turn-of-the-century edifice had a clock tower and cupola with a weathervane on top and its lawn was dominated by a towering stone War Memorial obelisk. As Chancery Judge, Francis presided in a grand, imposing temple of justice called the Ceremonial Courtroom, with a domed ceiling, huge chandelier, rich carpet, a balcony section with brass railings, and large cathedral windows. The bathroom had a marble sink with gold fixtures and a wooden water closet flushed by yanking a chain. One of the defense lawyers, Wayne Natale, saw it as a metaphor. *Soto* would be a colossal battle of enormous import that deserved to be played out in a big, majestic room.

The *Soto* hearing began November 28, 1994 and Judge Francis assumed it would be over by Christmas. So did State prosecutors. But the defense team knew better. A short trial would be a prosecution trial. They took a *Paul Masson* approach: *"No verdict before it's time."* But even they had no inkling of what was to come.

By this point, Buckman was under enormous strain. He was nearly broke and his wife was about to give birth to their second child. For five years he'd devoted more than a quarter of his time to *Soto* and hadn't earned a dime of compensation. Court-appointed attorneys traditionally waited for a case to end before billing the court for services rendered. Buckman had been paying his office rent and legal secretary from the other three-quarters of his practice. Now he would be devoting every minute to *Soto* for at least several weeks. He had no financial cushion and didn't know how he was going to feed his family.

Soto promised to be a landmark case. Pedro Soto and the other defendants wouldn't testify, no evidence about them would be presented, and after the first day they wouldn't even be in the courtroom. *Soto* would put the State Police on trial. The troopers were represented by Deputy Assistant Attorney General John Fahy, a lawyer in his early 40's whose confrontational style quickly set him on a collision course with the defense. For years, Fahy had been the State's point man on racial profiling, which had succeeded in Warren and Middlesex Counties largely by plea bargaining. Buckman suspected Fahy was so confident of triumph in Gloucester he'd convinced the Attorney General not to plea bargain *Soto*. By making a stand the State was taking a risk, but Fahy and his bosses apparently considered victory a virtual certainty. And with good reason, based on a decade of judges' rulings.

As momentous as *Soto* was, the hearing hardly registered a blip on the public's radar screen. The case was lost in the giant shadow being cast by the Super Bowl of all trials, one in which race would also be a vital element. As the prosecution and defense gathered in Judge Francis' stately but near empty courtroom, the O.J. Simpson murder case was kicking off 3,000 miles away in Los Angeles in the midst of one of the biggest media circuses in history. Everyone knew about O.J.; almost nobody knew of Pedro Soto. Buckman and the defense team certainly didn't exude the cachet of Simpson's legal Dream Team led by the swashbuckling Johnnie L. Cochran, Jr. They didn't wear Rolex watches or hand-tailored suits, their names were rarely in the newspaper, and Geraldo Rivera didn't obsess about them on TV. But *Soto* would ultimately have far greater implications for black America than the Simpson spectacle. (Ironically, it would also one day help make millions of dollars for Cochran and the Dream Team.)

Whereas O.J. Simpson's fate would rest in the hands of a jury, *Soto* would be decided by one man. The entire defense would be aimed at convincing Judge Francis that the New Jersey State Police were guilty of racial profiling. But it got off to a rocky start. After four years waiting for their day of reckoning, the defense announced it wanted to present an unorthodox opening statement—a tape of the WWOR-TV report *Without Just Cause*.

"It was our intention," Jeff Wintner told Francis, "to actually play this tape to the court since, in effect, this investigation represented a pretty concise representation of the case we intend to present."

Francis turned to John Fahy.

"I don't know, your Honor," Fahy said. "It's a unique proposition to show a videotape in lieu of an opening statement. It would all be hearsay."

"Judge," Buckman retorted, "we are making an allegation that something is very horribly wrong here in New Jersey on the Turnpike. *Without Just Cause* says that."

"No reporter," Francis said, "unless licensed to practice law in the State of New Jersey, can make an opening statement. Isn't that what you're asking me to allow?"

"Judge," said Wayne Natale, "the video is absolutely consistent with the evidence we're going to be presenting and I think it depicts visually for the court what you will hear verbally from witnesses."

"In my opinion its use in whole or in part as the opening would be improper," Francis said. "I'd rather hear it from the lawyers, not from a TV commentator."

The Ceremonial Courtroom may have been the most splendid courtroom in New Jersey but, with its high ceilings and the constant din from traffic outside, it had dreadful acoustics. As Jeff Wintner stood looking up at Judge Francis, perched on his elevated mahogany bench, he had to raise his voice for his opening statement to be heard.

"Your Honor, what we intend to prove, most defense attorneys practicing in this county and in many other counties know, what the news media have examined, and what I think a whole lot of black people know. And that is that the New Jersey State Police operating on the New Jersey Turnpike are conducting searches based on a racial profile."

Wintner promised defense studies would show an "overwhelming disproportion" of black motorists being pulled over.

"Statistically it is almost inconceivable. When we have completed presenting our case it will be clear to the court that we have established a case both statistically and from other evidence that these types of stops are taking place."

"The burden is not on the State in this situation," countered prosecutor Brent Hopkins, John Fahy's right hand man on *Soto*. "The burden is on the defense, and the case law indicates that it is a heavy burden. They have to present stark evidence statistically of some type of racial discrimination to show that people are being prosecuted based solely on their race."

Hopkins said the State had studies that indicated blacks were being stopped at a higher rate than whites not because of racial profiling by State Police, but because, in essence, they were worse drivers.

"They have to explain that, Judge. They can't," Hopkins said. "Not only is the State Police not involved in selective prosecution, but they are pulling over blacks in a percent which is justified, given the motor vehicle violations conducted by blacks."

Chapter 56

THE JUSTIN DINTINO ERA LASTED four years. For the apolitical
State Police Superintendent, the end was dictated by politics. Jim Florio
had proven to be an unpopular Governor. He was a decent, honorable
man, but was also blunt and humorless and had the personal magne-
tism of a trout. He'd succeeded the venerable Tom Kean, who—despite
his broad appeal—left behind a billion dollar budget deficit. Florio
responded by doubling the state income tax and slashing services to
the bone. *"Dump Florio"* bumper stickers were omnipresent.

Florio was ousted by a charismatic newcomer named Christine
Todd Whitman. In the age of Ronald Reagan and Bill Clinton,
Whitman had the same silky flair for convincing the electorate she
could transform vinegar into champagne. The Republican had never
held elected office beyond the county level, but politics was in her
blood. Her parents were prominent GOP fund-raisers. The Todd's
made their fortune building Rockefeller Center and restoring Colonial
Williamsburg. The Schley's—her mother's family—were New York
bankers who owned large swathes of New Jersey real estate. The future
governor grew up on Pontefract, her family's idyllic 230-acre estate in
the rolling hills of Jersey's horse country. One of her childhood play-
mates was Steve Forbes, heir to the *Fortune* magazine fortune.

Christie and Steve stepped into the national spotlight together at
age 8 when they stood with President Dwight D. Eisenhower on stage
at the 1956 Republican Convention. Seventeen years later she was escorted to Richard M. Nixon's inaugural ball by John R. Whitman,

the grandson of a former Governor of New York. Romance blossomed and Todd and Whitman married.

Christie Whitman had a regal presence. With her feathery blonde hair and captivating smile, she bore a striking resemblance to Princess Diana, the Duchess of Wales. The look served her well in the political arena. In 1982 she won a seat on the Somerset County Board of Freeholders. In 1988, Governor Tom Kean appointed her president of the State Board of Public Utilities. In 1990, Whitman shocked the political world when she came out of nowhere and got within a whisker of snatching the U.S. Senate seat of Bill Bradley, the celebrated Oxford-educated former New York Knicks basketball star.

Whitman was suddenly a hot political property and in 1993 she narrowly defeated Florio after an 11th hour pledge to slash state income taxes. After Whitman's victory, her campaign manager, Ed Rollins, inexplicably claimed he'd paid black ministers to discourage their congregations from voting for Florio. Rollins later recanted, but New Jersey blacks remained wary of Whitman.

After the election Justin Dintino announced his retirement. He had no regrets. The State Police was a mess when he took over as Superintendent. Because of his swift action, complaints of brutality and racial profiling had quickly subsided. There had been bumps in the road—such as the Black Radicals disparaging the State Police in front of Congress—but overall the Outfit was back on track. Most of Dintino's reforms had come in his first year in office and since then he'd become somewhat bored with the job. At age 65, he was ready to enjoy his golden years on the golf course.

But even though the tumult had faded, all was not well in the Outfit. It was a fractured agency. Dintino had long ago banished Clinton Pagano's top lieutenants, but a sizeable faction of troopers remained who had made their bones under Pagano. They bit their tongues when Dintino scaled back highway drug interdiction and brought in the ACLU and NAACP to lecture them about sensitivity. But they were still there.

Dintino was replaced by Carl Williams, a 30-year veteran who began dreaming of joining the State Police as a starry-eyed youngster after a trooper visited his elementary school and spoke to safety patrol guards. Williams certainly was not considered to be the brightest light in the organization. He had a vanilla personality, was not very articulate, and came across as somewhat of a rube. Fellow troopers nicknamed him *Opie*. Williams never distinguished himself in any particular area of police work and nearly retired before Whitman's election. Dintino talked him out of it, never imagining he'd be picked to succeed him.

Christine Todd Whitman wanted someone who could mend fences between the Dintino and Pagano blocs. Williams was well-liked and non-controversial and would be palatable to both camps. His school safety patrol story was so mom-and-pop-and-apple pie, the new governor decided he'd be the perfect man for the job.

For some, Williams' appointment was almost laughable. But for others it was an opportunity to return to the glory days, to a time when the Black Dragon was a gauntlet where drug traffickers feared to tread, a place where the State Police was respected, and a place where legends were made.

Chapter 57

As PROSECUTION AND DEFENSE LAWYERS in the *Soto* case wrangled over evidence before Judge Robert Francis, the first witness—Fred Last—paced the large, otherwise vacant courtroom, waiting to testify. After 20 years as a defense lawyer, sitting on the witness stand would be a new experience.

"Mr. Last," Francis said finally, "I can appreciate your nervousness, but I tend to follow you wandering around the courtroom. I find you staring out the window, wishing you were someplace else, and feel I'd like to be someplace else, too. Relax."

Soto had been pending for four years and here they were, at the threshold of the hearing, still squabbling over evidence.

"You would think by now all discovery issues would have been resolved," Francis said. "Why you've all waited 'til now is disturbing."

From the early stages Bill Buckman had been grumbling that prosecutors were stonewalling the defense. *Brady vs. Maryland,* the landmark U.S. Supreme Court ruling, established that prosecutors must turn over all evidence beneficial to defendants. Buckman accused the State of shirking its *Brady* responsibility. It hadn't produced State Police search data, training material, or the Pagano Report, the confidential analysis put together in response to *Without Just Cause* that Clinton Pagano had shown to reporter Joe Collum five years earlier. John Fahy denied such a report even existed.

"This is an organization that prides itself in its investigative abilities, its ability to amass evidence, its ability to maintain statistics," Buckman said, "and suddenly this one key document has disappeared."

"I think they're becoming a little paranoid about things," Fahy said. "They're fishing. This is not some free-wheeling investigative tribunal."

Fahy was combative right from the starting gate and the defense lawyers fast developed a keen dislike for him. He came across as cocky and arrogant and never passed up an opportunity to denigrate them, constantly grousing that it was too easy to make allegations about profiling.

"What it's been reduced to is public defenders coming in and saying 'We've looked at our cases and we're suspicious.' If that's the standard it's virtually no standard at all."

"I hope we're through with surprises and new thoughts," Judge Francis said. "It's time to try the case. Now can we begin?"

"Yes, your Honor," Jeff Wintner said. "We would call Fred B. Last to the stand."

Last's role would be to lay the foundation of the defense case, explaining why the racial profiling challenge was filed and how they'd gone about building their evidence.

"Beginning about 1987," Last testified, "we began to note that when we got cases from the Turnpike the defendants were invariably black. This was different from other limited access highways where troopers would bring in black folks, white folks, Hispanic folks."

Last detailed the *Soto* team's two big studies, the Turnpike Census and Violator Survey. By standing on the roadside with binoculars and eyeballing 42,706 cars, they determined 13.5% of Turnpike travelers were black. In the Violator Survey, Last said he observed 2,039 vehicles on the Turnpike and found 98% were speeding and, thus, subject to being stopped. Of those, 15% had black occupants.

Fahy blasted the studies. How could Last possibly identify the race of passengers in cars racing by at 60 or 70 mph? But all he could do was criticize. The State hadn't performed *any* highway tests.

After Last laid the groundwork, the case started heating up. Dr. John Lamberth was called to answer the nitty-gritty questions. Lamberth cited U.S. Public Health Service statistics that said blacks and whites abused illicit drugs at almost identical rates (11-12% of their respective populations). Therefore, based on the Turnpike Census, one would logically expect blacks to comprise about 13.5% of Turnpike drug arrests. Instead, they made up 73.2%.

"It is highly, highly improbable that 73.2% of blacks would be arrested from a population of 13.5% black," Lamberth said.

"Apparently it happened," Judge Robert Francis interjected, "so it's not highly, highly improbable. Are you saying if it were random?"

"If it were random, yes," Lamberth said

Defense suspicions about Judge Francis were reinforced by some of his rulings. Jeff Wintner tried to put the arrest records of individual troopers at Moorestown Station into evidence. One trooper had a 95% black arrest rate and many others were over 80%.

"I'm hearing no contention by the State that if there is any profiling by race that it's done just by a few bad boys and gals," Francis said. "I don't want to take this case off onto an avenue that is sort of like 'Never Never Land.' Therefore I won't admit it."

The ruling kept some potent data out of the evidence, but the defense still had an ace-in-the-hole. The Violator Survey showed blacks accounted for about 15% of speeders, but 46.2% of trooper stops. The statistical imbalance was overwhelming.

"The probability of this outcome [occurring randomly] is substantially less than one-in-one billion," Lamberth testified. "Put bluntly, the disparities strongly support the assertion that the State Police have targeted the community of black motorists."

Buckman's carping about the State withholding evidence began to pay off. Prosecutors started turning over a windfall of new data. Buckman used a drunk driving report to bash the State Police, showing that blacks comprised 10.4% of DUI arrests statewide, but 50% of DUI arrests by troopers on the southern Turnpike.

"It is preposterous to think," Buckman argued, "that 50% of the people driving on the Turnpike south of Exit 3 under the influence were black, simply preposterous, when on the other roads of the State of New Jersey they're 10%."

Just as compelling was a discovery the *Soto* team made while analyzing traffic tickets issued by three different State Police units. Each unit had different degrees of discretion on who to stop. The Radar Unit—with the least discretion—gave 18% of its citations to blacks. The Tac-Pac—a traffic enforcement unit—had more discretion and gave 23.8% of its tickets to blacks. And the Patrol Unit—which had total discretion *and* a mandate to interdict drugs—issued 46.2% of its citations to black drivers.

"The study demonstrates overwhelmingly that it's trooper discretion that is causing black motorists to be stopped disproportionately," Wintner said.

But the defense lawyers needed to put flesh on the statistical skeleton it was constructing. That's why Kenneth Ruff was a potentially pivotal witness. He could talk about the State Police from the inside. Ruff, of course, came to the stand carrying very heavy baggage. John Fahy intended to make the sordid details about him allegedly being caught in a dress, wig and mascara a part of the record. But Ruff had never been formally charged with cross-dressing and the alleged incident was not given as a reason for his firing. Judge Francis ruled the information was irrelevant and wouldn't allow it into evidence. The sigh of relief from the defense table was almost audible.

"Tell us," Buckman asked Ruff, "the first incidence of profile training you received."

"It was during the third night in which I was transferred to the Turnpike," Ruff testified.

"Who was the trooper that you were assigned to ride with?"

"Trooper Nicholas Monticello."

"Objection," interrupted Fahy, whose challenges were growing more and more incessant and were often punctuated with biting criticism. "I think it's totally unfair to Trooper Monticello. I can start bringing in black troopers to talk about where white troopers made decent stops."

"Well, we'd appreciate it if you would," Jeff Wintner said.

Francis let Ruff continue his testimony. He recounted Monticello sitting at a U-turn facing traffic, shining his spotlight at cars, then chasing after one containing three black occupants.

"Did Monticello tell you he had seen any violation?" Buckman asked.
"No."

"Was this car going at a high rate of speed?"

"It didn't constitute a high rate of speed at all."

Ruff said Monticello stopped the car and ordered the motorists out then searched them and found 160 vials of crack on the backseat passenger. Monticello didn't radio the stop to a dispatcher until he had handcuffed the prisoners, he said, in contravention of State Police rules which required calling in the races of vehicle occupants before confronting motorists. Later Ruff received a letter of commendation from the Attorney General for *"an outstanding arrest."*

"Mr. Ruff, did you feel that stop was an outstanding arrest?" Buckman asked.

"No. I recognized it as being wrong."

"Are you talking about a racially-motivated profile?"

"Absolutely."

When Fahy began cross-examining Ruff, the defense lawyers decided to give him some of his own medicine and started objecting at every opportunity. Fahy produced Monticello's arrest report which said he *"paced"* the car in question for one mile and determined it was speeding.

"You know for a fact that car was not going 64 miles an hour?" Fahy asked Ruff.

"I would object," Buckman said.

"Object, that's not what he said," Justin Loughry said.

Now Judge Francis was annoyed. "Every time I start to make a note you get into a fight."

"Well, every time I'm going to ask a question I get five people objecting," said Fahy, his frustration showing.

Chapter 58

THE PREDICTION THAT *SOTO* would be wrapped up by Christmas 1994 proved to be fantasy. The defense presentation lasted until January. John Fahy's rants about his opponents prolonging the proceedings were becoming routine.

"To quote Ronald Reagan: 'Here we go again!'" was a frequent dig. In early January, Judge Francis asked Fahy when he would call his witnesses. "Probably in 1996, the way this is going," he said with a flip of the hand and his voice dripping with sarcasm.

Fahy had one big advantage. He didn't need to win. A tie was as good as victory. The burden was on the defense to prove its case. If it fell short, the State Police would prevail. But the defense presentation had been formidable. Fahy had choices to make. One option was to end it all by offering Pedro Soto and his co-defendants plea bargains. The possibility hung over Bill Buckman and his associates like Damocles' sword. Five years of painstaking labor would be wiped out. Had Buckman been in Fahy's shoes, he'd have cut a deal. It just made sense. But to his enormous relief—and utter bafflement—Fahy didn't.

The question became what trial tactic he would adopt. Fahy could take the high road and bring in a procession of troopers—tall and straight and beyond reproach—to say: "No, your Honor, the State Police absolutely, positively do not racially profile." Judges had always bought the line, so why not Francis? Or he could blast away at the defense evidence until it collapsed like a house of cards. Fahy chose

217

to attack. He took dead aim at the defense's weakest links, Kenneth Ruff and Kenneth Wilson.

"The State will call Detective Karl Douglas," he announced.

Karl Douglas was a 17-year State Police veteran. He was also a black man of Jamaican descent. In 1989 he taught a course at the Academy, attended by Wilson and Ruff, about the Jamaican Posse, a vicious organized crime group that was a major player in the cocaine underground.

Posse members were known to travel through New Jersey and Douglas showed troopers a video and slides on the gang. Wilson and Ruff said they were struck by two photographs, one of a Posse member wearing dreadlocks and colorful Jamaican garb, and another of the same man with short hair dressed in a business suit, who looked like a middle-class black businessman. The ex-troopers testified the message the exhibit conveyed to them was that troopers should suspect all black people and they had carte blanche to stop dark-skinned travelers.

"Did you ever instruct troopers to pull over persons by race in an attempt to find Jamaican Posse members?" Fahy asked Douglas.

"No, I did not."

The defense had been asking for State Police training materials for more than a year, but hadn't seen Douglas's Jamaican Posse tape. To Buckman it was another *Brady* violation.

"What occurred with the videotape?" Buckman asked Douglas on cross-examination.

"I still have a copy."

"Were you questioned by the AG's office concerning training materials?"

"Yes."

"Did they ask you for copies?"

"Yes. I was asked to bring it in. However, I did not."

"You decided that it was not relevant?"

"No."

"Objection," Fahy shouted, jumping out of his seat. "This is becoming argumentative."

"Who in the AG's office asked you to bring this in?" Buckman said to Douglas.

"Jack Fahy."

"Objection," said Fahy.

"Judge, we were supposed to get training materials," Buckman said.

"You are silly people, I'll tell you," Fahy chided.

"Gents, let's—Gents, let's stop," said Judge Francis.

"Is there a reason you didn't want the defense to see these materials?" Buckman asked.

"No," Douglas replied. "I was just waiting for someone to say bring them in."

Judge Francis, always careful not to insult the attorneys, spoke up nonetheless. "I, in no way, have nor am questioning your integrity, Mr. Fahy. However, from our experience with Detective Douglas, it leads to my suggesting that you, at your convenience, double-check with any witnesses you expect to call to insure they have produced whatever they may have within their possession which has been requested by the defense."

It was as close as Francis came to reading the riot act. The next day Douglas brought the Jamaican Posse videotape to court. To a reggae music soundtrack, the "training" tape consisted of television news clips about drug posses, rioting in Jamaica, and a scene of a black man with a switchblade viciously slashing the face of another black man. To Justin Loughry, something about the tape looked curiously familiar.

During the noon break the lawyers convened at Café Nina's, a little luncheonette across the street from the courthouse and a favorite haunt of judges and lawyers. The *Soto* team had become regulars. Jack Fahy and Brent Hopkins typically sat several tables away, glaring at the defenders, who were often laughing hysterically at one of Buckman's fiendishly exact imitations of Fahy or one of his witnesses. Loughry said he recognized a clip on the Jamaican Posse video. It had been 20 years, but he remembered seeing those very scenes as a college student in a theatrical film called *The Harder They Come*, starring the legendary reggae singer Jimmy Cliff as a violent drug kingpin. The State Police were using movie clips to train troopers about drug smuggling. It was like teaching them about the Mafia by playing *The Godfather*.

"This is really great," Buckman said. "How do they teach troopers about the Hispanic profile? Show old Lucy and Ricky re-runs with

Ricky saying: 'Lucy, my conga drum is bery, bery heavy. What you got in there? You got a lot of 'splainin' to do now.'"

The lawyers howled as Fahy eyed them warily. When court reconvened Loughry got right to the point.

"Sir, have you seen a film called *The Harder They Come?*" he asked Detective Douglas.

"Yes."

"There's an excerpt on that tape of that film, is there not?"

"Yes."

"Detective Douglas," Wayne Natale asked, "*The Harder They Come* was a total fictional film. Is that not correct?"

"Yes."

"You took that movie and took sections of it to put it on your video to show troopers?"

"Yes."

"Why'd you do that?"

"I wanted to illustrate the violent nature of Jamaican Posse members."

"So you used a film as an accurate factual representation of the violence of Jamaican Posses, though you knew it was fictional."

The *Soto* team had turned Fahy's first witness to its own advantage and quickly realized that for every punch Fahy threw at them, they could counter-punch to devastating effect. They soon got another chance when Fahy called Trooper Nicholas Monticello. Tall and dark with chiseled good looks, Monticello strode into the elegant courtroom looking cool and confident in his crisp, clean State Police uniform. He was there to rebut Kenny Ruff's testimony accusing Monticello of making a racial profile stop on the black trooper's third night at Newark Station.

"Trooper Monticello, what caused you specifically to notice the car?" Fahy asked.

"Well, at first, I observed that the vehicle was traveling at a high rate of speed."

"Did you know the race of the occupants of this vehicle when you pulled out?"

"No. I got behind the vehicle and conducted a speedometer pace, which lasted approximately one mile."

Monticello said he clocked the car going 64 mph, nine miles above the speed limit. He pulled it over and observed a vial on the floor that looked like crack cocaine, then searched the three passengers and found 160 vials of crack on one of them.

"Did Mr. Ruff ever make any complaint about your conduct that evening?"

"No, he did not."

Fahy accomplished his objective. It was a case of "he said-he said." Monticello's testimony nullified Ruff's. Tie went to the prosecution. Satisfied, he offered up the trooper for cross-examination.

Wayne Natale was licking his chops. Like his fellow defenders, Natale was a dyed-in-the-wool idealist. Born and raised in Camden, New Jersey, his mother had been a card-carrying Socialist and his father a union organizer. Natale didn't get a look at Monticello's arrest report until the trooper took the witness stand. While he testified, the attorney scoured the document word-by-word, looking for something, anything, to hang his hat on until, finally, a small detail jumped out at him.

"Your police report says the vehicle was stopped at mile post 110.8?"

"That's correct," Monticello said firmly.

"Now let me see if I can get this straight. You were in a dead stop at mile post 111.8; got behind that vehicle and paced it for approximately one mile, stopping it exactly one mile down the road at mile post 110.8. Is that your testimony, trooper?"

"Yes."

Natale had set the hook and began to reel in his catch. In a long, painstaking examination, he dissected the stop second-by-second, first forcing Monticello to admit it had taken him at least 10 seconds to go from a dead stop to 60 miles an hour. In that time he would have traveled an average of 30 mph while the other car continued going 64 mph.

"I place a 500 foot distance between you and this vehicle after 10 seconds," Natale said.

"No," Monticello disagreed.

"You were closer to them?"

"I believe so. To the best of my…"

"Then they couldn't have been traveling 64 miles an hour," Natale said.

He did the math. If Monticello's car was moving at 30 mph—or 44 feet per second—he would have covered 440 feet in 10 seconds. If the other vehicle was traveling 64 mph—or 93.3 feet per second—it would cover 933 feet in the same time span—a 493 feet difference.

"That would have placed you nearly 500 feet behind that vehicle?" Natale said again.

"Yes," Monticello finally conceded.

"Can you pace at that distance?"

"No."

"So, I see, we've traveled nearly one-fifth of a mile and you're not even in a location to pace." Suddenly Monticello didn't seem so confident. "You believe the car was doing a little more than the speed limit, which is basically what 64 is, correct?"

"It's nine miles over the speed limit."

"When you cruise up and down the Turnpike what kind of speed do you travel at?"

"On routine patrol, 55 miles per hour," Monticello said.

Judge Francis interrupted: "Let me get this straight. Are you saying you're required to obey all the traffic regulations that every other motorist is obligated to obey?"

"Yes," Monticello said.

"I must confess that shocks me. I have never seen a trooper within the speed limit."

A jolt of electricity shot through the *Soto* team. Anyone who drove the Turnpike knew troopers routinely cruised at well over the speed limit. But the revelation was that Judge Francis called Monticello on the fiction. The lawyers wondered if they were making progress.

Natale continued. He maintained that, after reaching cruising speed, it would take Monticello another eight seconds to close the gap between the two vehicles and begin pacing.

"I don't recall," the trooper said.

"You don't recall? I'm asking you to use your mind, trooper. I'm asking you to think about whether you would have caught up to him in anything less than 18 seconds," said Natale.

"I don't know, sir."

By the time he was done, Natale had demonstrated that—between catching up to and stopping the drug car—Monticello would have burned at least 33 seconds and traveled more than 3000 feet. Thus, his official account that he'd paced the vehicle for one mile was a physical impossibility. Monticello became hesitant, his self-assurance disappeared, his dark eyes got wide and he began having trouble answering the rapid-fire questions. To Natale, the trooper looked like a deer in jacklights.

"Therefore, you did not pace that vehicle for a mile?" Natale said.

"That's correct," Monticello said finally.

The trooper had been called to expose Kenneth Ruff as a liar, but accomplished just the opposite. The implication was clear. If Ruff was telling the truth about Monticello not pacing the car, what was the justification for the stop? Maybe Ruff also told the truth when he said it was the color of the occupants.

Natale had turned another of Fahy's witnesses to the defense's advantage. The *Soto* team was batting two-for-two.

Chapter 59

AFTER JUSTIN DINTINO TOOK OVER as State Police Superintendent, narcotics arrests on the Jersey Turnpike plunged and minority complaints evaporated. Dintino and civil rights advocates believed racial profiling was a thing of the past. But it had only gone into a dormant stage. By the time Dintino retired in 1992, the practice was already coming out of hibernation.

Darryl Beard saw it firsthand. One of the surviving Black Radicals, Beard was transferred to Moorestown Station in 1992. At first, the South Jersey assignment didn't seem nearly as bad as Newark Station had been. Then he began noticing things. As the renowned New Jersey philosopher Yogi Berra once observed, "It was like déjà vu all over again."

Even though Dintino de-emphasized highway drug enforcement, some of those instrumental in its development still held positions of authority. When Sgt. Brian Caffrey arrived at Moorestown, he was still a State Police legend with his full cluster of ribbons and reputation as the king of interdiction. Word soon spread that Caffrey was unhappy that the station wasn't producing arrest numbers like it did back in his heyday.

Beard began seeing *ghost stops,* troopers stopping and searching cars without calling them in unless they found contraband. When he stopped to back up white troopers he was routinely waved off, only to discover later that other white troopers had stopped and helped search the cars—which invariably were driven by minorities. Beard went to his supervisor and complained that troopers were racially profiling again. Not long after, the supervisor called Caffrey into his office and told him about Beard's grievance.

"Darryl is absolutely wrong," Caffrey protested. "He doesn't know what he's talking about. He chooses not to contribute to the criminal program."

Beard overheard the discussion and stuck his head in the doorway. Caffrey waved him in and began lecturing him.

"It's a vital necessity to stop drug dealers, Darryl," he said. "You should be happy we're targeting people who are bringing crack and cocaine into your community."

"I think you've said that so much you actually believe it," Beard said, trying to contain his anger. "What you're doing is a self-fulfilling prophecy. Everyone is using drugs in America, but all you do is target one group. So the group you pick is the group you're going to marginalize."

"Well, that's what you see," Caffrey said.

"You're not talking to a rookie. I know everybody in the station that's profiling."

"It's not racial profiling," Caffrey said, becoming emotional. "It's good police work."

"You try to make it seem like science," Beard said. "All your boys are doing is stopping people with dark skin. I see absolutely no science in that."

"You need to come out with me," Caffrey said.

"I'm not coming out with you because I'm not going to racial profile."

Chapter 60

As THE *Soto* HEARING DRAGGED through its second month, it had become a grind on all involved. Every morning at 7:30, the defense team plodded into the Public Defender's office to begin strategizing. It was the same routine day after day. Jeff Wintner began calling the group *Team Groundhog,* after the Bill Murray movie about a guy who kept reliving Groundhog Day. "Hi, Groundhogs," became Wintner's daily salutation. At 8:30, Team Groundhog walked one block to the courthouse while a PD investigator loaded boxes of evidence into a car and drove them over. Court convened at 9:00 a.m.

"Well, guys, are we gaining on it?" Judge Francis would say every day.

"Yes, your Honor, we're gaining on it," the Groundhogs would reply, trying to sound sincere.

No one had a more grueling agenda than Francis. While he was hearing *Soto,* he was still presiding over other Chancery Court cases, including a complex stock derivatives trial that involved some of the biggest law firms in New Jersey and New York. The judge rarely left the courthouse before 8 p.m. Nonetheless, he remained unfailingly polite and didn't let other pressures short-circuit the *Soto* inquiry.

At the same time, John Fahy seemed to be growing more frazzled. The defense team was showing him no quarter, pouncing on every opportunity to argue and object and the pressure seemed to be driving Fahy to distraction. A more ominous trend for him, though, was his witnesses. Fahy called another trooper, Timothy Grant, of the

Drug Interdiction Training Unit, who rebutted Kenneth Wilson's testimony that he'd patrolled with Grant one day when the trainer stopped and searched six motorists, five of whom were black. Grant denied everything and refused to say anything to help the defense. But the *Soto* lawyers were concocting resourceful ways to use Fahy's witnesses to bolster their case. One was called *The Blue-Haired Lady from Wenonah Hypothetical.*

Wenonah was a wealthy South Jersey community. Jeff Wintner described a hypothetical scenario in which two vehicles were speeding down the Turnpike, one driven by an elderly rich white woman from Wenonah, the other a rental car from Dade County, Florida driven by a black man.

"Isn't it a fact," Wintner asked, "that you would be more likely to pull over the rental car from Dade County than the blue-haired old woman from Wenonah?

"I don't know that," Grant said. "If I'm stopping cars, then I'm going to stop both cars."

"Trooper, is it your testimony that you never take into account such factors as whether the vehicle is a rental car registered in Dade County?"

"Well, first off, if there was a motor vehicle violation..."

"Address yourself to the question," Wintner said.

"That was a slap at the witness," Fahy objected. "A little respect can be shown."

"Well, let me interject," Judge Francis said. "Which one do you stop?"

"Well, there are a lot of other factors..." Grant said.

"You've now paced these cars for a mile," the judge persisted. "These fools don't see you and continue to drive 70 miles an hour. Which one do you stop?"

"Is this purely hypothetical, your Honor?" Fahy asked.

"Of course it's hypothetical. Do you think I'm not making this up?"

"A car from Dade County stands out a little more than the in-state car," Grant said.

The defense got its hands on another videotape called *Operation Pipeline,* about a drug interdiction program in New Mexico. The film's credits said it used "techniques" developed by the New Jersey State Police. Sgt. Brian Caffrey had used it to train Jersey troopers.

When the handsome, broad-shouldered trooper entered the Ceremonial Courtroom, one of Judge Francis' clerks—an attractive, middle-aged woman—was captivated. She thought he looked like a god. But the *Soto* lawyers considered Caffrey one of those responsible for the Turnpike problem. His charisma and self-confidence had been used to help sell drug interdiction as sophisticated science. To Bill Buckman it was gobbledygook and he lampooned Caffrey at Café Nina's.

"How dare you, sir," Buckman said, impersonating Caffrey. "You can't talk to me like that. You see these medals? This means I have training and experience."

The defense lawyers guffawed as Fahy glared at them from a few tables away. Caffrey, however, was a formidable witness who didn't concede one iota to the defense. At the end of the direct examination, Wintner asked Francis' clerk how she felt.

"Oh, I think he's very credible," she said.

Under cross-examination, Caffrey denied the State Police employed a racial profile. He denied the 73.2% black arrest rate by Turnpike troopers was a sign of bias. He even denied the Drug Interdiction Training Unit was meant to train troopers to interdict drugs. Caffrey claimed he'd been qualified as an "expert witness" in 30 drug-related criminal cases, but when pressed by Jeff Wintner he could remember almost nothing about them.

"Are you able to give me the names of any of the defendants you testified against?"

"No, sir."

"The names of any of the defense attorneys?"

"No, sir."

"The names of the judges that qualified you as an expert?"

"No, sir."

Wintner confronted him with the *Operation Pipeline* video. The tape prominently displayed Hispanic-looking drug couriers and ended by stating that the program had resulted in the arrests of 84 Hispanics.

"So, how would the general road patrol trooper utilize that information?" Wintner said.

"It's something for him to be aware of. I don't see it as a tip-off," Caffrey said.

Later, Wintner asked one of the defense experts, Dr. James Fyfe, a former New York City police officer, about the video.

"The only characteristic I saw had to do with ethnicity," Fyfe said.

"How could a police officer use that information in his day-to-day policing?"

"What it does is encourage officers to use ethnicity as a cue."

Caffrey spent seven days on the witness stand. At the end of his cross-examination, Wintner approached the female clerk again.

"Do you still feel that way?"

"Oh, no," she said. "I don't know if I like this guy."

By February, Bill Buckman was suffering from insomnia. The mental and physical demands of *Soto* had been draining. Worse, the case had all but destroyed him financially.

Buckman still hadn't been paid for thousands of hours of work on *Soto* going back five years. He was barely able to support his family and keep his practice afloat. For nearly three months now he'd been working exclusively on the racial profiling case and had no money coming in. His savings were gone and he'd run up more than $15,000 in credit card debt. There was no end to *Soto* in sight and Buckman was so broke he couldn't sleep, racking his brain over where his next dollar would come from.

On February 10th his wife, Shellie, gave birth to their second child, a girl they named Emily. It should have been a joyous event but instead it nearly pushed them over the edge. The pressure on Shellie leading up to the birth had been enormous. Buckman was almost never home and she'd gone through her pregnancy raising their 3-year-old son Ethan by herself. Emily's delivery was difficult and Shellie contracted toxemia. Buckman could only take off two days from the trial. The day she came home from the hospital he picked up her and the baby, took them home, then rushed back to court. He felt miserable. He knew it was no way to live. Shellie had always been very optimistic and never nagged him about money or his grueling work schedule. But that day she cried. The strain only got worse.

One night he came home late and exhausted. He went to bed, but the new baby was screaming. Sleep was impossible and Buckman snapped.

He started yelling at Shellie: "What's wrong with her? I need to get some sleep. I'm getting out of here." He left home and went to a hotel.

John Fahy was having problems too. Like Buckman, he was nearing a meltdown. In retaliation for his constant stream of snide remarks and denigrating attitude, the *Soto* team was showing him no mercy and it was taking its toll. In February, Fahy asked to speak with Judge Francis and one member of the defense team. Jeff Wintner was picked.

"I need a recess," Fahy said, "at least for a week or two."

"Why?" Francis said, looking at him with surprise.

"I'm going nuts. I can't take the adversarial nature of this. I can't take the argumentative battling and the contentiousness. I've never been involved in anything like it. I've been to a counselor and he wants me to take some time off."

Wintner had the impression Fahy was on the verge of a nervous breakdown.

"Just calm down, Jack," Francis said. The judge was clearly concerned about Fahy's welfare, but he refused to delay the hearing. "I'm going to ask the defense to be easier on you. We've got a long holiday weekend coming up for President's Day. Relax and take it easy and let's see how you feel when we return."

One reason for Fahy's anxiety may have been that the *Soto* team was clobbering him with his own witnesses. And they'd uncovered a series of smoking gun documents. One was a checklist from the Drug Interdiction Training Unit. The defense had been trying to get its hands on DITU records for months, but were told they didn't exist. Eventually, to their surprise, the State turned over hundreds of DITU checklists trainers used to grade troopers. One contained a narrative written in 1989 by a trainer named Geleta about a Trooper Fash.

"Trooper Fash…has become a little reluctant to stop cars in lieu of the Channel 9 News Report. He was told as long as he uses Title 39 he can stop any car he wants."

The implications of the memo leaped out at the lawyers. Why would Trooper Fash be reluctant to stop cars over a news report about racial profiling? If he wasn't profiling, why was he concerned? The note also showed troopers were being told they could stop "any car" they saw violate Title 39, the New Jersey Traffic Code. The defense had already demonstrated that virtually everyone on the Jersey Turnpike was speeding. If troopers could stop anyone, why were blacks being stopped at a rate five times higher than whites?

The dramatically disproportionate stop rate was Fahy's biggest conundrum. Too glaring to ignore, he had to attack it. The center-piece of his assault became: *Are blacks stopped more often because they drive worse than whites?* Fahy had no independent evidence blacks drove faster or more recklessly, but the defense didn't either. They hadn't even addressed the possibility. If he raised *blacks drive worse* as a theory for the elevated black stop rate, it might defuse the cataclys-mic impact of the defense statistics on his case.

Fahy broached the premise to Dr. John Lamberth. "Your census does not make demarcations, distinctions between a speeder going 75 miles per hour versus a speeder going 61, correct?"

"It does not differentiate," Lamberth said.

"So it doesn't differentiate by race when you're looking at the vari-ous speeds people travel on the turnpike, correct?"

"There is no evidence in the data that we looked at that would indicate that blacks are going slower or faster when they are stopped than whites."

"You cannot tell this court the percentage of blacks speeding at rates in excess of 70 miles per hour, can you?"

"No."

Bill Buckman was outraged. To imply that blacks were somehow inferior drivers compared to Caucasians was morally repugnant. There was no basis to even raise the issue. But Judge Robert Francis seemed to attach some importance to Fahy's posit.

"If that data were to show," Francis interjected, "that all blacks that were stopped for speeding were doing an average of 89 miles per hour and all whites were doing an average of 66 miles per hour, would that make any differences to your conclusions [that troopers were tar-geting blacks]?"

"It might," Lamberth admitted.

Justin Loughry thought Fahy was grasping at straws and decided to at-tack his premise head on by again using Fahy's witnesses against him.

"There's nothing, is there Trooper [Donald] Nemeth, about the way blacks drive that made them more noticeable than the way whites drive?" Loughry asked.

"I haven't found any," replied Nemeth, a former DITU trainer.

"Has it been your experience," Loughry asked Trooper Timothy Grant, "that any particular ethnic or racial group commits more traffic violations than any other group?"

"No," Grant said.

"Is there any racial or ethnic group that are worse drivers than any other group?"

"No."

"Your Honor," Fahy said, jumping to his feet, "I'm going to object."

But Francis let the testimony stand and the *Soto* lawyers began asking every trooper the same question. They all said the same thing: There was no difference between the driving habits of blacks and whites.

Chapter 61

VICTOR COOPER WAS WORKING THE MIDNIGHT SHIFT when he heard another trooper report over the radio that he'd stopped two men on the Turnpike 14 miles north of him. The trooper said the men were Caucasian and he'd sent them on their way.

A short time later, Cooper—an African-American—stopped a car for speeding. The license plate number seemed familiar.

"You got me," the agitated driver said as soon as Cooper reached his open window. "I know I was speeding. I'm just trying to get the hell out of this state."

Cooper realized why the license number was familiar. The other trooper had called in the same number a few minutes earlier. But these couldn't be the same people. The trooper said the car contained two white men. These men were black.

"I just got stopped by your guys," the driver said. "They searched us, trashed our car, then they wet in my trunk."

"What do you mean they wet in your trunk?" Cooper said.

"Yeah, they wet in my trunk," the man said, reaching down to his groin and giving the universal gesture of a man urinating.

"Oh," said Cooper, flustered. "They pissed in your trunk. Oh, boy! I see, I see."

"This is ridiculous," the man said, growing more furious. "I want out of this damned state."

"Okay, calm down," Cooper said. "Maybe you should go to the station and report this."

"Which way is the station? Is it on my way?"

"No, it's back," Cooper said, pointing north.

"No, I'm not going back. I'm going home. I just want out of here."

Cooper couldn't blame him. He'd been seeing more and more of what appeared to be racial profiling. His squad leader had been pushing his troopers hard to make drug arrests.

The sergeant vowed to ride the midnight shift with each of his men and personally school them on how to interdict drugs. When Cooper's turn came, his sergeant drove while he explained that their emphasis would be Hispanics in cars from out of state. They spent part of the night parked, with their spotlight pointed at eye-level at passing vehicles, or driving up the left lane examining car tags. If the license was from outside New Jersey, they'd check out the driver. If it was a Latin-looking male, they'd stop him. The sergeant searched a couple of cars, but came up empty. Most of the stops were not called in. About three o'clock in the morning, he asked Cooper what he thought.

"It's totally illegal and we shouldn't be doing this. And I'm not doing it," Cooper said.

"We're done for the night," the sergeant said.

With that, he parked the car beside the Turnpike, put his head back and went to sleep.

Chapter 62

ARCTIC WINDS BLEW SEVERAL BLIZZARDS into New Jersey the winter of '95, burying the Garden State under a blanket of snow. The Ceremonial Courtroom was so chilly in the morning that a female reporter from a local newspaper took notes wearing her mittens. Judge Francis joked about burning paper to get warm. But by afternoon the courthouse furnace would kick in and the sun poured through the tall south windows and the big room got so stuffy the lawyers sometimes had to struggle to keep from dozing off.

The defense team found the best antidote for fatigue was laughter and they vented their acidic humor daily. The butt of their jokes was invariably the opposition. They concocted absurd songs revamped from old TV programs. One ditty composed by Bill Buckman was about prosecutors Jack Fahy and Brent Hopkins, sung to the theme song from *The Patty Duke Show*, a 1960's sitcom about a pair of identical cousins.

"Here's Jack who's been most everywhere,
From Bergen County to Hamilton Square.
But Brent has only seen the sights
A prosecutor can see from Woodbury Heights.
Oh, what a crazy pair."

Prosecution witnesses were not immune to some of the most stinging parody. In early March, Major Alexander Tezsla took the stand and said flatly: "We do not practice racial profiling on the New Jersey Turnpike." Tezsla was the State Police Turnpike commander in 1989

235

when *Without Just Cause* was broadcast. Buckman grilled him on what he did to investigate the TV report's charges.

"You didn't initiate any investigation to see if the allegations on the tape were true?"

"The Colonel [Pagano] was handling the WOR allegations," Tezsla said.

"It didn't pique your interest to say 'Maybe I ought to look at this'?"

"No. I was satisfied that the Colonel was handling it."

"That's interesting," Buckman said. "What was the Colonel doing?"

"The Colonel was doing what he felt was right and proper."

"Did you talk to the Colonel about this?"

"No, I did not."

"So you don't know if the Colonel was doing what was right and proper?"

"I don't know where you're leading," Tezsla said.

"Where I'm leading is up to me," Buckman said.

Later, at Café Nina's, Buckman did a take-off of Tezsla as Sergeant Schultz from *Hogan's Heroes,* the television comedy about a World War II prison camp.

"Tell me, sergeant, did you do anything about the reports of atrocities?"

"That vould have been the Colonel's job," said Buckman mimicking Tezsla as Schultz. "I see nothing! I hear nothing! I know nothing!"

Around that time, Buckman and his cohorts came to a startling realization. They'd gone into *Soto* expecting to fight the good fight, but not anticipating victory. Yet their statistical evidence had been powerful and they were making great headway cross-examining prosecution witnesses like Major Tezsla and Sgt. Brian Caffrey. And Judge Francis seemed to be getting what they were saying. One day one of the defense lawyers blurted out a shocking statement.

"You know, we could win this thing."

They looked at each other and realized it was true. The State doggedly refused to admit the defense allegation contained even a morsel of truth and Buckman prayed Judge Francis would see through their blanket denials.

The prosecution's last best hope was Dr. Leonard Cupingood, a gangly man with a prominent Adams Apple who reminded the defense lawyers of Ichabod Crane. Cupingood was the State's chief statistical expert. But before he even began testifying, the *Soto* team spent two days roughing him up over his Curriculum Vitae, which they demonstrated was puffed up and misleading, in several instances failing to credit co-authors of scholarly papers. It was like sacking an opposing quarterback early in a football game to take the starch out of him.

Cupingood came to the witness stand with one message—the defense statistics were hogwash. He castigated everything about the *Soto* team's numbers. The Turnpike Violator Survey was invalid because it was conducted during daylight hours, he said, testifying that troopers gave blacks more tickets at night when they couldn't see a driver's color and therefore had to be acting in a race-neutral manner.

Jeff Wintner asked Cupingood if he was familiar with *spotlighting*, where troopers parked their cruisers perpendicular to the Turnpike and shined their light at eye-level, giving them a clear view of occupants.

"No, I was not," Cupingood said.

"If that premise is correct, then the standard which you set forth is an invalid standard, is it not?" Wintner said.

"It definitely would call into question the whole alternative analysis, yes."

Cupingood also championed the prosecution's *blacks drive worse* theory. The Violator Survey recorded the races of drivers traveling 61 mph or faster.

"We know nothing of those going say 80 to 90 miles per hour, and, of those, what is the racial mix."

Wintner asked him if he knew several troopers had testified there was no difference between the driving habits of whites and blacks.

"I was not told that," said Cupingood.

"Doesn't that encompass the concerns that have just been expressed?"

"That's exactly the type of data that I had been—you know, I had been looking for."

Cupingood performed a series of purportedly complex calculations, one called the *Mantel-Haentzel Analysis* and another called a *Chi Square* computation, which concluded troopers were stopping only a few more black drivers than should be "expected." The defense attacked his conclusions as "gibberish" and accused Cupingood of "winnowing" data and massaging his numbers until they were meaningless.

By now the hearing—predicted to last one month—was in its fifth month and the *Soto* team's gallows humor had reached new depths. The jokes were getting more and more perverse. At the time, the news was full of reports of genocide in the African country of Burundi. Hundreds of thousands of people were being slaughtered. Bill Buckman began regaling his cohorts with the "Cupingood Burundian Principal of Expected vs. Non-Expected Massacres."

"Assume there's this hypothetical country, we'll call it Burundi," Buckman said during a mock cross-examination. "People are finding dead bodies all over the place. I take it then that your testimony would be that if the average number of dead bodies per Burundian village is 20, you don't see any problem until we reach 25 dead bodies per village."

Over lunch at Café Nina's, Justin Loughry crooned about Cupingood's analyses, to the tune of *"I Get A Kick Out Of You."*

"I get no kick from Chi Square.
Mantel and Haentzel don't take me anywhere.
But Lenny Cupingood
We get a kick out of you."

Judge Francis also seemed dubious about Cupingood's calculus. After the statistician struggled to explain one of his laborious mathematical equations, the judge ended the session with a portentous remark: "For what it's worth to the State, I don't follow that, but I'll let you worry about that later."

As testimony neared its end, one State Police witness still had not been called to testify. More than five years had passed since Clinton Pagano's ouster from the State Police, but his spirit hovered over the hearing like a wraith.

John Fahy had avoided calling Pagano, as if he was some barmy uncle to be hidden from the neighbors. Cupingood was supposed to be Fahy's last witness, but he'd been a disaster and the prosecution was standing on very wobbly legs. It got even more rickety when Judge Francis acquiesced to a defense motion to admit into evidence Pagano's videotaped remarks from *Without Just Cause*—several of which, in retrospect, seemed reckless, particularly his response to a question about whether the rights of minority travelers were *"of serious concern."*

"It is of serious concern," Pagano said at the time, "but nowhere near the concern I think we have got to look to in trying to correct some of the problems found with the criminal element in this state."

Drug interdiction was Pagano's spawn and all the glory or guilt that flowed from it ultimately traced back to him. Judge Francis didn't say so outright, but by allowing the video into evidence he was putting Fahy on notice that he needed to pull a rabbit out of his hat. Pagano was the only rabbit left.

When he took the witness stand on May 17, 1995, Pagano was not a man at the peak of his powers. Now in his mid-60s, he *was* making a lot of money. Unlike Justin Dintino, after leaving State service Pagano had leaped into the gambling industry, helping found a company that built and managed Indian casinos. Yet, he still sounded like the man once known as the "J. Edgar Hoover of New Jersey."

"There is no dispute," Pagano said from the witness stand, "that the highways of this State are used regularly by criminal offenders of every ilk. Every form of human debauchery is occurring on the Turnpike."

Pagano recounted traveling through New Jersey during the 1980s, listening to minority communities beg him to stop the drug plague and how that led him to make drug enforcement his number one priority.

"I had a very simple standard. No work, no eat. I would expect that every trooper patrolling the Turnpike would make criminal apprehensions."

Pagano called the profiling allegations "alibis." He noted that Bruno Richard Hauptmann claimed the State Police arrested him for the Lindbergh baby kidnapping because he was German. He recalled when blacks began moving into New Jersey with "the advent of the so-called Great Society, a common alibi was that they were being arrested not because they were guilty, but because they were black. I don't ever remember a court that accepted the alibi. It was then and is now wrong."

During cross-examination, Jeff Wintner posed a variation on his question about the *Little Old Blue-Haired Lady from Wenonah*.

"Let's say that this trooper on the Turnpike sees a car that has Judge Francis operating it going 65 miles an hour and at the same time he sees another motor vehicle going the same speed and it has a driver who appears to be Jamaican."

"If, in fact, your Honor," Pagano said, "I saw them both from behind and could tell the identities as Mr. Wintner has portrayed it, I, as a patrolling trooper, might very well stop the one I think is occupied or operated by the Jamaican."

Every other State Police witness had waffled on the question and the defense lawyers were pleasantly surprised by Pagano's candor. Their cross-examination remained polite and courteous. It was Judge Francis who interjected some of the most pointed questions.

"Before the WOR series was aired, Colonel, had you heard any general complaint by blacks about supposed targeting?" the judge asked.

"Specifically blacks, yes, your Honor. But we could only accommodate them on the basis of a specific complaint. You can't scatterboard and say 'We're going to investigate every action taken against a black member of our society.'"

"How would an investigation of an individual complaint prove or disprove a general claim of selected enforcement?"

"It would not, your Honor," Pagano said.

"What, if anything, did you do to look into that?"

"I don't remember ever actually looking into a general complaint or, for that matter, having the need to look into a general complaint. It's up to the courts to decide whether or not that kind of activity has been occurring."

Just before Pagano took the witness stand, the State finally produced the Pagano Report, which John Fahy had been denying existed. The 11-page analysis Pagano had pulled out during his second interview with reporter Joe Collum after the airing of *Without Just Cause* concluded that 76% of trooper Turnpike arrests were of blacks—as the TV story had reported. But it also rejected the profiling allegations because they were based on *arrests* rather than *stop* data, which the report maintained was the true measure of profiling.

"Was there any attempt to gather that stop information?" Wintner asked.

"Not that I'm aware of," Pagano said. "I know of no inquiry that was made."

Chapter 63

"HALLELUJAH!" JUDGE ROBERT FRANCIS SHOUTED, throwing his arms into the air. The hearing that was supposed to last one month was finally over—six months after it began. *Soto* had consumed 72 days, 30 witnesses, 200 pieces of evidence, and 15,000 pages of testimony. The judge and lawyers shook hands, smiled, and engaged in some friendly conversation. The defense team was even cordial to John Fahy.

"We're glad it's concluded," Fahy said. "It certainly has been a long and, at times, strongly adversarial proceeding."

"Who's going to lead the hallelujah?" Francis said again.

The judge retired to his chambers and lit a cigarette. The marathon was over, but there was still work to do. Written summations were due in two months, followed by oral final arguments in the fall. Then Francis would decide whether the New Jersey State Police were guilty or innocent.

Yet, for Bill Buckman the conclusion hadn't come a moment too soon.

By the end of May 1995, he was burned out and broke and had decided to change the direction of his life before it destroyed him and his young family. A couple of years earlier, he'd attended a legal seminar in Vermont and someone from the Public Defender's Office there offered him a job running the PD's Rutland office. He and Shellie started talking about it. *Soto* had been such an excruciating pressure cooker the urge to pack their bags and head north to the clean air and tranquility of the Green Mountains became overpowering.

As the trial neared end, Buckman announced he was leaving New Jersey to go hug trees in Vermont. The other defense lawyers were stunned. He knew they suspected he'd lost his mind—and that they may have been right. But he owed it to Shellie and the children to get away. He wanted a lifestyle that allowed him to come home at night after work and play with the kids on the lawn. They sold their modest house in New Jersey and bought a country home on 10 acres outside Rutland. It was one of the best moves Buckman ever made. The pace of life in Vermont was infinitely more serene. He put the brakes on the destructive track of endless hours of work, stress, and nights lying awake worrying. The first summer he built an addition onto their house. After five years of craziness the manual labor was perfect therapy.

When Buckman left New Jersey he had no plans to return, but he did have an agreement with the Vermont Public Defender that he could continue working on *Soto* until the case was finished. Via FedEx and fax machine, he helped his colleagues construct the written summation and, in November, returned one last time for oral summations.

"Your Honor," he said, "I remember my remarks when this litigation started almost a year ago. And my very brief opening statement was that something's horribly wrong on the New Jersey Turnpike. Something *is* horribly wrong. It is of an alarming nature. We are struggling with the soul of the constitutional government in Jersey itself because we are talking about the State Police."

Buckman spoke of the State's attempt to cover-up evidence and of the defense's powerful statistical case that showed troopers stopping blacks on the Turnpike at outrageously elevated rates that could only be explained as racial profiling.

"They carry the day. They are a disgrace on the government of New Jersey. It's probative of government that has run amok. Why? If everyone from Clinton Pagano down to the lowliest trooper say that blacks do *not* drive worse than anyone else, why should they be stopped *five times more* than other people?

"Look what Clinton Pagano said. Even after *Without Just Cause,* a powerful, powerful documentary, did he take the time to research it? He sloughs it off with a constitutional sneer. There is such an overwhelming constitutional cynicism afoot that it cries for no other reasonable explanation other than they knew what they were doing. We are smug, 200 years after the Founding Fathers wrote the Constitution. We talk of tyranny as if it's some type of antiquity. We've seen in New Jersey a modern-day, budding tyranny. No fair state can tolerate that."

His final argument complete, Buckman returned to his family in Vermont and awaited the verdict.

Chapter 64

THE CONFRONTATIONS BETWEEN DARRYL BEARD and Victor Cooper and their commanders were a turning point. Black troopers at Moorestown Station were fed up with what they saw as a return to racial profiling.

Citizen complaints jumped from 140 in 1993 to more than 250 in 1995. In September of '95, Beard, Cooper, and several Moorestown troopers went to the African-American sergeant who supervised Squad #6 at the barracks.

James E. Smith was keenly aware of the racial divide inside the State Police. Eight years before, he'd been at an Affirmative Action workshop when a white sergeant came up to him wearing a Ku Klux Klan costume. Smith's superiors had brushed the incident off as a joke. Now Cooper, Beard and the other black troopers asked him to plead their case to the hierarchy. Smith took the matter to Moorestown commander Lt. Bernard Gilbert.

"Let me make some calls," Gilbert told him.

The issue went up the chain of command and, in November, the lieutenant came back and told Smith: "Talk to a couple of your guys and write me a special [report]."

Smith took statements from 14 minority troopers. By the time his report was written Moorestown Station was awash in hostility. Everyone knew something was coming and white troopers were confronting black troopers.

"I heard you said I was profiling," a trooper told Beard.

"How could you hear anything about a secret conversation I had with the lieutenant?"'"

"Well, I'm just saying that's what I heard," the trooper said. "It's out there in the air."

"Well, leave it out there," Beard said.

On January 10, 1996 Smith turned in a one page memorandum entitled *"Improper Patrol Procedures at Moorestown Station."*

"Minority troopers feel that several Moorestown Station personnel are using improper patrol procedures when stopping motorists."

Smith quoted Beard claiming that *"racial profiling was being used by several [troopers]."* Trooper Roger Wilkins accused a white trooper of conducting *"an illegal search of a black motorist's vehicle."* Trooper Mark Stephens complained about *"ghost stops."*

The black troopers believed the memorandum would force HQ to send a truckload of Internal Affairs investigators to Moorestown. At last, something would be done. Finally, the brass would get to the bottom of things. But they couldn't have been more wrong. Instead of investigating the racial profiling allegations, the black troopers were sent into exile.

Beard was transferred to Red Lion Station. A short time later Victor Cooper was gone, too. And Sgt. James Smith soon followed. Eventually almost all of the black troopers at Moorestown Station who had complained were picked off like tin ducks at a shooting gallery.

Chapter 65

As Felix Morka drove through the night of January 16, 1996, a mantle of snow illuminated the countryside flanking the Jersey Turnpike. The car's heater wasn't working and his friend, Laila Maher, sat in the passenger seat with her hands stuffed in her coat pockets. Morka and Maher were lawyers, he the director of the Social and Economic Rights Action Center in Takoma Park, Maryland; she a poverty law specialist in Washington, D.C.

Morka was Nigerian, Maher an Egyptian-born American citizen. Both were dark-skinned. They were headed to New York to see Morka's sister, who had just arrived from Africa for a meeting at the United Nations. In the icy conditions, Morka was careful to stay with the flow of traffic. By 2:30 a.m. they were halfway through New Jersey when Morka saw flashing lights in his rearview mirror. He eased the car onto the highway shoulder and waited until two state troopers walked up. One looked into the passenger window at Maher.

"Show me your hands," he said and Maher raised her arms. The other trooper ordered Morka to produce his driver's license. His wallet was in his left pocket, but he was wearing a seat belt and had difficulty reaching it.

"I said give me your driver's license," the trooper repeated, then suddenly reached through the window with both hands and grabbed Morka by the collar and began slamming him back and forth between the seat and steering wheel, his grip so tight Morka began to choke

246

until he reached up and managed to squeeze his fingers between the trooper's hands and his throat so that he could breath.

Morka gasped. "What have I done? What have I done?"

"When an officer tells you to do something, you better do it," the trooper shouted.

He dragged Morka from the driver's seat while a stunned Maher jumped out to see what was happening to her friend. The trooper forced Morka to the ground and Maher laid down to look under the car. When she looked up again, a pistol was pointed at her forehead.

"Get back in the car or I'll arrest you," the trooper screamed, the muzzle of his gun mere inches away.

"We're lawyers, we're lawyers!" she yelled, weeping. The trooper grabbed Maher's right hand, twisted it behind her, slammed her against the car, then forced her back inside the vehicle.

Eventually the troopers gave Morka a ticket for speeding.

"Officer, what is your name?" he demanded, but the trooper refused to answer. "You are public officers. Why don't you just tell me your names?"

"Look, you came this close to getting arrested," the trooper said. "People like you shouldn't be on the road anyway."

The troopers returned to their patrol car and, before they pulled away, Maher looked back at them.

"Felix," she said, "can you believe it? They're laughing."

Chapter 66

WHEN THE THUNDERBOLT STRUCK, Bill Buckman was sitting at his desk in Rutland, Vermont. It was March 4, 1996, exactly six years to the day since he'd filed the first motion in what became *State of New Jersey v. Pedro Soto et. al.* Buckman had made his closing argument five months before and, still, there was no verdict.

Not that Buckman had high expectations. When he left New Jersey in November after his summation he did so with a sense of calm elation. The experience had been torturous and had compelled him to abandon New Jersey, but *Soto* had also been the most satisfying experience of his career. He and his colleagues had made an excellent case and, in Buckman's mind, proved the State Police guilty of racial profiling. Even so, for a guy who made his living tilting at windmills, he was pragmatic. He harbored no illusion they would overcome the institutional pressures on Judge Robert Francis. Siding with the defense would send shockwaves through the State. Prison floodgates would be thrown open and police, politicians, and the public would scream bloody murder. It would take a remarkable act of courage that Buckman simply did not expect.

Not because he didn't respect Francis. Quite the contrary, he'd developed tremendous esteem for the judge during the 72-day marathon. He was a true gentleman who allowed them to make their case and Buckman genuinely liked him. In fact, he worried Francis' career might already be jeopardized by the extraordinary amount of time he'd given them.

Then the telephone on Buckman's desk rang. On the other end of the line, Wayne Natale was calling from New Jersey.

"Bill!" Natale screamed. "You won't fucking believe this!"

"What?"

"He granted our motion."

"What do you mean?"

"It means we won!"

"What? We won! My God!" Buckman said, screaming now too. "I can't believe it."

"Bill, we fucking won!" Natale bellowed.

"We won!" Buckman repeated, trying to absorb the news. "God bless him. God bless Robert Francis. He had the guts to do it after all."

Buckman ran to the fax machine, hooting to everyone within earshot that they'd won the New Jersey racial profiling case. The first paragraph of the 16-page ruling said it all.

"After a lengthy hearing, I find defendants have established a prima facie case of selective enforcement which the State has failed to rebut."

Holy shit, Buckman thought, *it's true!*

They'd done it. They'd proven the State Police guilty of racial profiling. Francis's decision was based principally on the *Soto* team's statistics. The judge accepted the finding of defense experts that blacks were 4.85 times more likely to be stopped by troopers than whites. He cited the disparity between troopers with little discretion—the State Police Radar Unit that issued 18% of its tickets to blacks—versus patrol troopers who exercised complete discretion and gave blacks 46.2% of its tickets.

Francis lambasted the State's chief expert, Dr. Leonard Cupingood, calling his statistical analysis "defective" and "worthless." He gave no credence to Cupingood's claim that blacks drive worse, citing trooper testimony that blacks and whites drive the same. He discussed Sgt. Brian Caffrey's testimony that race was *never* a factor in deciding which cars were stopped. Yet, Caffrey condoned a comment by a DITU trainer that a trooper was "reluctant to stop cars in lieu of the Channel 9 News Report."

"Why would a trooper who is acting in a racially neutral fashion become reluctant to stop cars as a result of a news story charging that racial minorities were being targeted?" Francis wrote. *"More telling, however,*

is what Colonel Pagano said and did, or did not do, in response to the Channel 9 exposé entitled Without Just Cause…He said to Joe Collum of Channel 9 that '(violating the rights of motorists was) of serious concern (to him) but nowhere near the concern that I think we have got to look to in trying to correct some of the problems we find with the criminal element in this state' and 'the bottom line is that those stops were not made on the basis of race alone.'"

"*Defendants have proven at least a de facto policy on the part of the State Police out of the Moorestown Station of targeting blacks for investigation and arrest. The statistical disparities and standard deviations revealed are indeed stark. The utter failure of the State Police hierarchy to…investigate the many claims of institutional discrimination manifests its indifference if not acceptance. Against all this, the State submits only denials and the conjecture and flawed studies of Dr. Cupingood.*"

"*The eradication of illegal drugs from our State is an obviously worthy goal, but not at the expense of individual rights. As Justice Brandeis so wisely said dissenting in Olmstead v. United States: 'Experience should teach us to be most on our guard to protect liberty when the government's purposes are beneficent. Men born to freedom are naturally alert to repel invasion of their liberty by evil-minded rulers. The greatest dangers to liberty lurk in insidious encroachment by men of zeal, well-meaning but without understanding.'"*

The decision was an astonishing document that left Buckman stunned. Judge Francis could not have been more emphatic and he'd left no doubt the *Soto* team had more than proven its case. Buckman could feel himself well up. They had worked so long and hard for this; nobody knew how hard. Certainly not for money, but because they believed a grave injustice was being perpetrated. The ruling went so far beyond what he expected that it was hard to fathom.

Buckman thought of Sheri Woliver, the pioneering Public Defender who launched the first attack on racial profiling eight long years ago, and faxed the ruling to her with a note attached: *"Sheri, this would not have come about without your foundational work in Kennedy."*

Buckman's next thoughts were of Marsha Wenk, the attractive young blue-eyed blonde who had been Sheri Woliver's fellow Public Defender on the first profiling case in Warren County. Wenk went on to become Executive Director of the American Civil Liberties

Union in New Jersey. She lent the ACLU's support to the *Soto* team as a friend of the court.

Wenk was dying of terminal cancer. Buckman telephoned her family, who put him through to her. He told her about the ruling as she lay on her death bed.

"Oh, God, Bill, that's fantastic," she said.

Buckman could tell she had little strength. He read her the decision and she told him how happy she was, each of them playing to the fiction that she was going to recover.

"Okay, sweetheart," he said. "I've kept you on the phone too long. I wanted to share this with you, of all people. We'll celebrate when you get better."

A few days later Marsha Wenk died.

Chapter 67

A LATE WINTER FROST NIPPED AT THE SYCAMORES emerging from hibernation along the Delaware River. Across Route 29 on the expansive campus of State Police HQ, the tranquility was being shattered by wails of disbelief from flummoxed troopers as news of the *Soto* ruling spread. State Police Superintendent Carl Williams cried foul.

"The profile scenario as well as the baseless allegations are simply untrue," Williams said in a press release and predicted *Soto* would be overturned on appeal.

Shortly after the bombshell exploded, Sgt. David Blaker walked down a hallway of the second floor and dropped a copy of the Francis decision on the desk of Detective Sergeant Thomas Gilbert.

"Take a look at this and get back to me and the Superintendent," Blaker said. "Tell us what you think about what the ramifications are and where we should be going."

Gilbert was in his late 30s, six feet tall with short brown hair and a lean athletic build. He was smart, competent, and had an honest presence about him. A 17-year veteran, Gilbert had worked his way up the chain of command, including a stint patrolling the Turnpike. Now he worked in Division Services, an adjunct to the Superintendent's office. Gilbert had paid little attention to *Soto* or the allegations of racial profiling. That was about to change.

It was much the same story in the New Jersey Attorney General's Office, which had always treated racial profiling more like a rash than a cancer. During her two years in office no one had ever bothered to warn Attorney General Deborah Poritz that the State Police might be engaged in a vast abrogation of law.

With her owlish spectacles and untinted gray hair pulled back in a bun, Poritz was a prim-looking woman, so tiny she had to stand on a footstool when she spoke in front of crowds. Despite her diminutive size, however, Poritz had the aura of a woman of substance. A college English professor, she hadn't obtained her law degree until age 40, after which her star rose fast. When Christine Todd Whitman was elected New Jersey's first female governor she appointed Poritz the State's first distaff Attorney General. And now there were whispers she'd soon be the first female Chief Justice of the State Supreme Court.

The *Soto* ruling hit Poritz like a bolt of lightning on a sunny day. Racial profiling had not even been a back-burner issue for her and she'd been only vaguely aware of the Gloucester County case. Now she had 15 days to get up to speed on *Soto* and decide whether to appeal. Poritz turned to her husband, Dr. Alan B. Poritz, a world-renowned mathematician whose pioneering treatise, *"Linear Predictive Hidden Markov Models and the Speech Signal,"* had been instrumental in paving the way to computer voice recognition technology. Poritz brought Judge Robert Francis's decision home and asked for his opinion. He was less than impressed. The *Soto* defense team's statistical studies didn't seem plausible and proved nothing. They were, he said, "junk science."

Over the next few days there was much scurrying in the hallways leading to Poritz' eighth floor office in the Hughes Justice Complex as she pow-wowed with senior staff.

John Fahy came in, distraught at being ground up like sausage by the Gloucester gang. His trial strategy a colossal blunder, Fahy desperately wanted the ruling reversed, but even he conceded overturning *Soto* was improbable. He harshly criticized Francis, but thought an appellate court would likely disregard the judge's errors to "eradicate the evil of racial selective enforcement." Even so, he recommended an appeal.

Debra Stone's telephone rang and she was ordered to fetch Anne Paskow and come upstairs. It had been 8 years since the two Appellate Division attorneys had warned against the use of "drug courier profiles," predicting they would lead to racial targeting (the term *racial profiling* wasn't even part of the lexicon in 1988). Stone was now head of Appellate and Paskow worked under her. Their portent had been spurned then and now they were again being petitioned for guidance.

Stone read the *Soto* ruling and realized the case had been a disaster for the State. The trial record was a mess. Fahy's witnesses—particularly Clinton Pagano—had been dreadful. An appeal, she said, could dredge up more incriminating evidence and plunge the State Police into an even deeper morass. Anne Paskow had a more pressing concern.

"Are we confident this is not going on?" she asked the Attorney General.

"The State Police assure me they are not," Poritz said. "I take them at their word."

Nonetheless, for the first time since Justin Dintino retired, the State Police and Attorney General's Office were transitioning from a perpetual state of denial about profiling to a potentially more painful state of introspection. A think tank was organized to brainstorm on the unfortunate turn of events. The thinkers quickly conceded one truth as enunciated by Fahy: "The issue is not going to go away."

Soto was like a bucket of blood hurled into a swarm of sharks, or, in this case, defense lawyers. The great dread was of a feeding frenzy. Seven new lawsuits had already been filed and Public Defenders were brandishing the Francis ruling in courtrooms around New Jersey like evangelists waving Bibles. In the post-*Soto* world, judges could no longer be counted on to willy-nilly dismiss profiling claims.

"The tide has changed," said Ronald Susswein, one of the illuminati who had prevailed against Stone and Paskow in 1988 to make drug courier profiles part of the State Police marching orders. "There is now a chink in law enforcement's armor."

There was no accord on who to blame. Sgt. David Blaker accused the "knucklehead factor," a few troopers who didn't understand the law, or didn't care. Others thought it was bigger than that.

"The numbers are high," Captain Richard Touw of Internal Affairs said in one meeting. "Our people are probably stopping minorities more than they should be. There are just too many complaints coming in."

The room grew quiet. That a high-ranking officer would say such a thing was jarring. Talk turned to whether troopers were cutting constitutional corners to win the Trooper of the Year award. Touw mentioned a Turnpike trooper named John Hogan, who several defense lawyers had accused of profiling. Hogan had been a leading candidate to win the Red Ribbon until an audit found 95% of his arrests were of minorities.

It was clear the Attorney General's Office had blundered by *not* plea bargaining *Soto*. Now a new front in the profiling war was opening in rural Hunterdon County where the minority arrest rate was sky high on Interstate 78, an east-west route that bisected the county between Newark and Pennsylvania. The Internal Affairs jackets of the most active troopers there were thick with racial bias complaints. No one wanted another courtroom showdown. Prudence dictated taking the path of least resistance and Fahy urged the local prosecutor, Sharon Ransavage, to offer plea deals to defendants who alleged profiling.

Ransavage wasn't happy. "I'm going to take a lot of heat for dismissing first-degree cases," she said.

The think tank also concluded that a fatal omission in the Gloucester County case was the State's failure to rebut profiling allegations with its own documentation. Studies were quickly initiated, but when the results came in, they only cast a new pall over the Outfit. One audit found minority Turnpike stops by troopers in south Jersey actually *exceeded* the numbers uncovered in *Soto,* which the State had vehemently denied. Yet, no action was taken on the new evidence. Nor was it turned over to the *Soto* defense team.

Chapter 68

At the close of the 20ᵗʰ century, Camden, New Jersey, was the most wretched city in America. It had once been a vibrant industrial hub, home of Campbell's Soup, RCA Victor, and a ship building industry that employed tens of thousands. Walt Whitman, the great white-bearded poet, lived and died there.

But Walt Whitman's Camden existed in the 1890s. Camden of the 1990s was the province of Christine Todd Whitman—no relation to the bard. When Whitman was elected Governor of New Jersey, Camden was like a third world country. Its smokestacks had long since gone cold and its bleak streets were lined with whitewashed windows and more than 200 liquor stores, but not one supermarket or movie theater. The city was a cesspool of poverty and crime, drugs were everywhere and the murder rate was soaring.

In January 1996, Whitman launched what she called the *Camden City Initiative*. State troopers moved in like an occupying army, swarming the streets with few restraints, raiding drug dens, and stopping and frisking people at will. A siege mentality prevailed.

"It was just a show of force," said one trooper.

In May, Whitman came to take a first hand look at the war zone. The Governor was a fervid supporter of the State Police. Constantly surrounded by a security detail of troopers and—a tomboy at heart —she enjoyed a spirited relationship with the lawmen, often throwing darts and shooting baskets with them. Troopers learned she was not above jabbing a sharp elbow into their ribs under the hoop. The evening before her arrival several troopers were eating pizza, drinking beer and talking about the impending visit. They hoped Whitman's support would help insulate them from criticism for their aggressive tactics. One of the captains in charge of the operation offered a week's vacation to any trooper who snapped a picture of the Governor "frisking a nigger."

Whitman arrived the next day, donned a bulletproof vest, and went with troopers into Camden's worst neighborhoods and crack dens. It was a great photo op and the press ate it up. About 10 o'clock that night, Whitman and six troopers pulled up to a corner where a group of young black men were gathered around the stoop of a shuttered bar. Troopers ordered them to stand with their palms against a graffiti-covered wall to be patted down.

When they'd finished, the troopers urged the Governor to pose for a photograph frisking one of the black men. Whitman agreed, but insisted on wearing gloves before touching the man. Eager to get the prize photograph, troopers quickly dug up a pair of black Kevlar gloves. Whitman was wearing a white jump suit. She slipped on the gloves and, with a big smile, patted down a 16-year-old kid named Sherron Rolax, who had already been searched by troopers and was found to be clean. As she did, Trooper Joseph Senatore pulled out an instamatic camera and began snapping away. At one point he offered a photo to the governor.

"Keep it as a souvenir," the Governor told Senatore. He did.

Chapter 69

THE RUMORS WERE TRUE. On June 13, 1996, Governor Whitman nominated Deborah Poritz to be New Jersey's first female Chief Justice of the Supreme Court. That meant the *Soto* appeal would be left in the hands of her successor. For the powerful position as New Jersey's chief law enforcement official, Whitman appointed her chief of staff, Peter Verniero, who at age 37 became the youngest Attorney General in State history.

Peter Gerald Verniero had had a meteoric career, due less to his legal acumen than his filiations. His political genesis could be traced back to 1976 when he was a precocious, right-leaning senior class president at Montville, New Jersey, High School. The Republican Party was in disarray in the wake of Watergate and the Nixon resignation when Verniero wrote a series of letters to *The New York Times* and other newspapers declaring that the setback was only temporary and the G.O.P. was *"neither dead nor about to die."*

"When the Republicans recover from the aftershock of the Presidential election," he wrote, *"perhaps they will discover that the fate of the G.O.P. lies with the family of young Republicans on the horizon."*

Verniero's missives caught the eye of a New Jersey Republican Congressional candidate who enlisted him as a volunteer campaign advance man. That led to a stint as a driver for Tom Kean during his 1981 gubernatorial campaign. Later, after graduation from Duke Law School, Verniero clerked for New Jersey Supreme Court Justice Robert L. Clifford, who recognized his young charge's political bent and dubbed him "The Senator." By the late '80s, Verniero was Executive Director of the New Jersey Republican Party, where he gained a reputation as a partisan bulldog willing to step on toes. He went on to work at the prestigious and politically-wired law firm of Herold & Haines. Verniero was not a courtroom lawyer and had never actually tried a case. But he did represent one noteworthy client whose skirt-tails he would ride to improbable heights.

When she met Verniero, Christine Todd Whitman was a wealthy housewife and part-time politician. A few years later, after she shocked the political world by being elected Governor of New Jersey, she brought Verniero along to Trenton as her chief counsel. Smart and smooth, ambitious and arrogant, Verniero was a humorless political operative devoid of the personality traits that generally signal success in matters of statecraft.

"Not a beer-buddy kind of guy," a colleague said.

Verniero quickly came to be viewed by many as Whitman's lapdog, but his fierce loyalty led her to promote him to Chief of Staff and then Attorney General.

The transition from Poritz to Verniero was hectic. The two didn't have much time to consult, speaking only at night on the telephone. Poritz didn't give Verniero a list of "hot issues," but did red flag racial profiling and the *Soto* case, telling him she had decided to fight Judge Robert Francis' verdict. Nevertheless, she said she had concerns. Even if the *Soto* ruling was flawed, it suggested a problem and Poritz recommended Verniero order a study to determine whether racial profiling was indeed real.

Chapter 70

JOHN HOGAN CONSIDERED THE UPROAR over racial profiling to be the height of hypocrisy. As a young trooper he'd been taught to profile, but in those days Hogan was patrolling the back roads of rural South Jersey where the priority wasn't drugs, but drunks. Older troopers taught him to stake out bars and honky-tonks in Fort Dix, Hightstown and Wilburtha, and wait for unsuspecting drinkers to get behind the wheels of their cars or pickup trucks, then swoop down on them. The drivers were always white.

It bothered Hogan that these poor guys lost their driver's licenses and got hit with thousands of dollars in fines and insurance premiums, yet no one made a hubbub about whites being targeted. But God forbid a trooper pull over a black guy with $20,000 worth of cocaine stuffed under his seat. He becomes a victim of racial profiling. Why was it wrong to profile a black dude running drugs, but nobody blinks when the same thing happens to some white chump? Hogan eventually refused to stake out bars.

In 1994, a year after becoming a trooper, Hogan was assigned to Cranbury Station on the Turnpike. He was ecstatic. Turnpike troopers had cachet and Hogan was eager to make his mark. But he was still green and veteran troopers treated him like a tenderfoot. Hogan knew his road to respect would have to be paved with drug arrests. But he wanted more. He wanted the kind of respect that only came with the Red Ribbon for Trooper of the Year. The kind of respect reserved for a select few troopers, like Sgt. Brian Caffrey.

Hogan began picking the brains of Cranbury Station's biggest *crime dogs*. They told him to look for two things—traffic infractions committed by minority travelers. That was reinforced by U.S. Drug Enforcement Administration *BOLOS* ("Be On Look Out for...") which highlighted blacks and Latinos as most likely to be transporting large quantities of drugs.

Hogan worked hard and learned fast. He mastered the art of the "rip and strip," dismantling car door panels and engines where drugs were commonly hidden. In 1995, he made 38 drug arrests and seized more than $300,000 worth of contraband. Only one year on the Black Dragon and he was already a primetime *crime dog* and a contender for Trooper of the Year. For such a young guy, the future certainly looked bright.

But not everyone considered Hogan a shining star. Despite the high regard he enjoyed inside the Outfit, he was gaining a reputation as a bad apple in other quarters. Defense attorneys in several drug cases had accused him of racial profiling. He denied the charges, but even his superiors were leery. The next year, 1996, he was again a leading candidate for the Red Ribbon until an internal State Police audit revealed that 95% of his arrests were of minorities. It was like a big flashing neon *D-A-N-G-E-R* sign hanging around his neck and the brass at HQ eliminated him from Trooper of the Year contention. Rather than kill his spirits, though, the setback only fueled Hogan's aspirations and made him more resolute than ever to one day capture the big prize.

Chapter 71

CHRISTMAS EVE 1996 was a quiet day at State Police HQ. Most had taken the day off or left early to do last minute shopping or go home to their families. In the early afternoon, Sgt. Thomas Gilbert was in his office when he looked up and was surprised to see the Superintendent of the State Police. It was a rare day when Carl Williams walked the 100 or so feet down the hall to Gilbert's humble space. But he wasn't delivering Christmas presents. Something was up.

"We're going to a meeting downtown," said Williams.

Gilbert was caught off-guard. In State Police vernacular downtown meant the Attorney General's Office in Trenton, about 10 miles away. Gilbert had never been in the office of the Attorney General and, any other day, he would have been honored. But it was Christmas Eve and Gilbert didn't want to get home late. He wondered how long the meeting would last.

There was little banter as they drove. Carl Williams was a nice man, but not much of a conversationalist. When he did speak it was in a slow mumble that sounded like his mouth was filled with marbles. The Superintendent simply didn't have much to say. He didn't even tell Gilbert what the meeting was about. They arrived at the Hughes Justice Complex and took a back elevator to the eighth floor. Gilbert had never met Peter Verniero and shook hands with the Attorney General, his chief deputy, Alexander Waugh, and John Fahy.

Verniero did the talking. A troubling situation had developed. In the wake of the *Soto* ruling, the U.S. Justice Department's Civil Rights

Division had opened an investigation of the State Police for racial profiling. It was the last thing Verniero wanted. This was an election year and the inquiry could cast a dark cloud over Christie Whitman's re-election. New Jersey might also be forced into a consent decree, leaving it at Washington's mercy. It was insulting.

Verniero said he'd traveled to Washington in early December to try to head off the investigation and assured Justice Department lawyers *Soto* was a flawed decision that would be overturned. He said racial profiling was not State Police policy and promised his full cooperation, but asked the DOJ not to categorize its probe as an investigation because it would create a bad impression.

Verniero handed Carl Williams a four-page DOJ data request form, then the meeting was over. True to form, Williams said almost nothing. Even more curious, no one, including the Attorney General, asked anything about whether racial profiling was real. The men exchanged Christmas salutations and Williams and Gilbert left. On the ride back to State Police headquarters there was no chitchat.

Chapter 72

THE JUSTICE DEPARTMENT PROBE HAD TURNED a manageable situation into a legal and political minefield for Peter Verniero. The *Soto* verdict had garnered sparse public attention and the appeal guaranteed racial profiling would be tangled up in court for years, perhaps until Christie Whitman graduated from the Governor's Mansion to the U.S. Senate or maybe even the Vice Presidency. Now, though, the DOJ was threatening to open a Pandora's box. Verniero needed to act fast to quell the threat. He asked John Fahy to draft a letter to Justice explaining New Jersey's position on racial profiling. But Fahy did not give the Attorney General what he'd anticipated.

"The State Police report to me," he wrote, *"that the number of stops involving black motorists in the southern portion of the Turnpike remains near the level reported in the Soto case. It is difficult for me to believe that despite a clear official policy prohibiting racial profiling that troopers assigned to one station would continue to reject it."*

What the *hell* was Fahy thinking? Verniero wanted to downplay the problem, but this letter was like putting a blowtorch to a tinderbox. The Attorney General took out a scalpel and excised Fahy's negativity, replacing it with the same story he'd told DOJ; that there was no "credible evidence" of profiling.

Even so, Verniero was jammed up. The State Police was finally doing a serious self-analysis that only confirmed the findings in the *Soto* ruling. God forbid word leaked out! If the *Soto* team or, worse, the U.S. Justice Department got its hands on the data there would be hell to pay.

But the picture just kept getting bleaker. Sgt. Thomas Gilbert had been threshing the data for months and was reaping a bitter harvest.

"The numbers are not good," Gilbert wrote to Superintendent Colonel Carl Williams in February 1997.

Gilbert had discovered the statistics were a lot worse than even the *Soto* defense team had presented.

One reason was the war against racial profiling had broken out in states beyond New Jersey and Gilbert found that new and more sophisticated standards for measuring the problem were being applied. For instance, while the *Soto* verdict had hinged on stop data, a judge in Maryland ruled that the true acid test was searches. The evidence there showed that 80% of searches by State Police patrolling Interstate 95 were of blacks, three times the rate they were searching whites, even though both races were being found with drugs at exactly the same rate. Maryland had been forced to sign a consent decree and was now under the microscope of U.S. Justice Department monitors.

Gilbert got the message. Searches were the new litmus test on racial profiling. The *Soto* lawyers had repeatedly requested search data from the State Police, only to be told it didn't exist. Yet it took Gilbert almost no time to find several file cabinets at State Police HQ filled with years of search records. He crunched the numbers and made a startling discovery. The situation was far graver than anyone suspected. Maryland's 80% minority search rate paled beside Central Jersey's, where an astounding 94% of searches were of blacks and Hispanics. South Jersey wasn't much better with 87% minority searches.

"At this point," Gilbert wrote to Williams, *"we are in a very bad spot."*

The Superintendent understood the enormity of Gilbert's findings. He ordered the sergeant to contact George Rover, who Peter Verniero had just tapped to replace John Fahy as Jersey's new designated driver on racial profiling.

Rover had been a strange choice for the job. He was a Deputy Attorney General, but more of a bureaucrat than a lawyer and had never handled a criminal case. His office wasn't even in Trenton. Yet, after years toiling at the periphery, Rover had been jockeying for a seat closer to the flame and was flattered to land such a consequential job.

Tom Gilbert told Rover that Jersey's search numbers were "in the same ballpark" as Maryland's and asked him to relay the news up his chain of command. He expected his findings to trigger a political earthquake in Trenton and waited for the tremors to reach HQ.

But there was no reaction. Not a ripple. Nothing.

Chapter 73

FOUR MONTHS LATER, THREE COPS AND four lawyers gathered around the large conference table in Peter Verniero's office to grapple with the U.S. Justice Department's increasingly incommodious snooping.

The evidence against the State Police was damning and the cops—Superintendent Carl Williams, Sgt. Tom Gilbert, and Sgt. First Class David Blaker—knew they were in grave peril. The DOJ didn't have all the dirt yet, but were closing in on it and the State Policemen feared Verniero would cave in and cut a deal with the Feds. They did not want a bunch of Washington strawbosses taking control of the Outfit.

The date was May 20, 1997 and Gilbert opened the dialogue by addressing the key bullet point on the meeting's agenda: *What to do about the DOJ's requests that New Jersey turn over its search data?*

Gilbert presumed everyone at the table was aware of the dilemma, including Peter Verniero. He didn't go into detail but explained that the Justice Department had already found Maryland guilty of racial profiling based on its search stats and New Jersey's numbers were as bad or worse than Maryland's.

Verniero didn't express surprise, didn't ask Williams why New Jersey's numbers were so high, and didn't question whether the State Police might actually be engaged in racial profiling. Instead, he vowed to fight the Feds.

"They'd have to tie me to a train and drag me along the track before I'd sign a decree," he said.

The troopers were gratified to hear the Attorney General take a strong stand. But what about the data? U.S. lawyers had already made three requests for their search numbers, but they were extremely explosive and nobody was eager to give them up. They looked at Verniero and asked what they should do.

He told them to stall. Don't send the search material—at least not *now.* If the DOJ asked *again,* they would produce it—*probably.* The Justice Department could not be ignored, but maybe it could be dawdled to death.

Chapter 74

ON VALENTINE'S DAY 1998, Trooper Emblez Longoria arrived at Cranbury Station in Central Jersey. For two years, the State Police had been in possession of alarming evidence that the station was a nest of racial profiling, yet no corrective action had been taken.

Cranbury's Assistant Station Commander was now Sgt. Brian Caffrey. When Longoria arrived, his sergeant informed him Caffrey was "a big numbers guy" who expected a lot of drug arrests.

Troopers who rang up the numbers had Caffrey's respect, and no trooper at Cranbury had better numbers than John Hogan. And, like Caffrey, he was well on his way to becoming a Turnpike legend. Cocky and intense, Hogan clearly relished his status, often strutting around the station bare-chested, his biceps pumped from hours in the gym.

Hogan's supervisors were touting him for Trooper of the Year and Longoria could see Hogan wanted the award more than anything. He'd been a top contender for the Red Ribbon in 1996, only to be shot down when HQ discovered his extraordinarily high minority arrest rate.

Hogan was disappointed again the following year when he was beaten out by Francis Burke, a behemoth trooper whose cranium was so immense his classmates at the State Police Academy nicknamed him *Big Head*. Alas, Burke's career turned to dust less than one year later when he was caught extorting Turnpike drivers for bribes.

But Burke's demise was not enough to mollify Hogan, whose obsession for the big prize only grew more intense. He kept a scrapbook of newspaper clips about his drug arrests and dolefully compared them to Burke's.

"Do you think [Burke] did something better than me?" he'd ask his fiancée, Christy Dittman.

Competition for the Red Ribbon was again as fever-pitched as it had been during the Clinton Pagano era. Longoria saw it every day: cars pulled over, luggage strewn on the roadside, troopers rifling through trunks, most of them unreported *ghost stops*. Invariably, the travelers were black or Hispanic. With Big Head out of the picture, Hogan had the 1998 Trooper of the Year award all but wrapped up. His minority arrest rate was 86%, but no one seemed to notice.

Longoria wanted nothing to do with it all.

"What's going on out here is bullshit," he said at morning squad meetings. "You guys are breaking the law to enforce the law."

"Give them what they want," his sergeant advised him, "and they'll leave you alone."

"No fucking way. I don't care. I know the Constitution."

Everyone knew Longoria wasn't a player. He handed out a lot of traffic tickets and was a crackerjack accident investigator, but made few arrests. Soon he was being treated like a bête noire; it was as though he was carrying the Ebola virus. Conversations would abruptly end when he entered a room and computer screen savers at the station had pictures of his head floating on a cloud.

Longoria was afraid that if he needed back-up, his fellow troopers might not be there for him. Then, in April, after only two months at Cranbury, he was transferred, much to his relief.

Two weeks later, Longoria was munching a sandwich and sipping a club soda at Kelly's Bar in Hightstown. His best friend, Vincent Belleran, was sitting across the table nursing a Guinness. Belleran was a 20-year State Police veteran who was once suspended after calling his sergeant a "racist bastard" for referring to minority troopers as "spics" and "coons." Just one month before, Belleran had won a federal discrimination lawsuit against the State Police, the judge ruling he had been subjected to a *"racially hostile work environment."* Longoria told his friend that Cranbury Station had reached the boiling point.

"I've never seen so much racism," he said between bites of his sandwich. "I didn't know if I was backing up troopers or protecting the public *from* the troopers."

The next morning, Longoria's telephone rang. Belleran was on the line.

"Have you read the papers yet?" he asked.

"No," Longoria said. "What's up?"

"You'll see."

Chapter 75

JOHN HOGAN FACED A CONUNDRUM. His bread-and-butter as a trooper was drug arrests and, as he'd been taught, the best way to make them was to target minorities. But his dilemma was how to make arrests without looking like a profiler. The answer, he learned in time, was subterfuge.

Ghost stops were one clever ploy. Another was phonying-up racial identifications in radio transmissions, using phrases like "he appears to be white" or "he looks white." Later, if an arrest was made and the *white* prisoner turned out to be *black,* nobody raised an eyebrow. The deceptions were so common among *crime dogs* at Cranbury Station that Hogan accepted them as part of the job. And they worked.

Hogan was in the midst of a monster year with 58 collars, including 21 in just the last two months. In April 1998, his commander wrote a glowing letter to HQ touting him for Trooper of the Year.

"These activities demonstrate Trooper Hogan's energetic, diligent, aggressive and alert approach to his patrol responsibilities," Capt. Ronald Franz wrote.

At about 10:30 p.m. on April 23, 1998, Hogan and Trooper James Kenna pulled over a vehicle driven by a law student from Temple University named Christopher Woodley. Hogan told Woodley they'd observed him making an unsafe lane change and released him with only a warning. The troopers called in the stop of a white man. Woodley was black.

Hogan and Kenna were not regular partners and had ridden together only a handful of times. They couldn't have been more unalike. Hogan—short, dark and intense— was the odds-on favorite to win the Red Ribbon. Kenna—tall, blond and laid back—was no *crime dog* and not even in the running for Trooper of the Year, despite having State Police blood running through his veins. His father, James, was a captain in the Outfit.

Kenna didn't make a lot of arrests and was reluctant to engage in deception. He actually filed consent forms every time he searched a car, as per State Police Standard Operating Procedure F-55. It was an order other troopers routinely ignored and they ridiculed Kenna for making them look bad, giving him so much grief he eventually stopped submitting the forms. Even so, more was expected from a captain's kid and, in an attempt to up Kenna's productivity, his supervisors moved him onto Hogan's squad, which had a reputation for big drug arrest numbers.

At the exact moment Hogan and Kenna pulled over a black student they reported to be white, a silver gray van was hurtling toward them. The sky had been black and a steady drizzle was falling when the vehicle emerged from the Lincoln Tunnel, curled up the long corkscrew helix past the dripping kaleidoscope of Manhattan's skyline, then pointed west, away from the city, away from the lights, into the darkness, and onto the Black Dragon.

The van was a chariot of destiny. Yet, as it rushed south through the swampy meadowlands of North Jersey, the four young men inside—three black and one Latino—were oblivious to the fate awaiting them. The Turnpike was their pathway to the Promised Land. They were chasing a hoop dream; basketball players on their way to a college tryout. Hip-hop music pounded on the stereo as they navigated past Newark Airport.

At the wheel was a quiet, mocha-skinned man named Keshon Moore, a 5 feet 9 inch tall point guard, too short to compete at most colleges. Yet he dreamed. Wedged into the seat beside him was his friend Danny Reyes. At 6 feet 7 inches, Reyes had been Mr. Big to Moore's Little Man at Curtis High School, where they had led their team to the Staten Island schoolboy championship four years earlier. Jarmaine Grant was stretched out asleep in the back seat. In front of him, on the center couch, Rayshawn Brown was dozing too, his right leg draped over the arm rest, wearing a black T-shirt with the inscription:

"I didn't have to use my A.K.
Today was a good day."

Traffic was heavy and rain spattered the van as Moore navigated past North Jersey's industrial skyline, steaming factories, giant tank farms, and air so rancid it smelled like an enormous fart.

The basketball players were headed for North Carolina Central University in Durham, a small school best known as the alma mater of the NBA superstar Scottie Pippen. The four friends planned to drive all night and each had kicked in $76 to rent the van and pay for gas and tolls.

Unbeknownst to the others, Moore was driving with a suspended license. So, as he entered the flatlands of Central Jersey, where industry gave way to suburbia which melted into gently rolling farmland, Moore was careful to set the cruise control at 55-miles per hour on the dot.

About 45 minutes after they entered the Turnpike, the van passed a police car parked in the median facing across the highway. Moore, driving the speed limit, didn't pay it much attention. A few minutes later the white squad car with blue and gold markings passed him in the left lane, then slowed down and let the van catch up. The troopers eyeballed its occupants. The four passengers were young dark-skinned men. If there was a racial profile, these *johnnies* certainly fit the bill.

Kenna and Hogan fit a profile too. Both were very skittish troopers. Each had survived near death experiences on the Turnpike.

Just a month before, Kenna was arresting a suspect who suddenly knocked him down, jumped into his State Police cruiser and tried to run him over. Kenna's gun jammed and he had to dive out of the way to avoid being crushed. The assailant was later captured and Kenna wasn't physically hurt, but there was psychological trauma. Yet, the young trooper received a grand total of 45 minutes of counseling and was sent back onto the Turnpike. He vowed to never lose control of a stop again.

Three years before, Hogan had almost been killed trying to arrest two men in a stolen car. The driver took off with Hogan clinging to the vehicle for dear life. He managed to pull out his service revolver and shoot both men. They survived and went to prison, but Hogan was haunted by the incident every time he stopped a car. "You're just waiting to see the barrel of a gun. That's the feeling as you approach a vehicle," he later testified.

On this night, Hogan maneuvered his cruiser behind the silver van and switched on his red and white overhead lights. Keshon Moore, the van driver, was confused. He wasn't speeding so the policemen couldn't be stopping him. He steered into the right lane to let the trooper pass, but Hogan shined his spotlight at the van and clicked on his public address system: "Stop the car! Stop the car!" Moore slowed and pulled off the road and onto the shoulder and stopped. Kenna, determined to take control of the situation, jumped from the cruiser before it even came to a halt and sprinted to the van, gun drawn, screaming: "Put your hands up! Put your hands up!"

Hogan rushed up behind the vehicle but, before he knew what happened, it started moving backward. Then he heard shots ring out and opened fire. Amidst a hail of gunfire, the van drifted backwards, bumped into the State Police car, and rolled slowly onto the Turnpike and collided with a Honda Accord speeding down the highway. The impact propelled the van forward and, as the troopers kept shooting, it coasted down an embankment. The vehicle came to rest in a thicket of trees and brush just as Danny Reyes felt a bullet strike him in the back. Eleven shots had been fired in a matter of seconds. The troopers raced down the hill and yanked the passengers from the van. Three of the four were wounded and bloody, but alive. They handcuffed them and radioed for back-up, then began searching the van, looking for the contraband they knew had to be in the vehicle.

They found bags of junk food, soft drinks, basketball clothing, and books—including a Bible—but no drugs, no guns. Before long a flood of state troopers had descended on the scene, quickly followed by the inevitable media mob. Jarmaine Grant and Danny Reyes were critically wounded and were helicoptered to a trauma center in Camden. Rayshawn Brown and Keshon Moore were taken by ambulance to a Trenton hospital.

Moore, the driver, was the only suspect who hadn't been shot. When State Police investigators came into his hospital room, he was shackled to his bed. The troopers told him he might be charged with attempted murder. Moore was petrified. He explained that when he stopped the van he'd accidentally put the gearshift into reverse. When the officer ran up screaming and waving his gun he must have taken his foot off the brake, causing the vehicle to lurch backwards. The detectives said his friends were fighting for their lives and asked him if he wanted to apologize. Distraught, Moore issued what could be interpreted as a confession.

"I would like to apologize for the incident," he said, "apologize to my friends, to the police officers. I can't blame anybody but myself. None of this would have happened if I'd just put the van in park."

The State Police hastily announced it had been a righteous shoot. The troopers "obtained a speed reading from radar" clocking the van doing 74 in a 55 mph zone. The "suspects" were "unemployed" New York City residents who attempted to run down the officers and escape. The troopers were defending themselves.

That was the official version, but the truth soon proved to be far more elusive. The troopers didn't have radar. Nor had they called in the stop. And Kenna didn't have an explanation for why he fired. Beyond that, the "suspects" were clean, students on their way to a college basketball try-out. They had no criminal records, no drugs, and no guns. So why would they try to escape? And why would they try to kill the troopers? The State Police version of events didn't add up.

In order to justify the shooting, Kenna and Hogan needed to get their stories straight. Throughout that night they conferred with dozens of troopers at the scene, at the hospital, and at Cranbury Station, who advised them to highlight certain points. The van was *speeding and driving erratically*. They saw furtive movement inside the vehicle indicating *something bad was happening*. They were taken into the station carport to examine the van.

After several hours they knitted together a story. Keshon Moore had told investigators he may have bent over for his wallet. So Kenna's story became that one of the occupants "bent over and reached toward the floor" as if he was going for a gun. Then the van's wheels started *spinning* and it jerked backwards. Kenna said he heard Hogan scream.

"I thought the driver intentionally attempted to run me over," Hogan said in his official statement. "I was scared to death that if I didn't stop the van I would be killed."

It was a patchwork of embellishments, exaggerations, and flat out lies concocted to justify a shooting that was not justifiable.

Chapter 76

JOHNNIE L. COCHRAN, JR. FIRST HEARD about the Turnpike shooting on the evening news. After 35 years practicing law, he wasn't shocked that minority kids had been shot by police. His surprise was that the incident was big news.

Cochran was at once America's most renowned and most notorious legal eagle, celebrated as a flamboyant and formidable trial attorney, yet detested by millions as the fast-talking lawyer who saved O.J. Simpson by playing the race card. Cochran had probably handled more police brutality cases than any barrister in America, most of them in Los Angeles involving African-Americans who'd had violent clashes with cops. But by 1998, he'd gone bi-coastal and had an office in New York City where he was immersed in a string of high-profile law enforcement abuse cases. One particularly lurid episode involved a Haitian immigrant named Abner Louima, who'd been sodomized with the handle of a toilet plunger by an NYPD cop, who then shoved it, covered with feces, into Louima's mouth, threatening: "I'll kill you and your entire family if you tell anyone." It was the type of nauseatingly scandalous affair that sent New York's media horde into paroxysms of tabloid bliss. The Turnpike shooting promised to rival it.

The day after the shooting, Cochran got a telephone call from a New Jersey lawyer named David Ironman, who'd been hired by Danny Reyes' family.

"I need your help on a really bad case," Ironman said.

The shooting introduced Cochran to a term he was not familiar with—racial profiling. Intrigued, he told Ironman he wanted to be involved. Cochran was retained by the parents of Jarmaine Grant, who was still in a New Jersey hospital bed with bullet wounds to his right shoulder, right triceps, left knee, and back. The slugs had also shattered his psyche.

"I am at the lowest point in my life," Grant told Jim Dwyer of the New York Daily News. *"Everybody who knows me knows I try to go to school, to play ball, and do the right thing. Any form of violent acts, it's not me."*

Cochran called Peter Neufeld and Barry Scheck, the Manhattan attorneys who'd been key members of the Simpson "Dream Team." During the trial Scheck gained national repute for his withering cross-examination of an LAPD criminalist that raised doubts about the integrity of the DNA evidence against Simpson. Cochran, Neufeld and Scheck had worked together on several cases since then, including Louima's, for which they eventually won an $8.75 million settlement.

Neufeld and Scheck were an odd couple; Neufeld—tall, gangly, and personable; Scheck—short, boyish, and intense. As a kid Neufeld had marched with his mother and father in civil rights demonstrations and later became an anti-Vietnam War activist at the University of Wisconsin, where he organized huge demonstrations and was a leader of the school's chapter of Students for a Democratic Society. He and Scheck met in the 1970s as idealistic young New York City Legal Aid lawyers representing indigent clients in the South Bronx, where they developed a keen interest in the nexus between law and science. Neufeld was one of the first lawyers to successfully use the *Battered Woman's Syndrome* as a murder defense and Scheck became a groundbreaking expert on DNA evidence. In 1991, they founded *The Innocence Project* at New York University's Benjamin Cardoza School of Law. In less than a decade they'd proven the innocence of more than 100 prisoners convicted of rape and murder, including many condemned to death.

In early May, Cochran, Neufeld and Scheck met with the Turnpike shooting victims at their office in the TriBeCa section of lower Manhattan, near the World Trade Center. Jarmaine Grant, who was out of the hospital but still carrying two lead slugs in his body, opened the meeting with a prayer. The victims' principal concern was that the two troopers who shot them be brought to justice. Cochran promised the Dream Team would do everything in their power to see justice served, but explained that they were not prosecutors and had nothing to do with the criminal case. He did tell the young men, though, that their case was an opportunity to attack racial profiling and the system that had allowed it to exist in New Jersey. The students liked that idea.

Chapter 77

THE DAY AFTER THE SHOOTING, *The Newark Star-Ledger* reported that John Hogan had a reputation among criminal defense lawyers as a racial profiler.

"He has a storm trooper quality, very arrogant," a Deputy Public Defender named Frank Farrell said. "He was just a time bomb waiting to go off."

Farrell said he'd accused Hogan of racial profiling in three different cases, each involving young black men driving cars with out-of-state license plates.

"Hogan is one name that repeatedly shows up on the bottom of the reports," said private defense attorney Robin Kay Lord, who'd lodged racial profiling allegations against Hogan in eight cases.

The day after the *Star-Ledger* article appeared, an investigator from the New Jersey Public Defender's Office headquarters came to Farrell's home and handed him an envelope. For speaking to the press without permission, he'd been suspended from his job for a week.

Chapter 78

THE *FREEDOM MOTORCADE*—all 135 cars and buses of it—trundled from the George Washington Bridge down the Jersey Turnpike 63 miles to the scene of the student shooting and pulled onto a narrow slice of pavement where 500 demonstrators stepped into the sweltering May morning chanting "Peace" and "Justice."

As new information emerged—particularly Trooper John Hogan's dismal 86% minority arrest record—outrage over the shooting was growing choleric.

"It's going to be sticky," one State Police investigator told *The Record* newspaper. "I'm going to be canceling my golf games for the next few months."

With police helicopters hovering above, a gaggle of news cameras jockeyed to record the scene while a bulbous black man with a pompadour hairdo descended into the grassy ditch where the bullet riddled van had come to rest. Traffic jammed the Turnpike 10 miles in either direction with drivers gawking as Rev. Al Sharpton spoke.

"There was a time in the '60s," he bellowed through a bullhorn, "when we had to ride through Alabama and Mississippi and Georgia. Now we have to ride through New Jersey."

Nobody threw a demonstration like Reverend Al. He was the consummate agitator.

Though he didn't possess the gravitas of Martin Luther King Jr. or the flowery eloquence of Jesse Jackson Jr., Sharpton was New York City's most influential African-American and its most irrepressible racial gadfly. When a black person was shot by a cop in Gotham, by six o'clock Sharpton would be standing next to the grieving family on TV, thundering about police brutality, demanding justice, grabbing all the face time. To some he was a self-promoting huckster; to others, an ebony guardian angel.

"I'm not an ambulance chaser," he said. "I'm the ambulance. People call me."

A new catchphrase had entered the national lexis: *"DWB—Driving While Black,"* and with it Sharpton had discovered a rich new vein of rage to mine.

"It seems to us that 11 shots are excessive,'" he shouted, mopping his brow with a white handkerchief. "We know the history of this Turnpike. We ask you to give us the strength to turn this history around."

Sharpton, the New Yorker, was filling a void. New Jersey had no dominant black voice, nobody to hold fire to the feet of officialdom. But the Turnpike shooting changed that when a husky, sharp-featured man stepped forward and took the bullhorn from Sharpton. He, too, was a minister and, from that day on, he would be the African-American that New Jersey power brokers would be forced to answer to on racial profiling.

"It's ironic," Reverend Reginald Jackson said in a slow drawl, "that other people can get on the Turnpike and go where they have to. African-Americans have to wonder if we're going to get stopped just because of the color of our skin."

Jackson was executive director of the Black Ministers Council of New Jersey, a loose alliance of 600 African-American clergymen. Historically, the council had been a toothless tiger dominated by a notion that, as a non-profit religious organization, it should avoid partisanship. Consequently, there was a vacuum in Trenton when it came to challenging racial injustice. Many clergymen were frustrated the Council wasn't baring its fangs. The situation came to a head after Christie Whitman's campaign manager, Ed Rollins, credited her stunning razor-thin victory in the governor's race to him having paid off black ministers to keep their flocks away from the polls on election day.

Rollins quickly retracted the claim, but black clergymen were cast under a cloud of suspicion. Soon after, Jackson was elected

Executive Director of the Council with a mandate to begin flexing its political muscles.

Ironically, Reverend Jackson supported Whitman in 1993. She had spoken passionately about racial profiling, calling it an unconscionable practice she would not tolerate. But since then she'd done nothing but deny its existence.

"Profiling is illegal," Whitman said after the Turnpike shooting. "I don't believe the State Police engage in illegal activity."

More than at any time since the 1968 Newark riots, New Jersey was in urgent need of a strong black voice. A reluctant Jackson stepped forth. Unlike the theatrical Sharpton, Jackson bordered on bland, preferring dialogue and reason to Sharpton's more confrontational style. Jackson wasn't a hothead who saw everything as black versus white. His brother was a Delaware state trooper. Jackson believed drugs were ravaging black communities.

"I'm just as vehement, if not more vehement, against drugs than racial profiling."

But Jackson was not naïve. He tutored young black males in his congregation at St. Matthew's African Methodist Episcopal Church in Orange, New Jersey, on how to conduct themselves during traffic stops: Don't fidget, keep hands in plain sight, and note the officer's name and badge number.

Jackson had recently been a target of what he considered racial profiling when a trooper stopped him on the Turnpike for allegedly speeding, even though his cruise control was set below the speed limit. When the trooper heard Jackson call the Governor's Office to let Whitman know he'd be late for their appointment, he let him go without a ticket. Later, Jackson told her what had happened. She nodded, but said nothing. After that, the minister began taking the train to Trenton.

"Whether profiling exists, as far as we're concerned, is not a debatable point," Jackson said. "The question becomes what to do about it."

Jackson demanded a face-to-face meeting with Whitman's Attorney General Peter Verniero and State Police Superintendent Carl Williams. After two hours with them behind closed doors, Jackson came out and called for an independent investigation into profiling.

"We do not believe the New Jersey State Police can investigate themselves in this matter," he said. "If they were effective at it, we would not be sitting here today discussing it after more than 10 years."

Chapter 79

NEW JERSEY'S DECADE-LONG DODGE on racial profiling began to disintegrate the day after the Turnpike shooting. State Police Lt. Colonel Robert Dunlop opened a red book he'd been handed by Sgt. Thomas Gilbert. It was a status summary on the *Soto* appeal and the contents startled him.

Dunlop was an imposing man, six feet five inches tall, a former Marine and Vietnam veteran, who some found intimidating, even scary, while others considered him conniving and Machiavellian. Even Dunlop's critics, though, respected him as a good cop; smart, tough, no nonsense. He'd just been appointed the right hand man to State Police Superintendent Carl Williams. Dunlop had earned his stripes as a detective rather than as a road trooper, yet had never been a critic of highway drug interdiction. Catching scumbag drug dealers was a good thing. But Sgt. Gilbert's red book revealed a dark side to interdiction and the numbers jumped out at him. Minority search and arrest statistics were high. Very high!

Debra Stone had been seeing some troubling data, too. After the shooting, the Attorney General's Appellate chief was assigned to the Hogan-Kenna investigation. She asked State Police Internal Affairs to send her all the information it had on the two troopers. Stone was stunned to discover Cranbury Station's 84% black and Latino arrest rate and that almost 9-in-10 of John Hogan's collars were of minorities.

"Why the hell am I finding this out now?" she asked Paul Zoubek, who was running the shooting probe for the Division of Criminal Justice.

Tall, square-jawed, with no hair on top and gray on the sides, Zoubek looked older than his years. He was a career prosecutor and former assistant U.S. Attorney recently hired by Peter Verniero as Director of Criminal Justice. As the #2 man in the Attorney General's office, Zoubek had not seen the State Police audit either and looked shocked and angry when Stone showed it to him.

"Paul, these numbers are very similar to *Soto's*," she said. Stone had advised against appealing Judge Robert Francis' verdict and argued now that the audit knocked the underpinnings from beneath the State's case. They had an obligation to either turn over the data the *Soto* defense team, she said, or drop the appeal.

But Zoubek wasn't ready to go along, saying he wanted to get a better picture of the evidence first.

Stone was not happy. Later she said: "I spent most of '98 and '99 pissed off."

Chapter 80

THE STUDENT SHOOTINGS HAD AWAKENED New Jersey's sleeping giant—*The Newark Star-Ledger,* the state's largest and most influential newspaper. For a decade the *Star-Ledger* had been largely silent on racial profiling. The same was true for other newspapers in-state and out, like *The Record* in North Jersey, *The New York Times* and *The Philadelphia Inquirer,* which had large circulations in the Garden State. But the *Star-Ledger* was Jersey's most powerful voice and the newspaper's apathy, along with that of the black clergy, had long allowed State leaders a free pass on profiling. If the issue didn't merit the *Ledger's* attention, maybe it wasn't really a problem.

After the shooting, however, the paper became engaged on profiling, prompted perhaps by a gaping chasm that had emerged between the races in New Jersey. That gulf was underscored by an opinion poll conducted in early May 1998 by Rutgers University's Eagleton Institute. On the question of whether the New Jersey State Police "treat all drivers the same regardless of race, sex, or age," 60% of whites gave troopers a positive assessment, while 72% of blacks responded negatively.

"I have never seen a schism as wide as this between any two groups in the electorate," Eagleton's Cliff Zukin said. "It is as though black and white New Jerseyans are living in different worlds."

Chapter 81

THE BIG THING JOHNNIE COCHRAN BROUGHT to a case was the spotlight. He got oceans of ink. He and his partners decided to use that power to fan the flames and make New Jersey decision-makers sweat. They wanted to turn racial profiling into a national issue and began talking about the shooting wherever they went—on college campuses, before bar associations, to *The New York Times* editorial board. Cochran met with U.S. Attorney General Janet Reno and urged her to initiate a federal civil rights probe.

"We think this is an important case, not only for the State of New Jersey, but for everybody in this country who is concerned about justice," Cochran told a throng of press people when he announced plans to file a lawsuit against New Jersey. "We are here to let the world know that a crime has been committed, not by the occupants of the van, but by New Jersey state troopers."

Cochran appeared to have a powerful case. Despite what he called a State Police attempt to "dirty up" the students, they had pristine records and were ideal plaintiffs. But the potency of the case hinged on a legal doctrine called *deliberate indifference.* If Cochran & Co. could show the State of New Jersey had turned a blind eye to racial profiling, the jury award could be enormous.

The Dream Team had tapped into a gusher of deliberate indifference. The failure of State Police to do anything about the *"de facto racial profiling"* found by Judge Robert Francis in the *Soto* case *"manifests its indifference if not acceptance,"* the lawyers alleged. Peter Neufeld got

289

his hands on the WWOR-TV exposé *Without Just Cause,* dating back to 1989, to which New Jersey's repeated response had been to deny, deny, deny. When it came to deliberate indifference, the case for the young basketball players looked like a slam dunk.

The Dream Team's strategy was paying off. The racial profiling ruckus was snowballing. The *Star-Ledger* ran a front page story quoting Trooper John Hogan's former fiancée, Christy Dittman, claiming that he exhibited overt racist tendencies in the months leading up to the shooting, including wearing T-shirts emblazoned with the inscription: *"KKK—The Original Boys in the Hood."* Dittman said Hogan would drive down the highway and point out black drivers.

"He'd call them 'johnnies,'" she said. *"'Two johnnies in a Maxima,' he'd say. 'I wish I was working. That would be such a good bust.'"*

The State Police seemed tone deaf to the din around them. Remarkably, months *after* the shooting, one of Hogan's supervisors recommended him for the Trooper of the Year award.

"Trooper Hogan has demonstrated that he is among the best that the New Jersey State Police have to offer," Sgt. Fred Gasior wrote to HQ in July 1998.

But by then Hogan was radioactive. His shot at the Red Ribbon had gone up in gunsmoke. He had become the new poster boy for racial profiling. Instead of accolades, the trooper was staring at a possible prison stint for attempted murder.

A crucial question revolved around the 11th and final bullet that Danny Reyes claimed hit him in the back after the van stopped rolling. When Reyes was released from the hospital, Neufeld took him to one of New York's top orthopedists, Dr. Stephen Nicholas, team doctor to the New York Jets.

Reyes was a mess. His arm was shot-up and he still had two slugs in him; one in his stomach and another an inch from his spine.

"My God," Nicholas said when he examined Reyes. Since the shooting the bullet in his back had migrated almost to the skin's surface.

"What can you do?" Neufeld asked.

"I guess I could take it out," Nicholas said.

"When was the last time you did that?"

"Twenty years ago, when I was a resident."

"Okay, here's what I want you to do," said Neufeld.

The lawyer suspected there might be fragments on the bullet which would tell a forensic pathologist if it passed through glass or upholstery or metal before it entered Reyes.

"What you need to do," said Neufeld, "is wrap up the slug, put it in a bag, and write your initials on it in my presence. We'll seal the bag and maintain the chain of custody."

Nicholas followed Neufeld's instructions. Sure enough, when he pulled out the bullet they could see foreign material on it that was not human tissue. The doctor handed Neufeld the bag and when the lawyer returned to his TriBeCa office he called Jim Gerrow, New Jersey's special prosecutor on the shooting.

Neufeld was impressed by Gerrow. He was a straight shooter. When the insurance carrier for the company that rented the van refused to cover the student's medical bills—claiming the injuries were a result of criminal activity—Gerrow wrote a letter certifying they were not perpetrators, but victims.

The State Police was not as obliging. Gerrow sent two investigators to TriBeCa. When they arrived, Neufeld gave them explicit instructions, but the detectives didn't welcome a defense lawyer telling them how to do their job and the encounter turned nasty.

"It's very important you don't open this," Neufeld said. "The first people that open it should be your hair and fibers laboratory."

"You don't tell me what to do," one cop said. "I want to open it here."

"If you open it you're going to compromise the integrity of the evidence," said Neufeld.

"Well, I'm not taking it out of here unless we open it right now," the detective said.

"Fine. You're not getting the bag. Get out of my office."

Neufeld called Gerrow, who agreed that he was correct and ordered the investigators to return to pick up the evidence and deliver it to the lab—sealed.

It turned out Neufeld was right. A tiny fragment on the slug matched material from the lower part of the driver's seat, suggesting that Danny Reyes had been shot in the back after the van stopped rolling. Ballistics found the bullet had been fired from John Hogan's gun.

Chapter 82

PETER VERNIERO HEARD A TANTALIZING RUMOR in early 1999. After 20 years on the New Jersey Supreme Court, Justice Stewart G. Pollock planned to retire. Verniero wanted the job. He was already the youngest Attorney General in state history. Now the middle-class kid from Montville could also become New Jersey's youngest Supreme Court Justice at age 39.

There would be opposition. His inexperience—especially never having tried a court case—would raise doubts. And, as Whitman's vinegary Chief of Staff, he'd left a harsh aftertaste with a number of lawmakers. But even critics acknowledged Verniero was exceptionally smart, some might even say brilliant, with a reputation as spotless as the starched white shirts he wore to work every day. And Republicans controlled the Senate. He would win approval. One nagging piece of unfinished business, though, could prove problematic.

Racial profiling was now a front burner issue. The press had locked onto the story like a pit bull. *The Philadelphia Inquirer* ran a piece quoting six unidentified troopers who claimed widespread racial profiling by New Jersey State Police. The troopers told reporter Douglas Campbell minorities were profiled not because they were *more likely* to carry drugs, but because their complaints were *less likely* to be investigated.

"If the same complaint came from a white male from Wall Street there would definitely be an investigation," one trooper said.

Three days later *The Newark Star-Ledger* published a front page article revealing that black motorists accounted for three-quarters of

Turnpike arrests, numbers almost identical to those WWOR-TV had uncovered a decade earlier. Little, it seemed, had changed. By noon, the startling news was being reported on TV and radio all over New Jersey and New York. Profiling had taken on a life of its own.

Verniero still had zero to show for his Turnpike shooting investigation. Reverend Reginald Jackson was calling for a federal probe. Al Sharpton was threatening massive protest marches. Johnnie Cochran and the Dream Team were putting the final touches on a huge lawsuit. And a crucial courtroom showdown loomed with Bill Buckman on the *Soto* appeal.

After two years in Vermont, Buckman had packed up his family and moved back to New Jersey. He'd grown bored handling nickel-and-dime cases and was now in full-tilt combat to keep the racial profiling verdict from being overturned. Verniero had to act swiftly or his fast track to the Supreme Court might be derailed—even before his nomination was announced. Suddenly, he seemed to undergo a metamorphosis, exhibiting a new urgency to get to the bottom of profiling.

"My office has embarked on an unprecedented review of State Police operations," the Attorney General announced. "Such a comprehensive review has never been undertaken at this level in the history of the State Police."

But Lt. Col. Robert Dunlop smelled a rat. The State Police review had been sprung on him and Superintendent Carl Williams without warning. They were called downtown and informed of the investigation the very day the *Star-Ledger* published its story. The whole thing seemed too hasty.

Criminal Justice Director Paul Zoubek was put in charge of the State Police review and moved swiftly to build a team. He recruited Appellate Division chief Debra Stone and it wasn't long before she made an alarming discovery—the Maryland State Police consent decree, which made search numbers the definitive test on profiling. New Jersey's statistics were not only far more egregious than Maryland's, the numbers also had a direct bearing on the *Soto* appeal.

The moment of truth was fast approaching on *Soto*. In one month a three-judge panel was scheduled to hear oral arguments on the appeal and Stone faced a dilemma. The Maryland information only bolstered her belief the challenge had been a mistake. Now she would have to send attorneys under her supervision to fight a battle in which she didn't believe.

In addition, the Attorney General's Office would face a harsh reprimand if the court discovered it was violating its *Brady* obligation to disclose exculpatory evidence to Buckman and the *Soto* defense. Stone was determined to see the appeal dropped. She and her longtime cohort, Anne Paskow, formed what they called the "nag patrol" and began tag-teaming Zoubek to give up the appeal.

Meanwhile, the *Star-Ledger* article was pouring gasoline on the already inflamed fury of New Jersey's minority community. Reverend Reginald Jackson demanded Carl Williams be fired.

"You cannot solve a problem unless you acknowledge there is a problem," he said. "The New Jersey State Police does not acknowledge there is a problem."

Williams responded at a hastily called press conference, posing before a phalanx of troopers, including several prominently-positioned black officers. "I am deeply hurt by the accusations," the Superintendent said. "There is no such thing as racial profiling in the New Jersey State Police."

Jackson got a telephone call from Peter Verniero, who asked him to come to Trenton for a "private meeting." When he arrived, the place was mobbed with cameras recording him being greeted by Verniero and Governor Christine Todd Whitman. He realized they were engaged in a public relations campaign and had used him as a pawn. Verniero promised the State Police review would be thorough and exhaustive and Whitman urged him to support the probe. But Jackson did not trust the State Police to investigate itself.

"I will stand in Macy's window at high noon," he said, "and say that the Justice Department needs to investigate the New Jersey State Police."

Whitman refused to relent, saying: "The day that government can't police itself will be a scary day in this state."

As that was happening, tea leaf readers were playing a popular Trenton parlor game—predicting the next Jersey judge to relinquish gavel and robe. Supreme Court watchers had been floating rumors that Justice Pollock was about to retire. He was an eminent jurist, who'd written many of the courts landmark decisions during his 20 years on the bench. On February 25th, he finally announced he was stepping down. At 7:30 the next morning Reverend Jackson's telephone rang. He couldn't believe his ears.

"I called to get your congratulations," Peter Verniero said cheerfully. "The Governor has just nominated me to the Supreme Court."

"Wait a minute," Jackson said, aghast. "You said this was going to be the most comprehensive investigation of the State Police ever and you were going to see it through. Now one week later you're calling to tell me you're leaving?"

"The Governor wants this done as soon as possible," Verniero said. "John Farmer, who is her chief counsel, is going to become Attorney General."

"Peter, that still doesn't answer why you can't stay until the report is due."

"I don't know why, but the Governor wants this done as soon as possible."

Racial profiling had become an incredibly incendiary issue in New Jersey and it occurred to Jackson that Verniero and Whitman were both eager to get out of town before the whole mess blew up in their faces; her to the U.S. Senate, him to the Supreme Court.

But, for many, the prospect of Verniero wearing the black robes of a high court justice was repugnant. New Jersey's Supreme Court was considered by some to be the foremost in America. *"The legal equivalent of the New York Yankees,"* it had once been called. The Court had a long history as an activist tribunal that had rendered a cornucopia of brilliant, groundbreaking opinions protecting the poor and underprivileged. Among its alumni were some dazzling legal giants, including William J. Brennan, Jr., who went on to become one of the great U.S. Supreme Court Justices. Verniero didn't seem to be cut from the same cloth.

"I think there's a huge stature gap," said Frank Askin, the noted Rutgers University law professor. "There's a great danger that this court's tradition will be undermined."

Bill Buckman was incensed. He considered Verniero a political hack utterly unqualified for the Supreme Court. His record on racial profiling alone nullified him, particularly his office's morally

reprehensible *blacks drive worse* theory. Buckman dismissed the State
Police review as a sham. He suspected Verniero was just trying to buy
time until his Supreme Court confirmation. Once he was approved
the State would return to business as usual and keep fighting on *Soto*.
To him, it was despicable.

Then it dawned on Buckman that maybe he'd misjudged. Maybe
the nomination wasn't so appalling. Perhaps this was an opportunity
to force Verniero's hand. It would be political suicide for Verniero to
publicly defend his office's assertion that blacks were stopped on the
Turnpike so disproportionately because they were lousy drivers. Even
Republicans would slam him. Suddenly Verniero's nomination didn't
seem so outrageous after all. Maybe it had opened a door that could
lead, finally, to a just resolution of *Soto*.

Chapter 83

APPELLATE DIVISION CHIEF Debra Stone was getting an earful—and the more she heard the more "pissed off" she became. Stone had put out word through minority investigators in the Attorney General's Office that she wanted to talk to troopers about profiling. She promised confidentiality and more than a dozen troopers responded, most of them black, none in uniform. The lawyer met the majority of them off state property, listening to their stories as she scribbled notes in shorthand decipherable only to her, which she destroyed after writing her scathing report.

"When you leave the Academy you are assigned a coach and his job is to teach you how to get ahead," Stone wrote. *"Trooper after trooper has testified that the coach taught them how to profile minorities. The perception among young troopers is that you are more likely to make a good arrest if you stop minorities. This is what they are taught by their coach, enforced by first-line supervisors and tacitly approved by upper management. The end does not justify the means. There is no program or discipline procedure in the event a trooper is found to have a high number of minority stops. This is a cocktail for disaster."*

Paul Zoubek responded in a memorandum: *"What do we do about our position in Soto? Can we still reasonably take the positions we have taken in Soto?"*

Chapter 84

Two DAYS AFTER PETER VERNIERO'S CAREER as a Supreme Court Justice was launched, Carl Williams' career with the State Police came to a crashing climax.

The Newark Star-Ledger published an interview with Williams on Sunday, February 28, 1999. Reverend Reginald Jackson made the mistake of reading the newspaper before he went into morning service. The headline said it all: *"Trooper Boss: Race Plays Role in Drug Crimes."* Jackson was flabbergasted.

"This is going to be a heck of a day," he told his church officers.

"Why?" one asked.

"I don't want to get into it. Read the paper."

"The Superintendent of the New Jersey State Police says he's told all of his troopers that racial profiling will not be condoned," the story began, *"but he adds that he believes most of the illegal cocaine and marijuana business in the United States is conducted by minorities."*

In one breath the Superintendent condemned racial profiling and in the next he blamed minorities for the drug problem.

"Two weeks ago the President of the United States went to Mexico to talk to the President of Mexico about drugs," Williams was quoted saying. *"He didn't go to Ireland. He didn't go to England. It is most likely a minority group that's involved with that. They aren't going to ask some Irishman to be part of their (gang)."*

Jackson looked out the church window. Several TV news vans were already in the parking lot.

"Today's Sunday," Jackson told his officers. "I don't want to deal with it today. Tell them I'll do all this tomorrow."

Christine Todd Whitman couldn't wait. The article was a public relations calamity at the worst possible time. Whitman was poised to make a run for the U.S. Senate and Peter Verniero was about to face Supreme Court confirmation and this could gum up the works for them both. She summoned Verniero and a few close advisers to Pontefract, her family's estate in Oldwick. Carl Williams, she told them, had plunged a dagger through the heart of his own career. He had to go—*now*.

Jackson was in the midst of services when he was handed a note. Leroy J. Jones, Jr., a black Assemblyman, was on the telephone. Jones was a member of the St. Matthew's congregation and Jackson wondered why he wasn't in church.

"I've called a press conference," Jones said. "Can you be there?"

"Well, I'm in church" said Jackson, realizing he couldn't avoid the issue, even on the Sabbath. "But I will stop by and make a statement after service."

When Jones stepped before the microphones his office was swarming with press.

"Williams' views are dastardly, his thoughts are ill and sickened, and he's unfit to hold such a critical, important office," said Jones. "He's a racist of the worst kind, because he doesn't even know it."

Rev. Jackson reminded reporters he had demanded Williams' resignation a mere two weeks before and now, he said, the newspaper article only validated his stand.

"It becomes clear to us that the problems facing the State Police are deep and pervasive," said Jackson. "It suggests to me that you have leadership whose perception is made up and they see no problem."

Late that afternoon, Governor Whitman put it all to rest, she hoped, in a statement announcing Williams' resignation after 34 years with the State Police.

"I have valued Colonel Williams's service, and his career record is an honorable one," she said. "However, his comments today are inconsistent with our efforts to enhance public confidence in the State Police."

But despite Whitman's effort to cauterize the Williams wound, blood continued to flow. The American Civil Liberties Union accused

Whitman of scapegoating Williams to save her Senate aspirations. Democrats demanded Peter Verniero's Supreme Court nomination be postponed until the State Police Review was complete.

Bill Buckman was encouraged. He wanted the political climate to get so hot that Whitman and Verniero would be forced to abandon the *Soto* appeal. But the State wasn't ready to throw in the towel just yet. At 3:00 o'clock on Friday afternoon, March 5th, Buckman's car telephone rang. It was Paul Zoubek. He wanted a 120-day extension in *Soto* until the State Police Review was finished. Buckman was taken aback. Oral arguments before the Appellate Court were scheduled for April 28th. Then it hit him: that would be right in the midst of Verniero's confirmation. This was another attempt to buy time.

"Paul, *Soto* has been pending for nine years," Buckman said. "This appeal has been pending for three years. I'll have to think it over. Give me until Monday morning."

Zoubek said he couldn't wait and, by the time Buckman got back to his office, Verniero had announced his delay request. Buckman realized he was at a crossroads. If Verniero won an extension, he'd be home free and the State would keep fighting on *Soto*. The courts, he feared, would eventually knuckle under to political pressure. He had to stop the delay or racial profiling could be permanently swept under the rug. Buckman had no idea someone inside the Attorney General's Office was also trying to keep that from happening.

Debra Stone was on the warpath. After her blistering memorandum she continued to interview troopers. Two weeks later, she wrote a second report so combustible flames were almost jumping off the pages.

"Racial profiling exists as part of the (State Police) culture," she wrote. *"You are taught that if you see 'Johnnies' in a 'good' car, they should be stopped and investigated. The assumption is made that minorities are drug dealers, and cops are encouraged to stop them and toss their cars. This is particularly true of 'Diggers' (suppressive troopers) who 'ride the Black Dragon' (the Turnpike). Failure of supervision is endemic. The bottom line is to make arrests and get drugs regardless of how that is accomplished."*

Chapter 85

THE VERNIERO NOMINATION INTRODUCED two old lions into the racial profiling conflict whose roars would eventually have a profound impact.

William Gormley was the powerful Republican State Senator from Atlantic City. Opinions on Gormley ranged from brilliant and gutsy to an obsessive bully. As Chairman of the Senate Judiciary Committee, he was gatekeeper to a thousand State political appointments, including the Supreme Court. And as a Republican, he was expected to shepherd Peter Verniero through the confirmation process. But Gormley was a maverick who often strayed from party lines. There was a running joke in Trenton:

Q: What do you call a Republican who votes with the Democrats?
A: Bill Gormley.

John A. Lynch, dean of New Jersey Democrats, was perhaps the only Senator equal in stature to Gormley. Lynch was widely regarded as the smartest man in New Jersey government. Gormley was right behind him.

The men were wily lords of the State's political jungle. They tangled occasionally, but had great respect for each other. Both came from Irish-American families with deep roots in public service. Gormley's father was sheriff of Atlantic County for 20 years. Lynch's father served 22 years in the same State Senate seat the son had now held for 17 years.

Gormley didn't hold Peter Verniero in terribly high regard. He certainly would not have nominated him to the Supreme Court. But no one was more opposed to the nomination than Lynch. He considered the Attorney General a glorified water boy for Christie Whitman, and there was no love lost between Lynch and Whitman. She once slashed $300,000 worth of State projects from his district after he voted against her budget. On another occasion, Lynch publicly berated the Governor for paying $175,000 in State funds to settle a sexual harassment lawsuit against a Republican official. Whitman retaliated by telling reporters that police had been called to Lynch's home to settle a domestic dispute between him and his wife.

But Lynch's animus toward Verniero went beyond Whitman. Lynch was a gifted trial lawyer, sixth in his class at Georgetown Law School, and had litigated hundreds of cases. Yet, he did not consider himself qualified to be a Supreme Court Justice and, in his mind, Verniero wasn't even remotely fit.

"His career predominantly consists of political assignments and positions in the Whitman Administration," Lynch wrote to the Senate President. *"The Whitman Administration and Mr. Verniero have fought to suppress evidence showing that racial profiling exists."*

Lynch demanded that the nomination be delayed until the State Police review was complete.

Chapter 86

Being Peter Verniero wasn't easy. These should have been the best of times for a man on the cusp of becoming New Jersey's youngest Supreme Court Justice. Instead, the walls seemed to be closing in on him.

Verniero was a lonely man, excoriated by black leaders, defense lawyers, Democrats, and newspaper editorialists. He tried to placate the critics, reminding them of his "unprecedented" State Police review, but succeeded only in painting himself into a corner. Now opponents were demanding he actually finish the job.

Verniero needed to do something dramatic, without looking too political. He called a meeting with his Criminal Justice Director Paul Zoubek, Appellate Division chief Debra Stone and James Gerrow, who was the Special Prosecutor on the Turnpike shooting case, and laid out the quandary—not mentioning his nomination. The public, he said, was losing confidence in the Attorney General's Office. Their credibility was at stake. Nearly a year after the shooting, they still had nothing to show for the investigation. Verniero wanted to know if Troopers Hogan and Kenna could be indicted for the shooting before the April 23rd anniversary. Gerrow gave him a thumb's down, saying his probe was still months from wrapping up.

What about the falsification case, he asked. There was a sudden wariness in the room. After the shooting, investigators discovered Hogan and Kenna had been lying about the races of motorists they'd stopped on the Turnpike, like Christopher Woodley, the black law student they pulled over the night of the shooting, who they reported to be white. The evidence was top secret. A falsification indictment, Zoubek explained, would create substantial risk of tainting the shooting grand jury. If one panel became aware Hogan and Kenna had been branded as liars by another grand jury it could create a bias. Any future indictment in the shooting could well be thrown out due to grand jury prejudice.

But Verniero persisted, despite having far less criminal court experience than the other three veteran lawyers. They explained to him that there was no statute of limitations concern, no pressing legal reason for a falsification indictment now, and Hogan and Kenna were not risks to flee. They could be charged later. Verniero was not swayed.

"Well, if it's ready to be presented, we should present it. I'm not comfortable suppressing an investigation. We have to bring this to closure in a timely fashion."

He ordered them to take the falsification case to a grand jury before the shooting anniversary "in the public interest," he said. Afterwards, many suspected his real motive was public relations. When they left Verniero's office, Zoubek called Stone and Gerrow aside.

"Look," he said, "we all have to be absolutely comfortable with this, given the risks entailed here. I want to hear from anyone if you're not comfortable with this approach."

Neither voiced an objection.

Chapter 87

"Beware the Ides of March!" the soothsayer admonished Julius Caesar in 44 B.C. Paul Zoubek might have stayed in bed had an oracle given him the same fair warning 2,043 years later.

On the morning of March 15, 1999, Sgt. Thomas Gilbert arrived at the Hughes Justice Complex with a red booklet entitled *"New Jersey State Police Statistical Analysis."* Gilbert went to a copy machine, duplicated the contents, and handed them to the Criminal Justice Director in an innocuous looking blue binder. But looks were deceptive.

Zoubek went back to his office, opened the blue book, and began reading. What he saw horrified him.

• A September 1996 analysis showing State Police minority stop levels worse than the defense put forth during *Soto.*

• A startling 1997 memorandum showing sky-high minority search numbers by various State Police barracks of up to 94%.

• A 1997-1998 monthly chart of "nonwhite" roadside searches ranging between 70-and-100%.

• Finally, Sgt. Gilbert's February 1997 memorandum to Superintendent Williams: *"The numbers are not good. We are in a very bad spot."*

Zoubek was livid. The blue binder contained all the evidence anyone would need to prove the State Police guilty of racial profiling. Debra Stone was walking past his office and heard the explosion. He rushed to the door and pointed at the binder.

"Have you seen this before?"

Zoubek seethed over her shoulder while Stone flipped through the book. No, she hadn't seen the paperwork, but immediately grasped the implications. The numbers added up to an open-and-shut case of racial profiling. Worse, some of the data had been sitting in State Police files for three years. Zoubek suspected a cover-up. He took the elevator to the 8th floor, stalked into the Attorney General's office and threw the binder on his desk. Verniero could see he was furious.

"Look at this," he said. "Have you seen this?"

"No," said Verniero.

"There's a document here from Sgt. Gilbert," Zoubek said, turning to *'The numbers are not good'* memo. "Have you seen this before?"

"No," Verniero said, not volunteering that although he hadn't seen these particular documents, he was familiar with the information. "Why haven't they been produced before?"

Still fuming, Zoubek promised to investigate. He returned to his office and telephoned Lt. Col. Robert Dunlop.

"Do you know about this?" Zoubek demanded. "Did you know about the Gilbert analysis?"

Dunlop was startled by Zoubek's ferocity. But even more by his intimation that the State Police had withheld information. The lawyer said somebody could be in big trouble and, before he hung up, raised the specter of criminal culpability for "obstruction of justice."

Then Zoubek's phone rang and his day went from bad to worse. The Appellate Court ordered him to make his oral argument on delaying the *Soto* appeal—*tomorrow!*

The Criminal Justice boss was reeling. The *Ides of March* 1999 had proven to be a most miserable day. Zoubek didn't need a soothsayer to tell him March 16th would be just as wretched.

Chapter 88

THE NEXT DAY LT. COL. DUNLOP TOLD Sgt. Thomas Gilbert that Zoubek was making noise about a State Police cover-up.

Gilbert was bewildered. He assured Dunlop that he'd been keeping the Attorney General's Office fully abreast of his findings on racial profiling for more than two years.

It wasn't long before Dunlop picked up another troubling piece of scuttlebutt. The Attorney General's Office was planning to turn Carl Williams into a sacrificial lamb and feed him to the U.S. Department of Justice. Williams would be indicted for obstruction of justice as the fall guy for the State Police cover-up of racial profiling. Dunlop placed a call to Zoubek.

"Paul, I wouldn't go there," he said. "You know, Attorney General Verniero had this information."

"What do you mean?" Zoubek said.

Dunlop told him about the meeting May 20th, 1997, when Sgt. Gilbert had informed Verniero that New Jersey's search rates were as high or higher than those of the Maryland State Police. Dunlop sensed Zoubek hadn't heard this before—and didn't believe it.

"There was even a comment made by the Attorney General," Dunlop continued, "in reference to not signing a consent decree that 'they'd have to tie me to a train and drag me along the track before I'd sign a decree.'"

Silence on the other end of the telephone suggested Dunlop had touched a nerve.

"I'll get back to you," Zoubek said finally and hung up. He went directly to the 8th floor and confronted Verniero.

"I'm hearing from the State Police that this Gilbert analysis was presented to you and there was a meeting in which all of this was completely and extensively reviewed."

"No," Verniero said. "I don't recall that happening."

Zoubek went back to his office and called Dunlop.

"I talked to the Attorney General. He doesn't recall a presentation of these statistics."

"That's what my people remember," said Dunlop. "What about Carl Williams?"

"We're not going there," Zoubek said.

Verniero was, to use Tom Gilbert's phrase, *in a very bad spot.* With the State Police now saying he'd been aware of incriminating evidence on profiling for years, the Attorney General needed to inoculate himself immediately or it would be him—rather than former State Police Superintendent Williams—facing a cover-up charge. His Supreme Court aspirations would be obliterated. Later that day he wrote a memo and inserted it in the Attorney General's Office file on racial profiling.

"Today I became aware for the first time of the existence of certain State Police documents concerning data and information relating to stops and searches of minority motorists not heretofore produced to us by the State Police. Director Paul Zoubek made me aware of the documents, which he said he himself only became aware of yesterday."

Verniero was adopting a simple posture: Deniability.

Chapter 89

BILL BUCKMAN'S MOMENT HAD FINALLY COME. After nine years, *Soto* had at last reached zero hour. If the defense lawyer played his hand right, New Jersey would be forced to throw in its cards and give up the case.

Peter Verniero was desperate for a postponement and Buckman was just as determined to stop him. A telephone hearing was held with a three-judge Appellate Court panel—Edwin H. Stern, Dennis J. Braithwaite, and David Landau. The judges were patched into a conference call with Zoubek, Buckman and *Soto* defense team member Justin Loughry.

Loughry could count on two fingers the times he'd opposed a delay request. But Buckman convinced him this was a transparent ploy by Verniero to buy time and one of those rare moments when they should say no. If they could stop a postponement, Buckman believed Verniero would cave in.

Judge Stern kicked off the hearing by asking Zoubek why he wanted a continuance.

"Well," said Zoubek, "we are looking into this issue of racial profiling. We are starting a study and we want to see where we are going with this appeal."

The words were barely out of Zoubek's mouth when Judge Braithwaite roared: "You mean to tell me that this thing has been pending all of these years and you are only now investigating?"

For several excruciating seconds the sound of silence echoed through the telephone lines while the judge's words resonated.

Zoubek finally managed to utter that the Attorney General's Office was beginning to see some disturbing statistical data causing them to reevaluate *Soto*.

"By the way, sir," barked another judge, "you realize this is a criminal proceeding?"

"Yes, your Honor," Zoubek said.

"What about your *Brady* obligations? If you're investigating this matter, you understand you have an obligation to provide your adversaries with discovery."

"Well, we recognize our obligations," Zoubek said.

"Have you given them anything showing you're looking into it?" the judge said.

That was Buckman's cue. He'd been listening quietly, relishing the moment as the judges skewered Zoubek. Now was the time to throw fuel on the fire, the moment he'd been waiting a decade for.

"I certainly would like to see any discovery the State has," he said. "We haven't been given anything indicating the State has looked into the allegations we proved in *Soto*."

The hearing turned into a tag-team match, with Buckman and the judges taking turns beating up Zoubek.

Judge Braithwaite chimed in. "What about your professional obligations not to prosecute a frivolous appeal when you don't have a basis for it?"

"Mr. Zoubek," Judge Stern said, "are you telling me that you feel you have some ethical issues as it relates to going forward?"

"Yes, your Honor," Zoubek said.

Buckman decided it was time for the coup de grâce. Peter Verniero was a neophyte compared to these three Appellate judges. Yet he was about to leapfrog them onto the Supreme Court. Buckman suspected that might be a sore spot with one or all of them and pushed the political button.

"Your Honors, Governor Whitman announced that Attorney General Verniero would be her nominee to replace a retiring Supreme Court Justice," he said. "Newspapers throughout the state have editorialized the nomination should be slowed while the issue of racial profiling is resolved. This appears to be an attempt to enlist this court's help in the resolution of the political and editorial problems faced by the Attorney General. We respectfully ask this court not weigh in on any political side."

That did the trick. The judges denied Zoubek's motion to delay *Soto*. They also warned him that the Attorney General's Office was treading on perilously thin ice and that Zoubek and Verniero better live up to their ethical obligations in the case.

Zoubek made his way back up to the 8th floor and informed the Attorney General that things had gone less than well. He said a decision had to be made to fish or cut bait on *Soto*. Zoubek recommended the latter. But Verniero wasn't ready for that. Before they dropped the case, he said, they needed to expedite the State Police Review Team and release a report before the Turnpike shooting anniversary. He didn't mention it would also be before his Supreme Court confirmation hearing.

Chapter 90

HOSTILITY TOWARD VERNIERO'S NOMINATION was becoming widespread and vitriolic. State troopers believed the Attorney General was using them as stooges in order to salvage his Supreme Court appointment. A flyer was circulated through the Outfit urging members to cast a symbolic vote of *"NO CONFIDENCE"* against Verniero.

The NAACP held a large rally outside the Statehouse and condemned what it called *"racist attitudes which prevail within the leadership ranks of the New Jersey State Police, including its present department head, Attorney General Peter Verniero."*

Even the New Jersey Bar Association ganged up on him. The Bar traditionally screened judicial nominees and gave the Governor its confidential recommendation. In 30 years its advice had rarely been rejected. Verniero had been trying to toady up to the Bar in a series of letters patting himself on the back for his actions on racial profiling.

"I have been second to no one in wanting to get to the bottom of these allegations. At every point where significant information or allegations were presented to me, I took appropriate action," he wrote. *"Not everything that is faced can be changed; but nothing can be changed until it is faced."*

But when Verniero *faced* the Bar it was a disaster. For two-and-a-half hours, a committee of seasoned lawyers roasted him over his lack of response to profiling and his scant legal experience. When it was over, the committee voted 17-to-6 to veto Verniero's appointment. The next day the supposedly hush-hush recommendation was all over the headlines.

With opposition growing, Verniero had to do something—fast. In early April he circulated the first draft of the State Police Review Team's Interim Report. In tough, direct language, the report explicitly rebuked the State Police for racial profiling.

"The study of consent searches was, quite simply, shocking. Interviews with troopers bears out the message made clear by the statistical data. Racial profiling is a practice undertaken by a group of aggressive troopers assigned to the New Jersey Turnpike."

The second draft was even more bilious, blaming the State Police not only for profiling, but also for covering-up evidence—especially on searches:

"This circumstance has seriously compromised the State's litigation posture, and also has needlessly delayed initiating appropriate remedies and reforms."

On Saturday, April 17th, Verniero and Paul Zoubek drove to Drumthwacket, the graceful Governor's Mansion in Princeton, and undraped the Interim Report for Christie Whitman. Beyond the toothy smile and wholesome Princess Di visage, a big part of Whitman's charisma was that she always *seemed* to be right and almost never admitted a mistake. But Whitman had steadfastly defended troopers on profiling. Now she was going to have to eat her words. And as Zoubek read from the eighth and latest draft, it became crystal clear those words were going to be hard to swallow.

"The problem of disparate treatment is real—not imagined. Our review has revealed two interrelated problems: (1) willful misconduct by a small number of State Police members who are bent, apparently, on harassing minority motorists and then tampering with State Police records to conceal their misconduct, and (2) more common instances of apparent de facto discrimination by officers who are influenced by stereotypes and thus tend to treat minority motorists differently, subjecting them more routinely to investigative tactics and techniques that are designed to ferret out illicit drugs and weapons."

Whitman asked a lot of questions, which Zoubek answered, and kept reading. Then a passage on Page 3 caught the Governor's ear.

"The most startling evidence of such a disparate treatment comes in the form of statistics that were compiled by the State Police as part of an internal audit, one not previously disclosed to the Attorney General's Office..."

"What was this?" Whitman demanded. "A cover-up?"

Zoubek explained that the State Police possessed several years worth of damning data that had been withheld from the Attorney General's Office until Sgt. Thomas Gilbert turned over his blue binder last month. That evidence would force Whitman to eat crow and admit to the state, and the nation, that she'd been wrong about the New Jersey State Police.

Chapter 91

NEW JERSEY HAD BECOME "the Mississippi of the '90s," as Rev. Al Sharpton branded it, the national symbol of racial profiling. But the Garden State had no monopoly on the issue. Racial profiling—or at least awareness of its existence—was spreading across the country like a virus.

New York City had been stained by the blood of Amadou Diallo—an unarmed black man shot 41 times by police on his doorstep as he pulled keys from his pocket.

Prominent African-Americans like movie star Wesley Snipes and O.J. Simpson prosecutor Christopher Darden claimed to have been profiled. Even the Justice Department's Eric Holder said he'd been touched by the practice.

Blacks constituted about 10% of the U.S. population, but 70% of stops on the Florida Turnpike, according to *The Orlando Sentinel*. In Maryland, they comprised 77% of stops and searches on I-95. In Chicago, minorities made up 90% of police searches.

The Justice Department had 10 active investigations into alleged racial discrimination by police. Federal monitors were already working "to identify and modify the behavior of problem officers" in Maryland, Pittsburgh, and Steubenville, Ohio.

Some police departments acted without being coerced. In California, San Diego and San Jose launched programs to track the reasons behind every traffic stop.

"It's the right thing to do," San Jose Police Chief Bill Landsdowne said. "There is a very true belief and perception in this community that law enforcement may be making car stops based on race, gender and dress."

Chapter 92

Something kept nagging Paul Zoubek. Things were moving too fast. The Turnpike shooting anniversary was four days away and they were about to release the Interim Report, which would pillory the State Police—enough to rattle anyone's nerves. But it was more than that. Since the meeting with Governor Whitman, the Director of Criminal Justice had been uneasy.

Accusing the State Police of covering-up *"the most startling evidence"* on racial profiling was a grievous charge. Zoubek wanted to be absolutely certain he was right.

The day before the report's release, he began sifting through boxes of documents George Rover, the Attorney General's liaison on racial profiling, had wheeled into his office two months before. Zoubek hadn't looked at them until now. He discovered several memorandums containing data very similar to the information in Sgt. Gilbert's *smoking gun* memo, much of it data already incorporated in the Interim Report. The more Zoubek read the more he realized Gilbert *had* passed the information to Rover, who had relayed it up the chain of command. The thing was, Rover answered directly to Peter Verniero.

Zoubek went upstairs to Verniero's office and told him what he'd found. The State Police had not covered-up. The Attorney General listened and then asked a single question: Did the files indicate that he, Verniero, received any telltale documents? It was a curious question. Zoubek said no, there was no indication of that. Then he went down to the 5th floor and revised the Interim Report.

317

Later that day, Verniero made good on his promise to charge Troopers John Hogan and James Kenna before the Turnpike shooting anniversary by announcing that both had been indicted for falsifying official reports by identifying black motorists they'd stopped as white. Hogan was accused of 17 specific violations and Kenna of eight. If convicted, they each faced up to 20 years in prison.

"It is always a sad day for law enforcement when a sworn officer is charged with a serious offense. Today is such a day," a somber-faced Verniero told the gathered press. "This conduct is intolerable and represents a serious breach of the public trust."

The troopers' attorneys immediately attacked the charges, claiming Hogan and Kenna were being sacrificed to save both Verniero's Supreme Court nomination and Governor Whitman's anticipated run for the U.S. Senate.

"These gentlemen are being thrown to the wolves for political expediency," said Hogan's lawyer, Robert Galantucci.

On the other hand, Johnnie Cochran and the Dream Team were ecstatic. They were putting final touches on a massive lawsuit and, before it was even filed, the New Jersey Attorney General had just given them the ammunition to wheedle an extra few million dollars—from his own state government. One Dream Team attorney summed it up with the understatement: "It certainly doesn't hurt."

Chapter 93

ON APRIL 20, 1999, GOVERNOR Christine Todd Whitman stepped to a microphone-encrusted pedestal. She was wearing a turquoise dress with a red and green scarf and gold earrings, but her trademark smile was absent.

"There can be no question," she announced, "but that racial profiling exists."

A crush of reporters scribbled furiously. After a decade of denial the State of New Jersey was finally admitting that racial profiling was fact and not fiction.

"I can only imagine how frustrating and humiliating it must be to be singled out simply because of the color of your skin," Whitman said solemnly. Peter Verniero stood beside her in a black suit and crisp white shirt as they unveiled the State Police Review Team's Interim Report.

"Minority motorists have been treated differently than non-minority motorists during the course of traffic stops on the New Jersey Turnpike," the report declared. *"We conclude that the problem of disparate treatment is real—not imagined."*

The 115-page report was a remarkable document—a confessional that did not repent. Instead, it recast sinner as saint, offering no apologies, but plenty of self-congratulation. In a single bound, New Jersey had hurtled past years of being transgressor and placed itself at the vanguard of the battle against racial profiling.

"We firmly believe that this Interim Report represents a major step, indeed a watershed event, signaling significant change [that]

will ensure New Jersey is a national leader in addressing the issue of racial profiling."

It was an astonishing U-turn. Only weeks before, Whitman had unequivocally denied the State Police profiled. Now she was not only admitting they did, but explaining why it had happened and how to fix the problem. Verniero was embracing facts his office had been renouncing in court for years and championing theories he'd hotly contested. The State—so recently oblivious—suddenly had all the answers.

The report could have been written by Bill Buckman and the *Soto* team. (Earlier in the day, Verniero had officially dropped the *Soto* appeal.) It condemned *spotlighting,* bashed *ghost stops,* and deplored the Trooper of the Year award for going almost exclusively to Turnpike drug-busters. The report blamed profiling on the stereotyping of blacks as narcotics offenders and *"the martial rhetoric of the 'war on drugs'."* It even embraced the *Soto* team's contention that trooper discretion led to racial profiling, which the Attorney General's Office had scoffed at during the hearing.

The true determinant of racial profiling, the report proclaimed, was search data—the same data the State had said would be too burdensome to produce during *Soto.* Now, it turned out, the State Police record on searches was "alarming."

"They are numbers that none of us had seen before," Governor Whitman said.

Verniero didn't blink. When his turn came to speak, he insisted racial profiling was not *official* policy, but rather the work of "a small group of hard-core profilers."

The Interim Report artfully tiptoed around several landmines that threatened to blow up on Verniero, among them a State Police cover-up. Harsher earlier versions had been watered down to a final draft that was so tepid the question of a cover-up barely drew notice.

Verniero also navigated around another potential storm about what he knew and when he knew it.

"These issues," he explained, "began to *crystallize,* particularly in my mind, as a result of the April 1998 turnpike shooting."

"Crystallize" was a nimble sleight-of-mouth that became Verniero's catchword for why he acted so late on profiling. The shooting had been like a bolt of lightning that made the blind man see. The eyes of New

Jersey's chief law enforcement officer were opened and, lo and behold, racial profiling was suddenly *crystal* clear. That was hard for some to stomach. A reporter tried to pin down the Attorney General on how long he'd known about the evidence in the Interim Report.

"Some of the data was gathered as a result of the Turnpike shooting case and some was gathered even more recently than that," Verniero said. The statement would come back to haunt him.

The Interim Report was not warmly received. Skeptics scorned Verniero's assertion that profiling was the work of a small band of renegade troopers.

"The problem isn't just a few bad apples," Rev. Reginald Jackson said at a packed press conference. "It's hard for me to believe the Governor can be surprised at the numbers of minorities stopped, then say that it's just a few people."

For Bill Buckman the day marked the end of an odyssey. He had finally won. He had trapped Verniero and left him no wiggle room, forcing him to make a choice: *Soto* or the Supreme Court. There was no contest. Verniero had dumped the *Soto* case like yesterday's newspaper. But Buckman's elation was tempered.

"While they've been stonewalling and avoiding their responsibility, how many innocent people have been victimized?" he said. "How many African-American families have been stopped and humiliated on the side of the road and been searched and treated like criminals? From our statistics in *Soto,* I can give you a guesstimate. It's been thousands."

Chapter 94

DESPITE THE INTERIM REPORT, Peter Verniero's Supreme Court appointment remained on shaky ground and demand intensified for Whitman to remove his name from consideration. *The New York Times* concurred in an editorial the day after the report's release:

"[Whitman] should withdraw her nomination of Mr. Verniero to the New Jersey Supreme Court because of his tardiness in rooting out racial profiling."

Verniero defended himself in a letter to William Gormley, the State Senate Judiciary Committee chairman.

"Until one sits in the Attorney General's chair, it is difficult to appreciate the vastness of the department or the breadth of the obligations of the office," Verniero wrote, claiming that profiling simply got lost in the shuffle of his office's 34,000 legal matters. He was confronted with his 34,001st on April 23rd, 1999—the first anniversary of the Turnpike shooting. This one was a whopper not likely to be lost in the crush of business.

Johnnie Cochran and the Dream Team filed suit against the State of New Jersey.

The lawsuit accused the State of *"deliberate indifference,"* ignoring more than a decade of evidence the State Police was infected by a *"pervasive and systematic...culture of racism"* which inexorably led to *"a bloody disaster on the New Jersey Turnpike."*

The suit didn't specify a dollar amount the students shot on the Turnpike would seek, but—between the Interim Report and the indictments of Hogan and Kenna—it had the ingredients to be the mother of all civil actions.

Chapter 95

THE SENATE JUDICIARY COMMITTEE convened for Peter Verniero's Supreme Court confirmation in a grandiose hall with 30-foot high ceilings, faux stone block walls covered with idyllic landscapes and large stained-glass windows depicting native Garden State fauna from wild turkeys to dinosaurs.

The SJC sat at a big U-shaped table ringed by 15 black leather chairs against a backdrop of United States and New Jersey flags. At the open end of the horseshoe, Verniero sat at a witness table topped with green leather. Behind him 100 hard-backed oak chairs were filled to capacity. Verniero began by proclaiming himself a pioneer in the fight against racial profiling.

"Racial profiling did not start with the Whitman Administration, but we have begun the process of ending it. The Interim Report represents a major step never before taken."

Verniero's testimony lasted two testy days, during which he alternately rubbed his chin and glowered at senators who gruffly drummed him about why he'd taken so long to act.

"You assume no personal responsibility?" pressed Republican Robert J. Martin.

"In all honesty I do not, Senator," Verniero said.

"I'm astounded!" said Senator Raymond Zane, another Republican.

"When you go back in time," Verniero said, "and you look at what I knew and what the circumstances were and you judge my actions, I acted appropriately."

By raising the question of what he knew versus when he acted, Verniero had opened the door to his harshest critic—Democratic Senator John Lynch.

"It appears that nothing really happened to examine racial profiling until it became politically expedient," Lynch said. "Why is it that the survey that you just conducted wasn't done when the early warning occurred after the *Soto* hearings?"

"Since I wasn't in the Office at the time frame that your question suggests, I don't know the answer to that question, Senator."

"And so there was no statistical analysis ongoing under your watch until sometime after the shootings in April of 1998, correct?"

Lynch had asked the million dollar question. Verniero was already on record saying the proof on racial profiling hadn't emerged until *after* the Turnpike shooting. In reality, analysis had been in progress for two years *before* the shooting. But if the truth came out, the uproar would have echoed from Atlantic City to the George Washington Bridge. Verniero zigzagged.

"If there was an analysis going on at that point in time somewhere in the Department of Law and Public Safety," he said, "I was not aware of it in July of 1996, no."

In a nifty bit of pettifoggery, Verniero answered a question that hadn't been asked. Lynch asked about *April 1998*. Verniero answered about *July 1996*. And no one noticed.

Verniero needed 21 votes in the Senate to win confirmation. All 15 Democrats were solidly against him, and several of the 24 Republicans hinted they might vote no—most prominently Senator John Matheussen. Despite reservations, the Judiciary Committee chairman William Gormley supported Verniero, comparing him to another supposed "political hack" named Earl Warren, who became one of America's most venerated Chief Justices of the U.S. Supreme Court.

When the vote came, three Republican senators joined the Democrats to cast 18 votes against Verniero. But thanks to some 11th hour arm-twisting by Governor Christie Whitman, he got the minimum 21 votes he needed, including Senator Matheussen's. So ended the most rancorous confirmation fight in the New Jersey Supreme Court's history.

"Peter Verniero's promotion to the Supreme Court after his performance as Attorney General sickens me," said Democratic Senator John H. Adler.

A few days later, *The New York Times* reported that Whitman had begun *"doling out political favors to some Senate Republicans who had major roles in helping save the nomination."*

She appointed a Superior Court Judge in Passaic County at the request of one senator; a prosecutor in Cape May County for another; promised another senator he could name the next two judges in Ocean County; and signed a pair of multi-million dollar bills into law sponsored by Senator C. Louis Bassano, one of the swing votes. Said Bassano: "It's a two-way street."

Chapter 96

SOMETHING ELSE HAPPENED around the same time Verniero was confirmed to the New Jersey Supreme Court. This, though, received no public attention. Judge Robert E. Francis was abruptly removed as Chancery Judge of Gloucester County and replaced by a former law partner of Senator John Matheussen, whose last minute vote tipped the scales for Verniero.

Francis' landmark ruling in *Soto* had been the single most consequential court decision of the 1990s in New Jersey. No other judgment triggered the legal, political, and social reverberations to match it. The sagacity of Francis's decision elevated him to the forefront of New Jersey jurists. A survey of 2,600 attorneys by the *New Jersey Law Journal* in 1999 ranked him 23rd out of 348 Superior Court Judges in the state and 4th among New Jersey's 20 Chancery Judges.

Nonetheless, without explanation, he was suddenly demoted to Family Court. As judicial posts go, Family Court was certainly an important assignment where judges handled divorce and child custody cases. But it was a grueling job usually assigned to newer jurists. No judge had been involuntarily removed from Chancery Court in New Jersey in more than 10 years. The relegation order was signed by New Jersey Supreme Court Chief Justice Deborah Poritz, who had been Attorney General when Francis ruled against her department in *Soto*.

For Francis it was a slap in the face. Although he never spoke about it publicly, his friends knew he loved Chancery Court, handling the most complex and intellectually challenging cases from the worlds of business and government. They knew he was devastated. Many in Gloucester County—including Bill Buckman—believed his ouster was retribution for *Soto.*

"I've always been concerned and troubled," Buckman said upon Francis' retirement in 2003, "that the untold story about Judge Francis is that after being a highly renowned Chancery Judge for 15 years, when he had the guts to decide *Soto,* suddenly he found himself transferred back to the Family Division."

Christie Whitman's glittering political star also dimmed after her racial profiling admission. Despite attempts to spin it to make her Administration look like an engine of reform, there was a widespread sense she was actually in the caboose.

Things deteriorated further when a photograph of the smiling Governor frisking a young black man in Camden popped-up in newspapers. In State Police possession since 1996, its release smacked of retribution for Whitman's perceived betrayal of troopers.

On September 7, 1999, Whitman dropped out of the U.S. Senate race.

Chapter 97

THE DAY AFTER WHITMAN QUIT the U.S. Senate race, and 17 months after the Turnpike shooting, John Hogan and James Kenna were indicted for attempted murder and aggravated assault. Lawyers for the troopers quickly blamed politics.

"Every time Governor Whitman runs into political difficulty she seems to indict Troopers Hogan and Kenna," said Robert Galantucci.

The indictment flatly rejected the troopers' claims that they had fired in self-defense and accused them of *"extreme indifference to the value of human life"* and *"attempting to cause death to Danny Reyes."*

From the beginning, prosecutors had pegged Hogan as the bad guy. They were convinced he was a coldblooded racial profiler who shot Reyes in the back unnecessarily as the van rolled down the hill. Conversely, they saw Kenna as something of a victim. His lawyer, Jack Arseneault, persuaded state prosecutor Jim Gerrow that Kenna was suffering from Post Traumatic Stress Disorder after nearly being killed by a drug suspect a month before the shooting. The State Police shouldn't have allowed Kenna back on the road, Arseneault argued. Gerrow agreed and made the trooper a tempting offer. He could walk away with a wrist slap if he testified that Hogan had intentionally tried to kill Reyes. Despite facing a possible 20 years in prison, Kenna refused, insisting it hadn't happened that way. To testify differently, he said, would be a lie.

Chapter 98

LT. COL. ROBERT DUNLOP—all 6-feet-5-inches of him—strode to the podium at Caesar's Hotel & Casino in Atlantic City to address the several hundred people gathered for the annual State Police Retirement Banquet. The Interim Report had been issued five months before and Peter Verniero was now sitting on the New Jersey Supreme Court.

"This has been a year filled with controversy and allegations of racial profiling and discrimination within the ranks," Dunlop said. "Allegations that are easily made and recklessly thrown about; allegations that are extremely difficult to defend when only one side of the story is presented. We that have dedicated our lives to the State Police and to the citizens of this State know these claims are not true."

The audience broke into thunderous applause. 1999 had been the worst year in the Outfit's illustrious history. The Carl Williams firing, the indictments, the investigations, and finally the tar-and-feathering of the Interim Report administered by—in the minds of many State Police—a politically expedient Governor and Attorney General. And, finally, the State of New Jersey was about to enter into a consent decree with the U.S. Justice Department to let a team of independent monitors come in to oversee the State Police on racial profiling, the ultimate insult troopers had fought vehemently to stop. Morale was at rock bottom. A record 81 troopers were retiring. Through it all, though, State Police brass kept silent. But, on this night, Dunlop was not pulling punches.

"The New Jersey State Police was mandated to aggressively interdict drugs on our state highways," he declared. "As one of the premier law enforcement organizations in the country we waged what politicians dubbed the 'War on Drugs.' Now this *'fight'* is not the *'good fight'* anymore and the politicians have cut ranks and run. I find their silence deafening and their lack of action inexcusable and unconscionable."

Most of the crowd erupted again. But at a front table, Verniero's successor as Attorney General, John J. Farmer Jr., and several members of his braintrust—including Paul Zoubek—squirmed.

Dunlop was now acting-Superintendent and the most respected man in the organization. Several other top State Police officials had recently taken cushy, high-paying jobs from the Whitman Administration that smelled suspiciously like payback for their acquiescence. Dunlop had also received a tempting job offer—rumored to be New Jersey's Inspector General—but turned it down, not wanting troopers to think he'd sold them out.

"Never hang your head when asked what you did for a living," Dunlop told the retirees. "Tell the people you meet that you were a New Jersey State trooper. I assure you that our continued dedication to the citizens of this State in preserving law and order and rendering aid and comfort to the injured will speak louder tomorrow than the political rhetoric which sounds so deafening today."

The assemblage rose to its feet in prolonged acclaim while the new Attorney General and his people sat red-faced and stunned, virtually at Dunlop's feet.

Chapter 99

THE DREAM TEAM COULDN'T have imagined a more perfect scenario. New Jersey was playing high-stakes poker against itself—a game it could not win. The State had become a modern-day Orthrus, the two-headed monster of Greek mythology, with each of its heads serving different masters. One was guarding the Treasury, trying to stop Johnnie Cochran from raking in an unprecedented pot of money, while the other kept dealing him aces, like the Interim Report and the indictments of the Troopers Hogan and Kenna. The only question was how swollen the pot would get.

The first hand was played on a big glass-topped table in the Teaneck office of Decotiis & Cole, the high-powered law firm New Jersey hired to represent the state in the lawsuit. Michael Cole, a stonefaced lawyer with a reputation as a tough-as-nails negotiator, invited Cochran to lay his cards on the table.

"Thirty million dollars!" Cochran said, dapper as usual in his hand-tailored suit and silk shirt.

A moment of silence while everyone absorbed the number.

"New Jersey doesn't pay that kind of money," Cole said finally.

The State had never paid out more than $5 million, that to the victim of a railroad accident who had lost a leg. The lawyer announced New Jersey would go no higher. Despite the gulf between them, Cochran was gratified to hear $5 million. He knew the number would go up, just as Cole knew the $30 million tender would come down. But the parameters were set. Settlement negotiations would proceed from there. If the State refused to dicker, Cochran had one more ace up his sleeve. He was ready to go to trial.

If ever a case stood to reap an astronomical jury award, this was it. A $100 million judgment was not unfathomable. Cochran knew it and the State's lawyers did, too. But New Jersey wasn't going down without a fight. The stakes were too high.

"We're not going to pay you anything," Cole said at a subsequent negotiation session. "We haven't done anything wrong."

"Look, you've indicted these cops," said Linda Kenney, Keshon Moore's lawyer. "Your own prosecutor said these kids were profiled. How can you now say they were not?"

In the dog fight that ensued, the Dream Team filed motions for discovery and Cole resisted, arguing that the plaintiffs should not get any information from the criminal cases because it was the product of a secret grand jury investigation. One State lawyer even argued that certain information should not be released because it would "embarrass" New Jersey.

But Cole was in a no-win situation. Cochran had him over a barrel. Then Christine Todd Whitman announced she was abdicating the governorship. Newly-elected President George W. Bush had appointed her Administrator of the U.S. Environmental Protection Agency. Whitman wanted to clear the slate on racial profiling before she left office.

In late November 2000, the lawyers for both sides met again in Teaneck. Cole plied his opponents with lunch and cookies, but they'd all been through hardball negotiations before and there were a lot of poker faces around the table as they whittled away at a settlement. By the end of the day they were still far apart. The State had upped its ante to $7 million. The Dream Team's demand had dropped to $15 million.

Chapter 100

THE SHRILL DRONE OF BAGPIPES pierced a crisp autumn morn as 500 New Jersey troopers marched to the State House in Trenton to decry 18 months of scorn. In a show of solidarity for their indicted colleagues, John Hogan and James Kenna, the troopers wore red lapel pins bearing the initials "H & K." The letters actually stood for Heckler & Koch, the gunmaker that manufactured the pistols most troopers wore and which donated the pins.

The crowd greeted a succession of speakers with cheers, jeers, kudos and catcalls as they took to a microphone and promised to stand by the State Police. Attorney General John Farmer vowed to try to heal the wounds of the agency he now controlled. But he didn't sound too convincing.

"I've had some difficult moments during my brief tenure as Attorney General," Farmer said to a chorus of boos, "and, given the nature of the issues that we're facing, there are likely to be many more."

The most clamorous applause went to Clinton Pagano, the long-departed State Police boss. Pagano symbolized the Outfit's glory days, days that now seemed so distant.

"I fear as a citizen that the underlying purpose of all the negative rhetoric is aimed at eventually changing the organization that I served for close to 40 years," said Pagano, condemning the Interim Report's profiling claims. "We want a fair hearing of the facts."

Bill Buckman was thinking about the facts, too. He was now recognized as one of the country's leading legal experts on racial profiling, and he wasn't taking his foot off the accelerator. If anything, he had the pedal to the metal. The Interim Report had produced a sea change in New Jersey courtrooms. For a decade, judges—with the exception of Robert Francis—had robotically sided with the State Police. Now, though, the State's credibility was zilch.

Buckman intended to exploit that. He'd never bought Verniero's story that evidence of profiling didn't materialize until *after* the Turnpike shooting. He believed a lot of big secrets were still hidden in State file cabinets and started making motions to flush out the evidence. Despite dropping *Soto* and issuing the Interim Report, the Attorney General's Office was still fighting him tooth-and-nail on his other profile cases. But judges had begun siding with Buckman and, before long, he was getting a treasure trove of documents that pointed to one conclusion—the State had known racial profiling was *"real—not imagined"* well before Peter Verniero claimed.

A 1996 Internal Affairs memorandum—written two-and-a-half years prior to the State dropping *Soto*—reported the number of minority stops at the south end of the Turnpike *"was dramatically higher than the 'expert' testified to in the Gloucester County trial."* Why, Buckman wondered, was he learning about that now? He made sure the memo didn't remain secret any longer and included it with a batch of documents in a public court file. In January 2000, the *Newark Star-Ledger* reported on the memo in a story headlined *"State Police Suspected Profiling as Early as '96."* The article marked the beginning of what was to become the unraveling of New Jersey's racial profiling cover-up.

In July, Buckman found his most tantalizing nugget buried in a bundle of paperwork the State Police was forced to turn over to him—Sgt. Thomas Gilbert's 1997 memo *"At this point, we are in a very bad spot."* Again, Buckman made sure Gilbert's *smoking gun* saw the light of day.

Sunshine was what William Gormley was after too, but of a different sort. On October 12, 2000, the senator was stretched out by the swimming pool of the Hotel del Coronado taking a long-awaited hiatus from the rigors of New Jersey politics. He'd always dreamed of staying at the legendary California resort, a favorite haunt of the likes of Marilyn Monroe, Ronald Reagan, and the Duke and Duchess of Windsor. The Garden State was 3,000 miles away and the furthest thing from his mind. His wife, Ginny, was lying next to him in a chaise lounge reading *The New York Times*.

"Bill," she said, "I think you want to read this."

Gormley examined the headline: *"Records Show New Jersey Police Withheld Data on Race Profiling."* What followed was a lengthy summary of the new evidence Bill Buckman had been dredging up and the press had been eagerly publicizing.

"As early as 1996, [State Police] internal audits had turned up evidence of widespread profiling along the New Jersey Turnpike, newly released police records show. Despite that evidence, senior commanders rejected aggressive steps to end the problem and instead pursued a strategy of withholding information."

The news was enough to wreck Gormley's vacation. It was starting to appear Verniero knew much more about racial profiling much earlier than he'd told Gormley's Senate Judiciary Committee during his Supreme Court confirmation. And his assertion that evidence of profiling didn't surface until after the Turnpike shooting sounded more like fantasy than fact.

No one could accuse Gormley of ramrodding Christie Whitman's hot potato through the Senate. Before allowing Verniero's confirmation he made sure profiling had been thoroughly vetted. The *process*—a word Gormley was fond of—was very deliberate. Everyone—particularly Verniero's arch-nemesis Senator John Lynch—cross-examined the Attorney General at length. They'd asked the right questions, but now it seemed Verniero *may* have given the wrong answers. Gormley remembered comparing Verniero to the great U.S. Supreme Court Chief Justice Earl Warren. He thought: *No, no, no, this is not what Earl would have done.*

Gormley's telephone started to ring. Reporters from the East Coast wanted to know what he was going to do. It didn't take him long to decide. He had to protect the integrity of the *process*. He called Attorney General John Farmer in New Jersey.

"John, it looks like we're going to have to have additional hearings," he said. "This time we're going to get *all* the information."

Skeptics figured the hearing would be another three ring circus. Call some witnesses, let John Lynch rant, put out a report, everybody's happy, but nothing happens.

Then Gormley announced that his ringmaster would be none other than Michael Chertoff.

Chertoff was a tall beanpole of a man with deep-set eyes, gray beard, balding pate and the gaunt body of a long distance runner. He was also New Jersey's pre-eminent trial lawyer. The son of a politically prominent rabbi, he graduated magna cum laude from Harvard Law School, then went on to become a federal prosecutor in Manhattan under then-U.S. Attorney Rudolph W. Giuliani. Chertoff spearheaded the celebrated "Commission" case, the most important Mafia prosecution in American history, which succeeded in locking away the heads of New York's Genovese, Colombo, and Lucchese crime families.

Chertoff developed a reputation as a dazzling trial lawyer, using a Gatling-gun interrogation style to eviscerate witnesses. *"He can make smart people look stupid,"* observed *The Weekly Standard.*

When Chertoff was appointed New Jersey's U.S. Attorney in 1990, Anthony "Fat Tony" Salerno, one of the mobsters he put away in the Commission case, said: "Give him a little message from Fat Tony. You tell that sonofabitch he owes me a thank-you note." As U.S. Attorney, Chertoff sent dozens of corrupt New Jersey politicians and white collar criminals to prison. Hiring him had given Gormley's Senate Judicial Committee investigation instant credibility. But Democrats remained suspicious.

Chertoff had also been chief counsel to the Republican-controlled Congressional Whitewater investigation, which spent years and tens of millions of dollars trying to nail Bill and Hillary Clinton, and ended up proving nothing. Whitewater was one of the few blemishes on Chertoff's record and stamped him as a partisan. Democrats couldn't help but wonder if the fix was in.

Chapter 101

A HUSH DESCENDED OVER the packed Trenton courtroom as Judge Andrew Smithson stepped to the bench on October 31, 2000. A crush of family and friends of John Hogan and James Kenna—including two dozen off-duty State Policemen wearing red "H & K" pins—were on hand to hear Smithson rule on a defense motion to dismiss attempted murder and aggravated assault charges against the accused. The judge didn't waste time.

"Members of society engaged in law enforcement deserve no less protection from the criminal justice system than that which is afforded to other citizens," he said. "In this case, that protection requires the most severe sanction—a dismissal of the indictment."

Gasps punctuated the silence as Judge Smithson scathingly enumerated why he was throwing out a case that took 16 months and $1 million to investigate. Without mentioning him by name, the judge lambasted Peter Verniero for making Hogan and Kenna "poster boys for racial profiling" by having them indicted on falsification charges while a grand jury was still investigating the shooting case. The action was "unthinkable," he said, and tainted the shooting grand jury.

"There was an intense, if not a frenzy, of public interest in racial profiling," Smithson said. "There existed powerful and intimidating forces driving the decision-making of the Office of the Attorney General. The motivation to allow the return of the indictments at that time was considerably more a matter of political expediency than of concern for the substantive rights of defendants Hogan and Kenna."

The courtroom exploded in applause. Kenna's wife wept as her husband hugged his lawyer, Jack Arseneault. Hogan, his flushed face streaked with tears, embraced his mother, father, and sisters. "I haven't smiled in three years," he said.

Hogan's attorney, Robert Galantucci, took the opportunity to rip Governor Christie Whitman one more time. "Her administration is coming to a close and, frankly, good riddance. She's left the State of New Jersey with a black eye with her conduct during the course of this case."

But while the troopers were ecstatic, New Jersey's minority community was outraged.

"It is interesting that the judge handed down this decision on October 31st," said Reverend Reginald Jackson. "It just happens to be Halloween. It does send an interesting message about the masquerade which has been taking place around the issue of racial profiling in this State."

Chapter 102

JUDGE SMITHSON'S HARSH WORDS lent credence to a long-harbored suspicion that Peter Verniero had played politics on racial profiling. The ruling incited a mounting fervor to get to the bottom of what Verniero knew about profiling and when he knew it.

Thanks in large measure to Bill Buckman, pressure was building on Attorney General John Farmer, Verniero's successor. Buckman kept turning up the heat by pushing for more State Police documents. And every time he hit pay dirt—which was frequently—the information was soon on TV and in newspapers. The Dream Team was also pressing for reams of data for its lawsuit. And now Michael Chertoff was demanding unfettered access to all evidence. Farmer finally yielded. After perusing State Police and Attorney General's Office internal files, Farmer seemed genuinely appalled.

"This may have been effective in law enforcement terms, but as social policy it was a disaster," he said. To restore public confidence and "pay a debt to the past," Farmer took the astonishing step of publicly releasing more than 100,000 documents on racial profiling in State files. The transparency was unparalleled. On the Monday after Thanksgiving 2000, dozens of lawyers and reporters huddled in a conference room at the Hughes Justice Complex and began poring over 185 three-ring binders containing the records.

"How many times in one's career," Bill Buckman said, "do you get to look inside government files to see that there was a vast cover-up of a vast unconstitutional scheme?"

The papers ignited a firestorm, as evidenced by the headlines:

"Memos Cast New Doubts on Verniero"
"Papers Show Delayed Reaction on Profiling"
"Peter Verniero's Curious 1999 Testimony"
"Then-AG Didn't Tell Senators of '97 Profiling Memos"
"Memos Confirm Profiling Awareness"

"The ugly secret of racial profiling in New Jersey is no secret anymore," stated an editorial in *The Record*. "Worse, it's even uglier than anyone could believe. How sad. How sick."

"Peter Verniero has a lot of explaining to do," Senator John Lynch said.

Lynch was about to retire from the New Jersey Senate. His heart wasn't in the job anymore. After nearly two decades in office, he'd become cynical, even bitter, about the political arena. As his last term was coming to an end, he'd all but vacated his post. Then came racial profiling redux and Lynch was alive again. People close to him saw it in his eyes. He was invested in his job in a way he hadn't been for a long time.

Lynch was offended that a political animal like Peter Verniero was now a Supreme Court Justice. He believed Verniero lied about racial profiling and orchestrated a massive obstruction of justice to cover up an egregious civil rights violation. This would be Lynch's swan song and he was reinvigorated by one last chance to strike a blow against his political enemies—Verniero and, by extension, Christine Todd Whitman.

The document dump had Lynch and fellow Democrats salivating to get Verniero back on the witness stand. As for Verniero, he was bleeding from the torrent of publicity. A few days later, he took an extraordinary step for a Supreme Court Justice by issuing a written declaration to the press.

"I testified truthfully before the Senate Judiciary Committee," his statement said. *"Reasonable minds may differ regarding the timeliness of my actions. We now have the benefit of a decade-long record, assembled in a single repository, on which to base a review of these issues. That record was not before me in 1996 and 1997."*

There was still plenty of skepticism about Gormley's investigation. Politically it made no sense. 2001 was an election year and an investigation could kill GOP chances to retain the Governor's Mansion and capture the U.S. Senate seat now up for grabs. But Gormley insisted he was simply trying to do the right thing and protect the *process.*

"No one is going to lie to the Committee," he said. "No one is above the law."

Gormley did open eyes by hiring Chertoff, who ran the New Jersey office of Latham & Watkins, one of the largest law firms in America with 1,500 attorneys. When the investigation began, Chertoff was involved in a trial and assigned Scott Weber from his firm to get things rolling. Weber was a bright young lawyer in his early 30s and a graduate of Boston College Law School.

When Chertoff and Weber met with Gormley, the senator gave them simple marching orders. He did not want a whitewash, he said. No stone was to be left unturned to determine who knew what about racial profiling. The vital question was whether Verniero committed perjury before the SJC in 1999, but Gormley didn't want a witch hunt. If the probe became a vendetta against Verniero, it would fail. The investigation had to be bigger than that.

While Gormley had Chertoff, Lynch had Democratic counsel Jo Astrid Glading. A big, blunt, tough-talking woman, Glading was a former Associated Press reporter who got into politics as press secretary to then-Governor Jim Florio. She was Florio's grenade-thrower during the 1993 gubernatorial race, lobbing verbal incendiary bombs at Christie Whitman. When Florio lost, Glading went off to law school and returned as staff attorney for New Jersey's Senate Democrats. Glading and Lynch didn't quite trust Chertoff or Gormley and decided to perform their own parallel investigation.

Chertoff and Weber put together a team of four young lawyers from Latham & Watkins and set up two tightly secured offices in the State House Annex in Trenton. Boxes containing the 100,000 newly released documents were stored in an adjacent room. Gormley had never been involved in anything so big and worried it was too big.

"Don't worry, Bill," Chertoff assured him. "It will all come down to three or four documents. It always does. People lie, documents don't."

Chertoff approached investigations like a storyteller. And the essence of the story was always those golden nuggets that drive the narrative and put everything in perspective. In this case, the nuggets would be made of paper. That meant slogging through all 100,000 documents, panning for gold or, as Scott Weber called them, "hot docs."

It was a grinding process. Three of the lawyers lived in New York City and took the train 70 miles to Trenton every day. Weber drove from his home in North Jersey, getting into his Audi every morning at 7 a.m. and not returning home to his wife and two children until late at night. Once he got caught in a blinding snowstorm, made a wrong turn, and ended up in Delaware.

While the Latham lawyers were doing their review, Jo Glading was doing her copycat analysis. Glading understood this was a singular moment in time. Nothing this big had ever been undertaken by New Jersey lawmakers and she was not going to let Gormley and Chertoff completely control the investigation. She and her assistant, a young attorney named Douglas Wheeler, scrutinized all 100,000 documents. By the time they were finished they knew all the important facts by heart and had composed a detailed timeline connecting the dots on racial profiling.

The dual document reviews lasted from late November into January 2001. By the time they were finished, the investigators had a vivid picture of what had happened. But, as the saying went, the rubber wouldn't meet the road until they could interrogate real people.

Sworn depositions were conducted in the State House Annex. Weber was the lead examiner, with Chertoff coming in to question a few key witnesses. Gormley and Lynch attended about two-thirds of the depositions, which was extraordinary. Senators never got that involved.

Sgt. Thomas Gilbert was the first and most important witness. Gilbert was an accidental hero. He'd been given an odious mission and—being a good soldier—performed it admirably. But doing so had put him in an awkward spot. To many inside the State Police, Gilbert had become persona non grata. When he was sworn in for deposition, he was visibly nervous.

The key issue was his February 1997 *smoking gun* memorandum. *"The numbers are not good. We are in a very bad spot."* The pivotal question was whether that message had reached the Attorney General.

Gilbert was a forthright witness and told the whole story, warts and all. By the end of questioning it was emphatically clear he had informed the Attorney General's Office of the bad news on profiling more than two years before it showed up in the 1999 Interim Report. That was in direct conflict with Verniero's sworn testimony. The rubber had met the road. That evening, on his long drive home, an excited Scott Weber called Chertoff.

"Mike," he said breathlessly, "you'll never guess what happened today..."

Jo Glading wasn't so much excited as she was scared. Glading had no litigation experience and the night before her first deposition she was petrified.

"Doug," she said to her assistant, Wheeler, "I don't know if I can do this."

Although younger, Wheeler had spent three years in private practice before becoming a government lawyer. He was also anxious, going into depositions with attorneys like Chertoff, Lynch, and Gormley looking on, but at least he had some experience. He tried to calm her.

"Jo, trust me. I know you can do it. You know this stuff cold." Her first deposition witness was the State Police's David Blaker, now a captain, who was with Sgt. Gilbert and then-Superintendent Carl Williams when they discussed the disturbing State Police search numbers with Verniero in May 1997.

"Captain Blaker," Glading asked, "is there any reason for you to believe anyone in that room was not aware of the similarity between the Maryland and New Jersey numbers?"

"No. No, ma'am."

Glading got Blaker to acknowledge it was his scribbling on an agenda recording Verniero's reaction: *"AG advised he would not consent to signing a consent decree. 'They'd have to tie me to a train and drag me along the track before I sign a decree.'"*

"It was awesome," Glading proclaimed afterwards to Wheeler. "I got him! I asked all the tough questions. I got him!"

Wheeler could see Glading's confidence grow. She started asking more questions at depositions and even Chertoff began picking up on her lines of inquiry. By the fifth or sixth deposition the Democrats and Republicans were working together like a well-oiled machine and suspicion between the two sides had evaporated.

After 160 hours of depositions and 4,000 pages of testimony, Chertoff and his band of lawyers had a keen insight into the racial profiling situation. One thing was evident. Under the watch of Governor Christine Todd Whitman, state officials were repeatedly put on notice about profiling.

The New York Times' Matthew Purdy summed it up: *"As cover-ups go, this one was about as effective as a washrag on a sumo wrestler. The ugly stuff was sticking out everywhere."*

Yet, Whitman's administration did nothing but ignore and deny the problem until the storm over racial profiling reached hurricane force. By the time she left New Jersey for Washington, Whitman was no longer the luminary she'd once been.

"She has failed us," Rev. Reginald Jackson said. "We have had not one achievement, no, not one."

Chapter 103

SETTLING A LAWSUIT is like buying a car. One side makes an overture and the other side takes the offer back to its manager—or, in this case, client—for approval. The negotiation goes back and forth like that, offer and counteroffer, until the sides meet at a mutual resolution.

By late 2000, the State and the Turnpike shooting victims were about $8 million apart. New Jersey was dangling a $7 million offer —more money than it had ever coughed-up to settle a lawsuit. The Dream Team was demanding $15 million. Over the next two months the sides gradually inched closer, the State sweetening their tender from seven, to nine, to 10, 11, and finally $12 million.

Johnnie Cochran was an old hand at negotiating. Until the other side came back and said, "We're not giving you any more money," he knew there was more money.

The Dream Team lawyers kept asking themselves: "Did you hear them say 'no more money'?" The answer was no. They advised the students to reject the offers.

"Trust me, Keshon," defense attorney Linda Kenney told her client, Keshon Moore, the student driving the van the night of the Turnpike shooting. "When I get nervous and say '*take it,*' take it. But we think there's more there."

Late-stage negotiations can get dicey. At crunch time, with an agreement looming, "settlement syndrome" often sets in. One side gets jittery and gives in, leaving money on the table. The Dream Team decided its bottom line was $13 million. By late January, the State had

346

upped the ante to $12.95 million. Cochran made several telephone calls trying to pry loose the last $50,000, but the State wouldn't budge. By then, though, it wasn't about the money. For New Jersey's lawyers it was a matter of public perception. $12,950,000 wouldn't look as bad in the headlines as $13 million.

"This is it," the lawyers finally told the students. "This is the number. You can reject it, but we don't advise it. We think we've squeezed the last dollar we can get out of them."

They could roll the dice and take the case to a jury, which *might* award them $100 million. But they could also walk away empty handed. It would be like throwing down $13 million on an Atlantic City roulette table. On February 1, 2001, the Dream Team announced the settlement.

The lawsuit was negotiated as a lump sum, but the students decided on a split based on the extent of their injuries. Danny Reyes, who suffered the most serious wounds, got 45%, or $5,850,000; Leroy Jarmaine Grant received $4,400,000; Rayshawn Brown $1,785,000; and Keshon Moore, who wasn't shot, took $912,000. But the students would end up collecting far more than that. Most of the money was invested in annuities that would increase the value of the settlement by many millions of dollars over the next 20 years. Johnnie Cochran and the other lawyers divided about $2 million in legal fees.

Despite the huge sum of money, Danny Reyes called the settlement "only halfway down the road to justice." Complete justice, he said, wouldn't come until Troopers Hogan and Kenna were tried on criminal charges.

Chapter 104

THE SENATE JUDICIARY COMMITTEE hearing was unlike anything that had ever happened in New Jersey, or perhaps any other state—a full-blown legislative inquiry that conjured memories of the Watergate hearings three decades before.

The hearing was held in the stately Committee room, with its stained-glass windows and large horseshoe-shaped table, where Peter Verniero had testified two years earlier. Chairman William Gormley sat at the center with Michael Chertoff to his right, Scott Weber next to him, then Senator John Lynch, the senior Democrat, and Jo Astrid Glading. Nine other senators filled out the U.

Chertoff—the grand inquisitor—would lead the examinations. The previous week new President George W. Bush had nominated him to pilot the U.S. Justice Department's Criminal Division, making him the second highest ranking law enforcement official in America.

But on March 19, 2001, his focus was on his first witness, Sgt. Thomas Gilbert. As Gilbert was sworn and took his seat, the 100 oak chairs behind him were packed with lawyers, politicians, civil rights activists and a large contingent of troopers eager to see history made. One trooper in the audience remarked that Gilbert looked like he was "shitting razorblades." Not surprising for someone about to be interrogated by a lawyer renowned for his take-no-prisoners style of cross-examination. Chertoff, however, was deferential to Gilbert and gently led him through the inquiry. In the crisp manner of a military officer, the sergeant explained how for three years he had compiled statistics on racial profiling. Nine television sets were scattered around the room and the lawyer displayed Gilbert's 1997 memorandum on the large-screens: *"The numbers are not good...we are in a very bad spot."*

"It obviously created a very troublesome perception," Gilbert said.

"Is it fair to say," Chertoff asked, "that the bottom line in this memo is—you could almost characterize it as explosive?"

"Yes, sir, it is."

The fundamental question was whether Attorney General Verniero knew about the data Gilbert was digging up. The essence of the *smoking gun* memo was that almost 9-of-10 Turnpike searches were of minorities. The trooper testified he personally transmitted that information to Verniero's liaison on racial profiling, George Rover. Gilbert also recounted the face-to-face meeting with Verniero and State Police Superintendent Carl Williams in May 1997 when he explained New Jersey's problems on search data. That was a year before the Turnpike shooting, when Verniero claimed the racial profiling problem began to *"crystallize"* in his mind, and two years before he admitted it was happening.

"Did anybody express surprise about that?" Chertoff asked.

"Not that I recall."

"Was there a point in time that anybody asked Colonel Williams, point blank, is there racial profiling going on?"

"Not that I recall," Gilbert said.

"Memorable meeting?" Chertoff asked.

"Yes, sir."

"Do you think it had crystallized by then?" Senator Raymond Zane asked. Gilbert didn't answer. He didn't have to.

Chertoff's blueprint was to start at the bottom and methodically climb to the top of New Jersey's law enforcement food chain. Gilbert was his foundation. Several other troopers testified they also collected reams of damning evidence on profiling, which was shared with the Attorney General's Office.

The hearing format offered Chertoff significant advantages over court trials. For one thing, there was no opposing counsel to object. And he could call multiple witnesses simultaneously.

On the second day Chertoff paired George Rover and John Fahy, who had been, over the years, the Attorney General's chief stewards on racial profiling.

During the State's crushing setback in *Soto,* Fahy's snide manner had earned him the deep enmity of *Soto* defense lawyer Bill Buckman and his colleagues. It didn't take Fahy long to make a similar impression on SJC members. Fahy seemed to be in disdain of the Committee, as if annoyed to be there. He responded to questions with long preambles, rambling answers, and protracted summations. Exasperated Committee members whispered that they now understood why the *Soto* hearing lasted 72 days.

"You've got to focus on yes or no," Gormley scolded Fahy. "We don't need the history of the Western world for every question."

When Chertoff asked questions, Fahy had an annoying habit of turning away from the Committee and addressing his answers to a row of TV cameras on the right side of the room. Irritated Senators and staff began looking at each other, wondering how long it would take Chertoff to react. They didn't wonder long.

"I have to ask, Mr. Fahy," Chertoff said in his serrated voice. "Is there some reason that in answering my questions you feel the need to look over to the press rather than looking at the Committee?"

Fahy swiveled right again toward the cameras. "No," he said, and the audience burst out laughing.

Chertoff drummed away at Fahy until a picture emerged of a man who had turned a blind eye on profiling. Fahy admitted being informed by Sgt. Gilbert that State Police audits were turning up statistics worse than the defense had presented in *Soto.* Chertoff asked Fahy if he would typically ask for a written report on such significant evidence.

"Always, sir. I'm not afraid of statistics or information. I'm a trial lawyer."

"So, did you ask Sergeant Gilbert, let me see some paper?"

"No," said Fahy.

With the Committee's ire aimed at Fahy, the hot spotlight was off George Rover. He acknowledged Gilbert had told him about New Jersey's problematic consent search numbers and that they were cause for serious concern.

"Did you report it to Mr. [Alexander] Waugh [Verniero's right-hand man]?"

"Yes, I did," Rover said.

"Did Mr. Waugh ask you to get any document?"

"No, sir, he did not."

"Just so we have the table set," Chertoff said, "you have the *Soto* case up in the Appellate Division, right? You have the Civil Rights Division in Washington knocking on your door, correct? So it's fair to say this is a front-burner issue?"

"Yes."

"Was there ever a discussion of finding out if we have a real problem?"

"That was not discussed."

The real problem for Verniero seemed to be not profiling but the Justice Department probe. Rover said he was ordered to withhold numerous damaging documents from the DOJ.

Chertoff flashed a succession of papers on the TV screens. One was an audit showing the preponderance of 1996 trooper stops and searches in South Jersey were of blacks. Rover said he didn't send it to the DOJ.

"Was it your opinion that it seemed that these documents were relevant?" Chertoff asked.

"Yes."

"So when you talked about this with Mr. Waugh, what did he tell you to do?"

"Don't produce it, but if they ask for it, then let me know."

"Do you believe that the directive was lawful?" Senator Raymond Zane asked.

"There was no legal obligation to provide anything."

"Do you think that it was moral?"

"I just don't understand moral," Rover said.

"You don't understand moral? Right from wrong?" Zane said. "Did it occur to you this might be obstruction of justice?"

"No, sir. I was following instructions from my superior and—."

"A lot of Germans in the Second World War were following instructions," Zane said.

Rover testified most of the information the Feds wanted was sitting in boxes in his office which he dispensed to Washington in small dollops over many months.

"I never saw it as pure delay, but I did see it as not initiating," he said.

"Do you think if we really wanted to solve the problem of profiling," another senator asked, "that we would have gone by the pace of the Department of Justice or we would have set our own pace?"

"Do I have to answer that?" Rover said.

"I think you did," the senator said.

Rover admitted telling the Justice Department he was looking for several years' worth of audits on stops and searches, when he actually had them in his office.

"It would be fair to describe the answer that you were told to give as a little bit misleading?" Chertoff asked.

"I don't want to use the word 'misleading,'" Rover said.

"I'll withdraw the question," Chertoff said. "You people can form your own impression."

Chapter 105

THE IMAGE OF THE New Jersey State Police underwent an intriguing transformation during the first days of the Senate Judiciary Committee hearings. Suddenly, troopers weren't the central villains on racial profiling anymore. The new bad boy was Peter Verniero.

Carl Williams felt like he'd been sacrificed, thrown into the volcano to save Verniero's Supreme Court nomination and was more than willing to stoke the flames lashing his ex-boss. The former Superintendent testified that Verniero was fully aware of the profiling evidence, but did nothing about it, reinforcing the perception of the ex-Attorney General-turned-Supreme Court Justice as malefactor. But Williams' hands were dirty, too, and Michael Chertoff refused to let him off the hook.

"The numbers certainly raise a big red flag, right?" Chertoff said.

"It showed that there's a flag out there, yes, sir," said Williams.

"Did you have someone investigate why the numbers were continuing to be high with respect to minorities being searched?"

"Not at that time, no, sir."

Williams was polite and seemed to be a nice enough man, but as he lumbered through his testimony it was evident he was uncomfortable with the spoken word, leading many to wonder how he'd ever gotten to be Superintendent of the State Police. Chertoff pressed him on what he'd done about profiling during his five years at the helm.

"Well I think it was an ongoing process," Williams said.

"Well, was there an endpoint to the process? Did you set a deadline?"

"No, I didn't have a chance to set that deadline."

"Why not?"

"I was still in the...in the fact-finding mode."

"Well, how many years did you envision you were going to go be in fact-finding mode?"

"We wanted to find out where the problem was," said Williams.

"And did anybody come up with an answer?"

"Not to my recollection."

"Did you push anybody for it?"

"Other than to continue what we were doing, no, sir."

"Nobody really lit a fire under you to come to grips with this until 1998, is that fair to say?"

"That's correct."

Chapter 106

NAYSAYERS WHO ANTICIPATED a whitewash had been taken by surprise. The inquest was the real deal. And it had been devastating for Peter Verniero.

"I think he's in a lot of trouble," Rutgers University law professor Frank Askin told *The Newark Star-Ledger*. "Unless he comes up with a credible explanation, he's going to end up leaving the bench—either voluntarily or involuntarily."

More than a century had passed since a sitting judge had been impeached in New Jersey. But there was a growing conviction Verniero had lied under oath about racial profiling. In addition, Michael Chertoff—about to become the number two man at the U.S. Department of Justice—had been hammering away at Verniero's stonewalling of the DOJ. The judge's reputation was hemorrhaging.

Four days before he was scheduled to testify, Verniero held a press conference, an extraordinary act for a Supreme Court Justice. Nibbling on a bagel, he sat with a small group of reporters inside the historic old Union Hotel in Flemington and sounded conciliatory.

"I'm human. I am susceptible to all the frailties of humanity," he said. "Looking back in hindsight, I wish that I had asked more searching questions of the State Police. I didn't. I didn't for good and valid reasons. I was their lawyer. I trusted them. I believed them."

Anticipation over the showdown between Chertoff and Verniero was like a championship prizefight—The Prosecutor vs. The Justice. Chertoff—steely and angular—was the hard-hitting knockout artist.

Verniero—doughy and officious—a lightweight by comparison. The buzz was whether The Justice could survive The Prosecutor's haymakers.

On the morning of Wednesday March 28, 2001, a cordon of television satellite trucks lined up outside the State House. Inside, cameras were trained on the door of the SJC meeting room. An adjoining room was crawling with reporters equipped with laptops and TV monitors.

The gallery was packed. Bill Buckman and Jeff Wintner, his colleague on *Soto,* were there, hoping to hear Verniero explain why critical evidence was withheld from them.

Emblez Longoria was one of many troopers on hand. Several young men from Newark attended, calling themselves *Blacks for Social Justice.* As the clock struck 9 a.m., Verniero made his entrance like a boxer, high-fiving people on his way down the aisle. Reverend Reginald Jackson was at the front of the room and when Verniero reached him they shook hands.

"The Committee will call Justice Peter Verniero," Senator William Gormley announced.

As the oath was administered committee members scrutinized Verniero. They all knew him and many did not like him. As Christie Whitman's Chief of Staff he'd treated legislators with disdain and his stilted personality had never endeared him to the State House crowd. He'd been confirmed by just one vote, thanks in large part to political favors. Beyond that, there was a general belief Verniero didn't have the gravitas to be a Supreme Court Justice. Gormley had voted to confirm him and gotten burned. This would be his self-administered tetanus shot for that mistake.

Verniero wore a navy blue suit, red tie, and his trademark crisp, white shirt. He began by reading an opening statement.

"I will get right to the point," he said, his voice tight. "I testified truthfully in all prior appearances before this Committee. I directed no person to conceal documents requested by the United States Department of Justice. I was assured by the State Police that profiling was not a problem. I began to question my assumptions after the April 1998 Turnpike shooting incident. I used the term *crystallize.* I take full responsibility for my actions as Attorney General. I wish that I had done more but would like to think that we made significant accomplishments."

It quickly became evident that witness Verniero would employ a master strategy for his appearance on the witness stand. Call it absentmindedness, memory lapse, amnesia, but as soon as Chertoff began asking questions, Verniero began not recalling.

When were you asked to become Attorney General?

"I don't have an exact recollection."

Did your predecessor, Deborah Poritz, advise you to investigate racial profiling?

"I don't have a specific recollection."

Tell us about the 1996 Christmas Eve meeting.

"I can't recall that meeting."

What about the April 22, 1997 memo from George Rover on consent searches?

"I don't recall specifically reviewing this document."

In the gallery, Trooper Longoria began counting every "I don't remember" and "I don't recall." But Verniero's faulty memory didn't deter Chertoff. He'd told Gormley the case would come down to a few key documents. Those "hot docs" had been identified and Chertoff began using them to confront the Justice. The first was the draft of a 1997 letter written to the DOJ by John Fahy in Verniero's name.

"Let's go to Page 8," said Chertoff, projecting the letter on the big screen TVs. It was a frank document, apparently too frank for Verniero, who had deleted all acknowledgments of racial profiling being a problem. "*'The State Police report to me that the number of stops involving black motorists on the southern portion of the Turnpike...remains near the level reported in the Soto case.'* You struck it out."

"I did," said Verniero. "I don't recall exactly why I did it. My best recollection is it was unverified information. *Soto* was based on junk science."

"This didn't raise a red flag to you?"

"It was not a red flag," Verniero said.

"Would you tell us, Justice Verniero, was there a single thing you did after getting this letter to ask questions about the information, one single thing?"

"I do not recall."

"And you understood, when you deleted this, this would mean the Department of Justice would be unaware that the State Police were accumulating information, right?"

"Presumably, yes."

The letter demonstrated Verniero was aware of the State Police audits in 1997, yet he'd told the SJC that damning evidence on profiling hadn't surfaced until after the 1998 Turnpike shooting. Chertoff called that testimony misleading.

"Well," Verniero said, "I disagree with your characterization."

"Now, let me show you a letter dated 4/22/97," Chertoff said, displaying a memorandum written by George Rover after Sgt. Tom Gilbert told him about the devastating search data. Rover had sent the memo to First Assistant Alexander Waugh, who forwarded it to the Attorney General. Verniero said he didn't recall ever seeing the document.

"Did you become aware that the Department of Justice was looking for consent to search data?"

"I don't recall, no," Verniero said for the umpteenth time.

"Perhaps you can help us," Chertoff said. "We've been through a series of documents. They're all in front of you. And yet, this document, which is an options paper discussing the status of what the DOJ is looking at—you have no recollection of reading?"

"I don't, Mr. Chertoff."

"Did you have an interest in knowing whether there was racial profiling going on?"

"Of course I had an interest, and whenever I asked the Superintendent whether racial profiling was an issue, I was told in very adamant terms that it was not an issue."

Chertoff projected another "hot doc" on the TV screens, this one a report revealing that two-thirds of searches by Moorestown Station troopers in 1996 were of minorities. Alexander Waugh had testified that he hand-delivered the document to Verniero and asked if he wanted it turned over to Washington.

"Do you remember seeing this?" Chertoff asked.

"I don't," Verniero said.

"Mr. Waugh testified speaking to you twice about whether you had made a decision, and your having said, 'I haven't focused on it yet, I'll get back to you.' Is it your testimony that didn't happen?"

"I just don't recall it happening."

Verniero didn't remember much about face-to-face meetings either. He drew a blank on the 1996 Christmas Eve meeting with Carl

Williams and Sgt. Gilbert. And he only vaguely recalled the May 1997 meeting with Gilbert, Williams, and Capt. David Blaker.

"Did the State Police make reference in any way, shape, or form in the meeting to the fact that they had some numbers relating to consent to searches in New Jersey?"

"I don't recall."

"So you're just a passive observer at this meeting?"

"Did I say I was a passive observer, sir? No."

"Are you taking the position before the Committee that in April and May of 1997, you had no idea there was any issue with consent to search in the State of New Jersey?"

"That's not my testimony. My position is that no one in this meeting said in any urgent way, 'We've got a problem.' They indicated that racial profiling was not a problem."

"I have to stop you," Chertoff said, his deep-set eyes boring in on Verniero, "because experience shows if the questioner doesn't insist that his question gets answered, then shame on him. This is my question —Do you now remember, in April and May 1997, that there was discussion that you had about consent to search numbers in New Jersey as compared to consent to search numbers in Maryland?"

"I have a vague recollection of someone making a general comparison. I have no recollection of numbers," Verniero said.

At about one o'clock, Gormley called a recess. By then Emblez Longoria had counted 136 variations of "I don't recall." Verniero ducked into a bathroom just as Chertoff was exiting. Verniero asked him when he should return from lunch.

"Oh, we're not breaking for lunch," Chertoff said. "We're going to keep going. You better get a candy bar or something and be back in 10 minutes."

Verniero had a shocked look on his face. He walked outside the State House Annex where he was greeted by a dozen or so black men carrying cardboard signs inscribed with *"Impeach Verniero"* and *"Racial Profiling Must Stop."* The Supreme Court Justice retreated down the sidewalk with the group chanting behind him: "I don't recall. I don't recall."

The Committee sat back and let Chertoff go after Verniero. Gormley looked over at the lawyer's note pad and saw he had only three sentences written down and was amazed at Chertoff's ability to weave through such a complex factual maze, rapid-firing questions like a boxer throwing jabs, always several steps ahead of his opponent.

Perry Mason moments—when a witness breaks down and confesses to some heinous crime—were rare events. Chertoff's method wasn't to destroy a witness so much as to expose him with relentless interrogation, each question stripping the façade until the deceit was plain to everyone. As the hearing progressed, Chertoff peeled away the layers of Verniero's story like the skin of an onion.

On his *Brady* obligation to turn over exculpatory evidence to the *Soto* defense: "I don't know if I thought about it at the time."

On whether he ordered the indictment of Troopers Hogan and Kenna for political purposes: "Politics did not infect any of my decisions."

But the crux of the matter was whether Verniero lied to the Senate Judiciary Committee at his 1999 confirmation hearing. His testimony had been carved in stone and Chertoff would not let him run from it. Four times Verniero had sworn the proof on profiling was gathered only *after* the 1998 shooting.

"Would you agree with me that, in fact, the underlying data in the Interim Report was being collected as far back as 1995, 1996, and 1997?"

"I was referring to the Troop D audit," Verniero said.

"But there is not a scintilla of data from the Troop D audit in the Interim Report."

"Yeah, I may have been mistaken."

"But then you came back to the same point again in response to questions from Senator Zane. *'The whole issue of profiling became crystallized and uppermost in my mind at around the time of the Turnpike incident.'*"

"I was obviously inarticulate in my response to Senator Zane."

"And it came up again later in the same hearing."

"And, Mr. Chertoff—my answer—my answer will be the same."

"Well, let's get it into the record, because I want to give you an ample opportunity to respond," Chertoff said, and read two more passages of Verniero giving the same story.

"The gist of what I was saying might have been unartful, but I believe it was accurate," Verniero said.

William Gormley bristled and Committee members shook their heads. Chertoff was pressing Verniero hard. Normally, a trial lawyer had to be careful not to push so hard that he turns a witness into a victim in the eyes of a jury. But with Verniero's memory blackouts and feeble explanations, there was no discernible sympathy for him in the room. Members were retreating to the coffee pot in an adjacent alcove for quick conversations: "Did he just say what I thought he said?"

In the gallery, Reverend Reginald Jackson had the sensation of trying to grip running water; he just couldn't get a handle on it. By mid-afternoon the examination was far from over and Chertoff was still hammering Verniero on stonewalling the Justice Department.

"I don't recall," he said.

Chertoff flashed up another document. Did Verniero remember the Justice Department request, addressed to him, for stop and search data in 1996-97?

"I don't have an independent recollection of that," he said.

Chertoff finally had enough. "Help me out. This is what I don't understand. This issue of racial profiling is huge. And yet, you don't have much of a recollection."

"I'm doing the best I can, with all the human frailties of memory, to answer your questions," said Verniero.

Chertoff finished his interrogation about 4 p.m. As Committee members began questioning Verniero, Chertoff's chief assistant Scott Weber turned to Albert Porroni, head of the Office of Legislative Services, which was coordinating the hearing and posting Verniero's testimony live on the internet.

"Albert, I need a transcript as soon as possible," Weber said. Twenty minutes later he had a copy. He handed it to Kalama Lui-Kwam, one of the Latham & Watkins lawyers. "Do a search of 'I don't know,' 'I don't recall,' and 'I don't remember.'"

Weber figured Verniero may have used the terms 75 or 100 times. When Lui-Kwam returned with the answer Weber couldn't believe his ears. He leaned over and whispered to Chertoff: "He answered 'I don't know' or 'I don't recall' 320 times."

Chertoff looked at Weber and turned to Gormley.

Gormley glanced back at Weber, and then turned to his left. The news made its way around the U-shaped table and Committee members were incredulous. This from a Supreme Court Justice! It was almost surreal.

"I hope his wife doesn't send him out to do the shopping," one senator quipped.

"He must have unfettered access to the State Police evidence locker," said another.

The hearing dragged on into the night, with each senator getting a turn to question Verniero. John Lynch had been waiting a long time for this. Lynch had a loud, raspy voice, like fingernails on a chalkboard. He began by attacking Verniero for sending the DOJ a letter with false information about consent searches.

"I suggest to you," Lynch barked, "the letter is an attempt to deceive the Department of Justice."

"I would disagree with that. There was no attempt, as far as I'm concerned…"

"You understand that's a misrepresentation?"

"Misrepresentation is an inflammatory term that implies an intentional misleading," Verniero said, beginning to sound weary.

Raymond Zane, a Republican who had voted against Verniero's confirmation, was as eager as Lynch.

"Justice Verniero, during your tenure as Attorney General what would you list as the biggest issue that you faced?"

"Racial profiling," Verniero said.

"Number one?"

"Number one issue."

"And it didn't crystallize, racial profiling, until 1998?"

"The Turnpike event marked a turn of my thinking for the reasons that I've enunciated."

"I'm having difficulty believing that. Tell me why I should. I find that incredible."

"I trusted the State Police," Verniero said.

"Justice Verniero, no witness so far in these hearings has testified like you have. I honestly can't believe that someone—I guess you're 42…"

"Forty-one, but growing older."

"You can't have that big a problem with memory. I'm very, very disappointed."

The hearing marched on late into the night and by 11:30 p.m. the gallery was nearly empty. Verniero had dark circles under his eyes and gray whiskers peppered his cheeks. He seemed to be holding on like a boxer just trying to stay on his feet until the final bell. He'd endured 13 hours of blistering interrogation, yet the worst was still to come. All the senators had had their shots—but one.

"I think I'll ask a couple of questions," William Gormley said.

Gormley had been sitting and listening all day and night. By now the man he was responsible for putting on the Supreme Court had repeated some variation of "I can't recall" a mind-numbing 579 times.

"This won't be lengthy," Gormley began, brusquely. "Aside from Hogan and Kenna, did you have occasion to have any other public relation indictments?"

"I do not accept the characterization, Senator, that they were public relations indictments."

"That's all they were," Gormley said abruptly. "Next question."

He confronted Verniero on his claim that the racial profiling investigation had begun only after the Turnpike shooting.

"I may have been mistaken," Verniero said.

"It could be construed that it was misleading," Gormley shot back.

"I…"

"Let me finish. Was it misleading, or was it a mistake?"

"Misleading suggests some intentional decision on my part to mislead the Committee, which I assure you, I did not have."

"Why should I not believe that that was misleading?" Gormley persisted.

"Because I did not intend it to be misleading."

"As of right now, I just find it hard to comprehend, and I'll tell you why. I wish I was the detail person you are. I mean, you're very focused, very bright—very bright. And on its face, it's misleading. It still is misleading. And I don't know how you get around that. Between mislead and mistake, at this moment in time, I fall to mislead."

It was an electric exchange and a mortifying public rebuke. A Supreme Court Justice accused of lying under oath. Verniero was shaken. He grasped for words.

"One thing I could suggest," he said unsteadily, "is to give me the opportunity to go through my recollection, and perhaps supplement with sworn testimony, an affidavit, which I could submit to this Committee to perhaps give a fuller explanation."

Gormley sat silent for several seconds contemplating Verniero's proposal, then leaned forward and spoke in a chilling near-whisper.

"My vote would be that you have to come back in. That's it for today," he said and slammed his gavel.

Chapter 107

PETER VERNIERO'S TESTIMONY HAD BEEN devastating. Senators, staff members, and the press believed he was lying through his teeth.

"Verniero Soiled Himself and the Court," announced one newspaper headline.

"Peter Verniero," opined *The New York Times* editorial page, *"gravely damaged his ability to continue serving effectively on the bench. His display of amnesia and his insensitivity to a key racial issue will inevitably diminish his authority as a judge."*

On the morning of April 3rd, Judiciary Committee members gathered in a small, windowless room in the basement of the State House in Trenton and listened to Michael Chertoff lay out the case for Verniero's ouster. It was not a tough sell. When Chertoff finished, William Gormley recommended a letter be written to the acting-Governor asking him to request Verniero's resignation. During that day's hearing, a letter was drafted and circulated in a small room behind the Committee hearing chamber for senators to read, make comments, and suggest changes. By the end of testimony, all but two senators had signed it.

Late that afternoon, the Committee marched en masse from the State House to the Governor's Office, besieged by an army of news cameras that followed them into the Governor's Reception Room. Donald DiFrancesco had been serving as acting-Governor of New Jersey since Christie Whitman left for Washington. Prior to that, he'd been the Republican Senate Majority Leader and had helped push through Verniero's confirmation. DiFrancesco waved the Committee into his office. Gormley held the letter in a manila folder while everyone sat around a big table in the conference room and listened to Chertoff.

"This is what we have and what we see as the major issues that lead us to a recommendation that Justice Verniero be removed," Chertoff said. He laid out several documents side by side and explained to DiFrancesco how they showed Verniero deceived the Senate Judiciary Committee in 1999.

Seated next to Gormley was Senator Norman Robertson, who had not signed the letter. "Let me see that folder," he said to the chairman. The letter inside the folder was a blunt instrument. Verniero, it stated, *"was derelict in his duty"* as Attorney General and *"chose to ignore"* substantial evidence on racial profiling which he *"withheld"* from the Department of Justice, then *"misled"* the Committee about what he'd done. Robertson scrawled his signature on the missive.

Chertoff's presentation lasted about 15 minutes. When it was over, DiFrancesco nodded and said he'd read the material and let them know his decision. The Committee members snuck out a back door. As they were leaving, Gormley called out: "Lou, Lou," and collared Senator Louis Kosco, the last holdout. Kosco signed the letter.

Two days later, in a searing speech, DiFrancesco announced his decision.

"I come to the conclusion that even if we give Justice Verniero every benefit of doubt, it is still clear that his original testimony withheld or misrepresented important information, thereby misleading members of the state Senate. We cannot allow that." The integrity of the confirmation process was violated, DiFrancesco said, because senators acted on Verniero's nomination without critical facts.

"Clearly, if the information known now about the status of the inquiry into racial profiling from 1994 to 1999 were known then, many senators, including me, would not have supported the Verniero nomination. Accordingly, I have called Justice Verniero and asked for his resignation. This is a very sad and unfortunate day for New Jersey. However, we have at stake the integrity of our government and the confidence of our citizens. Our Supreme Court has a well-deserved reputation for excellence. As long as Justice Verniero sits on that court, it will enjoy a reputation less than it is worthy of."

In a stunning proclamation, New Jersey's highest ranking official had branded Verniero a liar. It was the first time in State history that a Governor had asked a Supreme Court Justice to vacate his office. Verniero defiantly refused.

"My testimony before the Senate Judiciary Committee was truthful," he said in a written release. *"I responded candidly and to the best of my ability. The Committee's conclusions are unfounded and unfair."*

But Verniero was, by now, a solitary man. Other than former-Governor Christie Whitman—*"Peter has been very honest,"* she said from Washington—his only supporters were his family and his lawyer, Robert Mintz.

"No one has ever been removed from office in New Jersey for an alleged lack of candor. Who among us could withstand that level of scrutiny?" Mintz said.

It was an astonishing observation that drove Gormley apoplectic.

"When you raise your right hand in front of the Judiciary Committee," he said, "and you want to be a member of the finest court in the country, I would expect candor."

Chapter 108

On Monday, April 9th, Gormley stopped at a Chinese restaurant and bought several bags of steaming Oriental food and drove to a condominium in Lawrenceville, New Jersey, where Michael Chertoff and Scott Weber were staying during the hearings.

The SJC had heard testimony that day and now Gormley, Chertoff, Weber, Jo Glading, Doug Wheeler, and Albert Porroni from Legislative Services convened to draft Articles of Impeachment.

By the time the Chinese food arrived, Chertoff and Weber had changed into shorts and T-shirts. The group sat down around the dining table and dug in beneath a painting of a nude woman hanging on the wall. As Wheeler wolfed his *chow fun*, he knew he was about to take part in an historic event. Verniero had refused to resign and impeachment had become the only option. It required a simple majority vote in the 80-member Assembly—the lower house of the State Legislature. That would send the matter for trial to the Senate, where it would take a two-thirds vote by the 40-member body to remove Verniero from the Supreme Court.

When they finished eating, Wheeler pulled out his laptop and the group began banging out the Articles of Impeachment. Senator John Lynch—who'd just undergone prostate surgery— was not about to miss this and attended via speaker phone from his hospital bed. Wheeler and Glading had roughed out a list of issues, but Chertoff was running the show and they quickly saw they weren't on the same page. They'd counted about 20 offenses they considered impeachable, but Chertoff didn't want singles or doubles, only home runs.

The lawyers worked through the night, going over everything. After months consumed by the case, each of them knew every fact by heart. Glading, Wheeler, and Weber shared the typing, until Glading—the ex-reporter—finally said: "I'm the fastest typer. I'm typing." Nobody argued. Everyone proposed articles and Chertoff sculpted them.

"Why don't we do it this way?" he'd say, until it was just like he wanted it.

It occurred to Wheeler that this was the highlight of his young legal career. Five years out of law school and here he was sitting in a roomful of fine lawyers putting together an unprecedented document. Across the table sat one of the most brilliant attorneys in the country, totally focused, at the peak of his skills. Wheeler had been in awe of Chertoff from the start but, in the beginning, the other lawyer didn't even know his name. Now they were talking back and forth, exchanging ideas, Chertoff treating him like a colleague. Wheeler was euphoric.

By the end of the night they'd crafted an 11-page document accusing Verniero of lying to cover up his knowledge of racial profiling. The letter cited five specific impeachable offenses:

1.   *AG Verniero provided false statements to the Senate Judiciary Committee at his confirmation hearings pertaining to the status of the DOJ investigation.*

2.   *AG Verniero provided false statements to the Senate Judiciary Committee at his confirmation hearings pertaining to the "data" that was the basis for the Interim Report.*

3.   *AG Verniero provided misleading testimony to the Senate Judiciary Committee in connection with the Racial Profiling Hearing.*

4.   *AG Verniero misled the New Jersey Legislative Black & Latino Caucus in responding to a request for information.*

5.   *AG Verniero withheld relevant information from the New Jersey Superior Court and the litigants in Soto.*

The letter included nine instances that Verniero allegedly gave false or misleading statements.

"Accordingly, the Senate Judiciary Committee respectfully requests that the General Assembly consider appropriate Articles of Impeachment to be presented to the Senate forthwith."

The letter was addressed to a 900-pound gorilla by the name of Jack Collins, the Republican Speaker of the Assembly. As such, he possessed the power to make or break the impeachment with a single yea or nay. The Speaker had final say on whether the legislative body even voted on Verniero's ouster. For Collins it would be a profoundly momentous and historic decision—but also a political one. And the politicking began immediately. Telephones started ringing off their hooks. Can you support it? What are the dynamics of getting the Assembly to vote for impeachment? Can Verniero survive the storm?

On its face, it seemed ludicrous that Collins would sanction impeachment of another Republican. A Senate trial would drag the Verniero scandal into election season, long enough for the Democrats to skewer the GOP on its own petard. As *The New York Times* observed: *"New Jersey Republicans have turned into a dysfunctional family, but it's unlikely they'll actually torch their own house."*

On the other hand, a Republican acting-Governor had already, in essence, branded Verniero a counterfeit Justice. And William Gormley and six other Republican members of the Senate Judiciary Committee had unanimously voted for his removal. Nonetheless, the final decision was now in the hands of one man. If Jack Collins permitted the Assembly vote, Peter Verniero was almost a dead cinch to become the first New Jersey State Supreme Court judge expelled from the bench.

As the political waters roiled, the SJC hearings ambled toward a close. Bill Buckman testified, accusing the Attorney General's Office of violating its ethical obligation to turn over evidence to the *Soto* defense. Trooper Greg Sanders described the Newark Black Radicals' long battle over racial profiling, how he'd been accused of being a "rat" and a spy for the ACLU, and how watermelon had been stuffed into his locker.

"If a trooper can do this to another minority trooper and supervisors can take no action, you can understand why no one has done anything about racial profiling," Sanders said.

Carson Dunbar Jr., the black former FBI agent who had replaced Carl Williams as State Police Superintendent, complained that New Jersey's obsession with racism in the agency was over-blown.

"I can't deny there are problems, but it's not as one-sided a picture as has been painted," he said to a near empty room.

The reason Dunbar was being ignored was that Johnny L. Cochran Jr. was holding court in an adjacent room before a swarm of reporters.

"Carson Dunbar continues to reside in the 51st state, the state of denial," the super-lawyer announced. Cochran was now representing 13 black troopers who were suing the State Police for alleged discrimination. Always the showman, he brought props, holding up racist posters—including the *"Runnin' Nigger Target"*—that had once hung in State Police barracks.

But the real drama remained what Jack Collins would do. Collins was a college professor and a farmer from Salem County, home of the notorious Cocaine Alley. Pressure was building on him from every side and his deliberation turned into a two-and-a-half week cliffhanger. The pot was about to boil over when Collins—after spending three nights holed up in a hotel room to escape the stress—finally called the press into the ornate Assembly chambers.

"We will not be moving forward with this," he announced, providing only fuzzy political logic to rationalize his decision. Yes, he admitted, Peter Verniero did lie under oath. But Collins did not want the Assembly caught up in months of squabbling just because a Supreme Court Justice committed perjury. Verniero's deceit, he said, was a violation of the law and should be sent to the local prosecutor for criminal action.

"That fucking asshole!" Jo Astrid Glading shouted. The telephone call had just come into the Democratic Senate Counsel's office informing her and Douglas Wheeler of Collins' crushing decision. They were dumbfounded.

"That son of a bitch!" Wheeler said. "I can't believe after all the work we did and he's not going to let it go forward."

"How dare he!" Glading seethed.

The air had suddenly gone out of their balloon. After months of total immersion building an incontrovertible case against someone who bore false witness in order to win a seat on the Supreme Court, one man had single-handedly ended the impeachment movement and allowed Peter Verniero to continue sitting in judgment of all New Jerseyans.

"He has made a mockery of the Senate's process," Senate Minority leader Richard Codey, a Democrat, said of Collins. "He abdicated his responsibility to protect the reputation of the Supreme Court to spare the reputation of a political crony."

"This threatens the Senate's sacred obligation to ensure that nominees to high public office are people of integrity, good judgment, and fine character," William Gormley said.

Gormley was beside himself. He'd been responsible for reopening the racial profiling investigation and protecting the *process*. It was an unprecedented endeavor, the likes of which New Jersey had never seen. Gormley vowed to press forward to force an impeachment vote but, despite all the sound and fury, the battle was over. The Senate, in a 37-to-1 vote, passed a resolution accusing Verniero of perjury and calling for his resignation, but to no avail.

Chapter 109

TWO WEEKS AFTER PETER VERNIERO DODGED expulsion from the high court, the New Jersey Senate staged a love fest for Michael Chertoff. Senators on both sides of the aisle fell over themselves saying nice things about him.

"Michael Chertoff represents the best New Jersey has to offer in terms of his unwavering fairness and his tireless devotion to justice," said Senator William Gormley.

Chertoff's law firm, Latham & Watkins, declined to charge the State for its services. The fees for Chertoff, Scott Weber, their four young associates, as well as paralegals, would have totaled about $1.3 million.

"If my partners ever figure that out, I'm in big trouble," quipped Chertoff, who had already left the firm and taken over as second-in-command at the U.S. Justice Department.

Months later, Peter Verniero billed the State of New Jersey for his legal fees of $250,000.

Chapter 110

WHAT BEGAN WITH A HORRIFIC SALVO of gunfire that led to a national firestorm ended with a snivel.

Troopers John Hogan and James Kenna finally had their day in court. When they entered the Mercer County Courthouse in Trenton, each faced up to 20 years in prison.

January 15, 2002 was the final day of the Whitman/DiFrancesco Administration, and Attorney General John Farmer was anxious to tie up all the loose ends before he left office. Farmer had successfully appealed Judge Andrew Smithson's decision to throw out the shooting indictment against Hogan and Kenna for being politically motivated and the charges had been reinstated.

Since the shooting, Special Prosecutor James Gerrow's perception of the case had been altered radically. The State had originally focused on Hogan as the bad guy, viewing him as a gonzo racial profiler who had fired a last shot while the van rolled down an embankment and was no longer a threat, striking Danny Reyes in the back and nearly killing him. But Gerrow ultimately concluded the shooting was actually Kenna's fault. He had run up to the van, gun drawn, screaming, banging on the window, and fired the first shots, for no good reason. Hogan—who'd been on the far side of the van and couldn't see what was happening —had fired because he thought his partner was under attack.

The prosecutor also decided the "final shot" that Danny Reyes described was a phantom. Bullet trajectories from a re-enactment of the shooting showed no shots had been fired from behind as the van rolled down the hill. Two UPS drivers also came forward who said they had witnessed the incident and disputed the last shot theory. The conclusion was that Reyes was struck by one of Hogan's bullets early in the shooting—which lasted less than a minute—but didn't feel it until the van stopped rolling, a delayed reaction phenomenon known to occur in extremely stressful situations.

The small wood-paneled courtroom of Judge Charles Delehy was packed beyond capacity when the troopers entered. Kenna—tall and blond—and Hogan—dark, brooding, and much thinner than his pumped-up trooper days. The hearing was tightly choreographed. Gerrow had conducted extensive interviews with the defendants and had written allocutions, scripted questions-and-answers, in which the troopers would admit to lying about the shooting and racial profiling. Kenna's lawyer Jack Arseneault immediately rejected the prosecutor's dialogue.

"Fuck you," he told Gerrow. "Jimmy's not admitting this stuff."

Arseneault knew he had the upper hand. The State was determined to settle the case before the old Administration left office and just wanted to get it over with.

"Okay, give me your language," Gerrow said.

Arseneault ended up writing 95% of Kenna's allocution. In court, he and Hogan's lawyer, Robert Galantucci, said nothing. They didn't have to. Gerrow did all the talking, sounding more like a defense attorney than a prosecutor.

"An organizational failure on the part of the New Jersey State Police," Gerrow told Judge Delehy, "led to Jim Kenna being on the road that night and overreacting, causing his partner to overreact as well."

Gerrow led the troopers through their accounts. The testimony was not sworn. Hogan said the night of the shooting he had contact with up to 75 troopers advising him what to say and how to say it.

"There was great concern about why Jimmy fired the first shots," Hogan said, reading his script. "At the station Jimmy told me he wasn't sure why he fired. His actions needed to be justified. The falsifications were exaggerations. I was trying to protect my partner."

Kenna and Hogan admitted lying about the speed of the van, why they pulled it over, and what happened after the stop. And both troopers said they were taught to profile.

"Racial profiling was a routine practice," Kenna said. "From the State Police Academy through to on-the-job training with senior troopers it was repeatedly made clear that race was an appropriate factor in deciding which vehicles to stop and in some cases search."

"If you wanted to satisfy the demand for drug arrests we were led to believe as young troopers that we had to stop minorities," Hogan said. "It was so common I just assumed it was how it was done."

By the end of the hearing, the troopers—who for nearly three years the State portrayed as villains—had been recast as victims.

"These young men, through their supervisors and their training, were carrying out a policy that was more than inappropriate," Gerrow said.

Judge Delehy went along with the script.

"Troopers Hogan and Kenna acted out of misguided zeal," he said, "and misguided loyalty born of an indoctrination into an approach to law enforcement that can generally be described as Machiavellian— the end justifies the means."

Hogan and Kenna pleaded guilty to reduced charges of obstructing the shooting investigation. They were fined $280 each and agreed to never again serve in law enforcement in New Jersey. They not only didn't get jail time, they didn't get probation either.

Outside on the courthouse steps, Reverend Reginald Jackson summed up the stunning conclusion.

"What happened today was like a hit-and-run," said Jackson. "Not one superior officer has been named. Not one superior officer has been disciplined. Not one superior officer has been removed. This was not justice."

Where Are They Now?

The Newark Black Radicals:

Greg Sanders retired from the New Jersey State Police in 2003 and is Chief Security Advisor for International Programs at the United Nations. The State Police paid him $475,000 to settle a discrimination lawsuit.

Darryl Beard retired from the New Jersey State Police in 2003 and is Director of Security at the Pennsylvania Hospital at the University of Pennsylvania in Philadelphia. Beard received $425,000 from the State Police to settle a discrimination and retaliation lawsuit.

Anthony Reed was dismissed from the New Jersey State Police in 1991. He is the Director of Procurement Technical Assistance for Washington, D.C.

Glenn Johnson, fired from the State Police in 1996, lives in Newark, New Jersey and works for New Jersey Transit. Johnson sued the State Police for discrimination and a jury awarded him $675,000.

Kenneth Ruff is assistant school principal at a southern New Jersey middle school. He is married with two children.

Troopers:

John Hogan works as a salesman for an events production company in New Jersey. In 2005, his book *Turnpike Trooper* was published, Hogan's account of his triumphs and tribulations as a New Jersey State Policeman.

James Kenna is an iron worker in New Jersey and was working on his master's degree in graphic arts.

Clinton Pagano is retired from the casino industry and divides his time between New Jersey and Florida.

Justin Dintino is retired and living in New Jersey where he spends most of his time playing golf.

Victor Cooper retired from the New Jersey State Police in 2003. He spent five years as Director of Security for the Philadelphia Eagles and is now President of the Urban Family Council, a non-profit Philadelphia organization. He received $275,000 to settle his discrimination lawsuit against the State Police.

Robert Henig, dismissed from the State Police in 1991, was acquitted of all criminal charges lodged against him and is a schoolteacher and wrestling referee in Ocean County, New Jersey.

Student Shooting Victims:

Danny Reyes lives in New Jersey where he's raising his daughter. In 2001 he formed Red Eye Entertainment to promote music and sporting events. He was executive producer of *4 Chosen*, a documentary about the New Jersey Turnpike shooting which was released in 2006.

Jarmaine Grant lives in Queens with his wife and daughter and is partner with Reyes in real estate development.

Rayshawn Brown earned his Bachelor of Arts degree from Bloomfield College and now operates a recording studio in addition to being a personal trainer in New Jersey.

Keshon Moore lives in the Bronx, New York, and works for a nutrition company.

Attorneys:

William H. Buckman continues to practice law in the State of New Jersey and is recognized as one of the pre-eminent legal experts on racial profiling. He represents a number of minority New Jersey State Policemen and motorists.

Johnnie L. Cochran, Jr. died of a brain tumor in March 2005. He was 67. In addition to the New Jersey Turnpike student shooting case, his client list included Lenny Bruce, Michael Jackson, O.J. Simpson, and Rosa Parks. He also represented a number of New Jersey State

Police minority troopers before his death. He was widely considered America's most famous trial lawyer.

Peter Neufeld and **Barry Scheck** continue to run The Innocence Project at the Benjamin Cardoza Law School at New York University. Their work with DNA evidence had led to the exoneration of more than 250 men and women across the country wrongfully convicted of murder, rape, and other violent crimes.

Michael Chertoff became Assistant Attorney General of the United States after the New Jersey racial profiling hearings were completed and led the federal investigation into the terrorist attacks of September 11, 2001. Chertoff was appointed United States Circuit Judge for the Third Circuit Court of Appeals in 2003. Two years later President George W. Bush chose him to become Secretary of the U.S. Department of Homeland Security. After leaving the federal government, Chertoff founded the Chertoff Group, a risk-management advisor firm, and is senior counsel at Covington & Burling. His book, *Homeland Security: Assessing the First Five Years,* was released in September 2009.

Scott Weber served as Senior Counselor at the U.S. Department of Homeland Security under Chertoff from 2005-06. He is currently a partner at the law firm Patton Boggs and is a member of of the Advisory Board of Directors of the Chertoff Group.

Jeffrey Wintner and **Fred Last** continue to work for the New Jersey Office of Public Defender in Gloucester County. **Wayne Natale** retired from the Public Defender's Office in January 2006 to go into private practice. For their work on racial profiling, the three lawyers shared the 2001 Kutak-Dodds Prize, the highest award of the National Legal Aid and Defender Association.

Justin Loughry continues to practice civil and criminal law in southern New Jersey.

Judges:

Robert E. Francis retired from the bench in 2003. He died in 2008 at age 65. Francis never spoke publicly about his demotion from Chancery Court or its relation to his ruling in *State of New Jersey vs. Soto.*

Justice Peter Verniero retired from the New Jersey Supreme Court in 2004. His reconfirmation was expected to receive strong opposition. He is a partner in Sills, Cummins, Epstein & Gross, one of New Jersey's largest law firms. In 2010 he was appointed to the prestigious position of annotator and commentator for the Rules Governing the Courts of the State of New Jersey. In June, Verniero was named chairman of the Governor's Judicial Advisory Panel, which screens candidates for all state Superior Court judgeships and makes recommendations to the governor.

Justice Deborah T. Poritz retired as Chief Justice of the New Jersey Supreme Court in October 2006 after ten years on the bench and became a partner at Drinker, Biddle, a Princeton, New Jersey law firm.

Politicians:

Governor Christine Todd Whitman served as Administrator of the Environmental Protection Agency under President George W. Bush from January 2001 until June 2003. She is currently president of The Whitman Strategy Group, a business and government consulting company. She is also the author of *It's My Party, Too,* published in January 2005.

Sen. William Gormley retired from the New Jersey Senate in 2007 and now practices law in southern New Jersey.

Sen. John A. Lynch retired from public office after 20 years in the New Jersey State Senate. Ironically—or perhaps not in New Jersey—the man so intent on exposing the corruption of Peter Verniero was himself indicted in 2006 for taking kickbacks from a contractor. Lynch pleaded guilty and served three years in federal prison. He was released in 2009 and returned to New Jersey.

Ministers:

Reverend Reginald T. Jackson remains pastor of the 2,000 member St. Matthew African Methodist Episcopal Church in Orange, New Jersey and continues to serve as Executive Director of the Black Minister's Council of New Jersey. He has received numerous awards for his fight against racial profiling. In 2000, he was named New Jersey's Man of the Year by New Jersey Monthly magazine. He is annually listed as one of the 25 most influential people in New Jersey.

Reverend Al Sharpton ran for the Democratic Presidential nomination in 2004 and remains one of the leading African-American spokesmen in America.

Author:

Joseph Collum retired from fulltime broadcast journalism shortly after the terrorist attacks of September 11, 2001, after spending several days reporting from Ground Zero. He and his wife Donna reside in Plantation, Florida, where he is a fulltime writer and contributes reports to PBS. His first novel, *Brady's Run,* was published in 2009 by Jigsaw Press. The sequel, *Et Tu, Brady,* is scheduled for publication in 2011. The Oxford English Dictionary credits Collum with coining the term *racial profiling.*

Visit Joseph Collum on the Web at **www.josephcollum.com** or contact him directly at **josephcollum.author@yahoo.com**.

Index

4th Amendment: 7, 56, 168-169, 179

14th Amendment, 169, 179

20-20 rule, 40, 42

ABSCAM, 154

ACLU, *see* American Civil Liberties Union

Adler, Senator John H., 325

America Online, 184

American Civil Liberties Union: Constitutional violations, 53; opposing interdiction, 95; deluged by complaints, 99-100; Buckman working for, 167; sensitivity training, 177, 210; Wenk lends support, 251; accuses Whitman, 299-300; Sanders accused of spying, 370

Arbuckle, Dr. Charles, 185

Andryszcyk, John, 60

Arnold, Benedict, 188

Arseneault, Jack, 329, 339, 375

Asbell, Sam, 149

Askin, Frank, 7-8, 295, 355

Atlantic City, N.J.: Dintino's raids, 23; casinos come to, 25; State Police banquet, 46; veteran troopers assigned, 49; Casino Association, 152; Dintino cuts casino staffing, 177; Dunlop addresses banquet, 330

Babick, Joseph, 44

Barnes, Leroy "Nicky", 27-28

Battered Woman's Syndrome, 279

Beard, Darryl: joins NJSP, 18-21; Ruff, 39-42; fishing holes, 62-64; racial targeting, 79-80; Black Radical, 94-95; *Without Just Cause,* 129-132, 142; accusation against Ruff, 170-171; *20* black troopers, 186-187; discrimination suit, 199-200; Buckman solicits, 201-202; transferred Moorestown, 224-

Beard, Darryl *(cont'd)*
225; transfer Red Lion, 244-245

Belleran, Vincent, 94, 270,-271

Belopolsky, Superior Court Judge Herman, 160

Bergen Record, 47, 282, 288, 341

Berra, Yogi, 224

Best, Tyrone, 106

Bias, Len, 29

Black Dragon, The: Turnpike as, 8; Ruff, 17; 3 years exp., 49; Wilson, 53; influx young troopers, 121; *Soto* Violators Survey, 198; return to glory days, 211; Hogan, 261; Turnpike shooting, 273; Stone's 2nd report, 300

Black Ministers Council of New Jersey, 283

Black Panther Party, 34

Black Radicals, *see Newark Black Radicals*

Blair, Dalton, 85

Blair, Delbert, 85-88, 102,-104, 162, 195

Blaker, 1st Sgt., Captain David, 252, 254, 267, 344, 359

Bordentown, N.J., 164

Boriello, Major Gary, 75

Brady vs. Maryland, 212, 218, 294, 310, 360

Bradley, Bill U.S. Senator, 210

Braithwaite, Appellate Judge Dennis J., 309-310

Brandeis, U.S. Supreme Court Justice Louis, 250

Brase, Pam, 56, 57

Brennan, Jr., U.S. Supreme Court Justice William J., 295

bridge sitting, 45-46

Broadhurst, Lt. Thomas, 11

Brown, Rayshawn, 273-275, 347

Brown, Stacy, 60, 74, 162, 173-175, 194

Brown v. Board of Education, 169

Bruncati, Trooper Peter, 87-88

Bruno, Angelo, 23

Buckman, Betty, 157-158

Buckman, Joseph, 157-159

Buckman, Shellie: 229-230, 241-242

Buckman, William H.: first concerns, 100; family history of, 157-161; first volley, 167-168; forming *Soto* team, 179-184; violator survey, 196-198; trooper to testify, 201-203; *Soto* hearing, 204-207; *Soto* case, 212-219, 228-231, 235-238, 241-243; *Soto* ruling, 248-251; return to New Jersey, 293-296; request for extension, 300; *Soto's* zero hour, 309-310; end of odyssey 320-321; Francis ousted, 328; flushing out evidence, 334-336, 340; at Verniero hearing, 356; SJC testimony, 370

Burke, Trooper Francis, 269-270

Burke, Trooper Wayne, 87-88

Bush, President George W., 333, 348

Byrne, Governor Brendan, 22, 24

Café Nina's. 219, 228, 236, 238

Caffrey, Trooper Brian: poster boy, 109-110; *Without Just Cause* aired, 129; interview, 139; at Moorestown, 224-225; *Soto* testimony, 228-229; prosecution witness, 236; Francis ruling, 249; Hogan, 260; at Cranbury Station, 269

Camden, New Jersey, 256-257

Campbell, Douglas, 292

Campbell, Trooper James, 46-47

Carmichael, Stokely, 37

Carr, Lynn and Nathan, 145-146

Carr, Captain Thomas, 75, 190

Cavott, Frank, 55-57

C.B., *See* colored boy

Charlie Bravo, *See* colored boy.

Charles, David, 145

Chertoff, Michael: SJC ringmaster, 337; access to evidence, 340; depositions, 342-345; Verniero hearing 348-366; articles of impeachment, 368-369; Senate "love fest," 373

Chesimard, Joanne, 80, 172

Chi Square, 237-238

Clifford, Justice Robert L., 258

Cleaver, Eldridge, 35, 37

Cliff, Jimmy, 219

Cobb, Paul, 35, 37

Cocaine Alley: Mastella, 46, 109; location of, 99; profit center, 115; percent arrests, 124; Disalvatore shot, 133; money seized, 149; cowboys patrolling, 152; Collins, 371

Cochran, Jr., Johnnie L.: Simpson, 206; Turnpike shooting, 278-280; oceans of ink, 289; civil suit, 293, 318; filing suit, 322; high stakes poker, 332-333; settlement, 346-347; black troopers, 371

Codey, Sen. Richard, 372

Cole, Michael, 332

Collins, Assemblyman Jack, 370-371

Collum, Donna, 137

Collum, Joe: discovers profiling, 76-78; tantalizing nugget, 90-93; investigating State Police, 97-101; Wells interview, 106-108; Caffrey interview, 109-110; drug dogs, 111-114; Hoerst interview 115-117; McLemore, anonymous trooper, 118-122; Pagano interview, 123-126; *Without Just Cause* aired, 129-132; Turnpike shooting, 134-140; troopers backlash, 141-142; Pagano second interview, 145-148; Pagano Report, 212, 240; *Soto* ruling, 250

Collum, Simon, 137

Colonel's Club, 165

colored boy, 41, 122

Congress for Racial Equality, 35

Cooper, Trooper Victor, 233-234, 244-245, 378

Coté, Meredith, 65-69

Council, The (black La Cosa Nostra), 27

crack cocaine: devastates community, 27-30; vials of, 40, 215; trooper shot, 136; Monticello testifies, 221; targeting, 225

Cranbury Station, 260-261, 269-270, 272, 276, 286

Crawford, Trooper Karlton, 61, 174

Crestmont Homes, 17

crime dogs: collective shudder, 3; Newark Station 40-41; biggest on Turnpike, 61; narco pups, 111; cold slap, 131; Hogan, 261; Hogan and Kenna, 272-273

Cupingood, Dr. Leonard, 236-238, 249-250

Darden, Christopher, 315

Darnell, Emerson Lippincott, 167-168

Davidson, Lt. Bill, 103

DEA, *See* Drug Enforcement Administration

Decotiis & Cole, 332

Delaware River, 134-135

Delaware v. Prouse, 168-169

Delehy, Judge Charles, 375-376

Del Tufo, Attorney General Robert, 151-154

democrats, *as slang,* 41

De Vencentes, Philip, 144

DiFrancesco, Acting-Governor Donald, 365-366, 374

digger, 3, 40, 52, 300

Dintino, Superintendent Justin: early career 22-25; protecting civil liberties, 48-51; white paper, 152-156; coming out party, 164-166;

Dintino, Superintendent Justin *(cont'd)* sensitivity training, 176-178; Henig fired, 193; retirement, 209-211

DiSalvatore, Trooper Anthony, 83-84, 133-135, 138, 140, 164

Dittman, Christy, 270, 290

DITU, *See* Drug Interdiction Training Unit

Douglas, Trooper Karl, 218-220

Drug Enforcement Administration, 47, 112

Drug Interdiction Training Unit, 109, 227-228, 230

Dunbar Jr., Superintendent Carson, 370-371

Dunleavy's, 203

Dunlop, Lt. Col. Robert, 286, 293, 307-308, 330-331

Dwyer, Jim, 279

Eagleton Institute, 288

East Brunswick Station, 53, 60, 75, 87, 103

Edwards, Attorney General Cary, 152

Edwards, Governor Edward I., 11

Edwards, John, 11

Einstein, Albert, 70-72

Farmer, Attorney General John: becoming AG, 295; State Police banquet, 331; difficult moments 334; call from Gormley, 336; pressure building, 340; last day, 374

Farrell, Frank, 281

Fahy, John: *Soto* hearing 206-208, 212-213, 215-223, 226-228, 230-232, 235, 238-241, 253-255; letter for Verniero, 264-265; SJC testimony, 349-350; DOJ letter in Verniero's name, 357

Fash, Trooper, 230

FBI, 26, 27, 47, 154

Fellowship Farm, 159

Ferencz, Brad, 127

fishing holes, 62-64, 202

Flemington Station, 20

Florio, Governor Jim, 151-155, 165, 209, 342

Francis, Judge Robert E.: *Soto* hearing, 205-207, 212-217, 219, 222, 226-228, 230-232, 238-241; *Soto* ruling, 248-250; demoted, 327-328

Franz, Captain Ronald, 272

Freedom Riders, 167

Fyfe, Dr. James, 229

Galantucci, Robert, 329, 339, 375

Gallo, "Crazy Joey," 27

Gambino, Carlo, 23

Gandhi, Mahatma, 15

Gardner, Barbara, 91, 97-98, 112, 119, 135

Gasior, Trooper Fred, 290

Gaugler, Trooper R.S., 55-56

Gerrow, James, 291, 303-304, 329, 374-376

Germantown, Maryland, 85, 103

Gilbert, Lt. Bernard, 244

Gilbert, Sgt. Thomas: *Soto* ruling, 252; meeting with Verniero, 262-263; smoking gun memo, 265-267, 317; accidental hero, 343-344; SJC hearing testimony, 348-350

Glading, Jo Astrid, 342-344, 348, 368-369, 371

Gloucester Public Defender's Office, 179

Gormley, Senator William: Verniero nomination, 301; Verniero letter to, 322; support of Verniero, 325; protecting the *process*, 335-337; meeting with Chertoff, 341-344; SJC hearing to recall Verniero, 348-350, 356-357, 359-361, 363-368; voting for removal, 370; battle over, 372-373

Gotcha Squad, 46

Grant, Leroy Jarmaine, 273, 275, 279, 347

Grant, Trooper Timothy, 226-227, 232

Greenblatt, Ron, 7

Gunnell, Captain Edward, 104

Hague, Mayor Frank, 11

Harley-Davidson, 9

Hartman, Francis, 162-163, 174-175, 188-190, 193-195

Hauptmann, Bruno Richard, 13, 239

Heckler & Koch, 334

Henig, Trooper Robert: Lowengrub arrest, 60-61; Barber shooting, 73-75; Blair arrest, 86-88; suspension and indictment, 102-105; new charges, 149-150; Hartman representing, 162-163; first trial, 173-175, 188-190; acquittals, 193-195

High Times, 47

Highway Drug Interdiction: SNAP, 30; army of bloodhounds, 43; king of, 46; Dintino not sold on, 48; legality of offender profiles, 66; newspapers touting success of, 90; Operation Coflame, 95; biggest cheerleader on, 115; Pagano reiterates importance, 138; showing signs of collapse, 149; Dintino criticizes, 153; no longer top priority, 156; de-emphasizing, 165; scaled back, 210

Hoerst, Frank, 115

Hoerst III, Frank, 115-117, 149

Hogan's Heroes, 236

Hogan, Trooper John: leading contender, 255; learning fast, 260-261; disappointment and obsession, 269-270; Turnpike shooting, 272-277; reputation, 281-282; Stone, 286; radioactive, 290-291; possible indictment, 303-304; falsification indictment, 318; further charges, 329; troopers march, 334; charges dismissed, 338-339; Verniero denies, 360; fined, 374-376

Holder, Eric, 315

Hoover, J. Edgar, 26

Hopkins, Brent, 183, 208, 219, 235

Hughes, U.S. Rep. William J., 47

Huntley-Brinkley Report, 158

Innocence Project, 279

Ironman, David, 278

J. Edgar Hoover of New Jersey, 25, 123, 152, 239

Jackson Jr., Reverend Jesse, 20

Jackson, Reverend Reginald: challenging racial injustice, 283-285; used as political pawn, 293-295; press conference, 298-299; on Interim Report, 321; Halloween, 339; not one achievement, 345; SJC hearing, 356; trying to grip running water, 361; not justice, 376

Jamaican Posse, 218-220

Jankowski, Major Richard, 153

Jennings, Trooper Alvin, 87

johnnie(s), 3, 41, 202, 274, 290, 300

Johnson, Trooper Glenn: driving prisoners, 79; Black Radicals, 94-95; say pervasive, 142; conspiracy to destroy Ruff, 186; suspended, 199-200

Jones, Nate, 14-16, 118, 130, 143

Kean, Governor Tom, 29, 209, 258

Kelly, Superintendent David B., 23-24, 44

Kelly, Jennifer, 85

Kenna, Trooper James: Turnpike shooting, 272-276; Stone assigned to investigation,, 286; falsification indictment 303-304; charges brought, 318; further indictments, 329; troopers march, 334; charges dismissed, 338-339; Verniero denies, 360; fined, 374-376

Kennedy, Curtis, 58

Kenney, Linda, 333, 346

King, Jr., Dr. Martin Luther, 15, 36, 158-159, 282

Kitchen, U.S. Dist. Court Judge John J., 7

Kosco, Senator Louis, 366

Krass, PhD., Dr. Alvin, 191

Ku Klux Klan, 79, 244

La Cosa Nostra, 25, 27

Lambda Legal, 177

Lamberth, Dr. John, 184-185, 196-198, 213-214, 231

Landau, Judge David, 309

Landsdowne, Sheriff Bill, 315

Last, Fred, 179-183, 196-198, 204, 212-213

Latham & Watkins, 342, 373

Laughton, Charles, 160

Law Enforcement Intelligence Unit, 49

Leck, Capt. John, 103

Lewis, Trooper Thomas, 171

Lindbergh, Charles, 13

Lisa, Judge Joseph, 180-184, 196, 204

load of coal, 41

Longoria, Trooper Emblez, 269-271, 356-357, 359

Lord, Robin Kay, 281

Loughry, Justin: joining forces, 179-182; software crash, 184; violator survey, 196-198; object, 216; tape looks familiar 219-220; Fahy grasping at straws, 231-232; crooning, 238; delay request, 309

Louima, Abner, 278-279

Lowe, Kim, 106

Lowengrub, Kenneth, 60-61, 73, 162-163, 173-175, 189, 194

Luciano, Lucky, 23

Lui-Kwam, Kalama, 361

Lynch, Senator John A.: animus toward Verniero, 301-302; Verniero's nomination, 325;

Lynch, Senator John A. *(cont'd)*
as arch-nemesis, 336; swan song, 341-344;
SJC hearing, 362; articles of impeachment,
368

Mafia, 22-25, 27, 49, 337

Maher, Laila, 246-247

Malcolm X, 37, 159

Manhattan, N.Y., 76, 107

Mantel-Haentzel Analysis, 237

Martens, Lt. Frederick, 44, 48

Martin, Senator Robert J., 324

Marvin, Walter, 70-72, 127-128, 150, 168

Maryland State Police, 265, 293, 307

Mastella, Trooper Andrew, 44-46, 109

Mastoris Diner, 164

Matha's Farm, 153-154

Matheussen, Senator John, 325, 327

McLemore, Trooper Paul, 34-38, 118-119, 143,
191-192

Meanor, U.S. District Court Judge Curtiss,
7-8

Merrill, Bruce, 59

Messerlian, Trooper Harry, 59

Mezzanotte, Sgt. Clement, 103

Microsoft Excel, 184

Middlesex County, NJ, 70, 74, 104, 127-128, 150

Mintz, Robert, 367

Monkey Drills, 12, 19

Monticello, Trooper Nicholas, 40, 215-216,
220-223

Moore, Christopher, 60, 174, 194

Moore, Keshon, 273-276, 333, 346-347

Morris, Veronica, 85

Moorestown Station: Disalvatore at, 133; arrest records of, 214; Beard transferred to,
224; special report at, 244-245; *Soto* ruling, 250; SJC hearing, 358

Morka, Felix, 246-247

mother lode, 40, 62

Mount Trashmore, 39

Murray, Bill, 226

NAACP, 15-16, 35, 177, 312

Narco Avenger, 43

Natale, Wayne, 205, 207, 220-223, 249

Nemeth, Trooper Donald, 231-232

Neuborne, Bert, 135

Neufeld, Peter, 279, 290-291

Newark Black Radicals: christening of, 94-95,
primary suspects, 142; looking up to Ruff,
170; magnitude of Ruff's dilemma, 186-187;
Ruff terminated, 192; termination of, 199-
200; in front of Congress, 210; Beard, 224;
Sanders at SJC hearing, 370

Newark, NJ: Crestmont Homes, 17; transferred to, 21; riots, 36-37; Wells, 106-107;
two officers from city, 170-172; Ruff denies being in, 186-187; complaint filed,
191-192

Newark Star-Ledger: Hogan's reputation,
281; engaged on profiling, 288; quoting
former fiancée, 290; front page article on
profiling, 292-294; Williams interview
298; State Police Suspected, 335; Askin
quoted by, 355

Newark Station: Ruff at, 17; 20-20 rule at
39-40; war at, 42; syringes found at, 59;
Beard at, 62-63; powder keg, 79-81; not
only one, 94; *Without Just Cause* aired,
129-131; fallout, 141-142; Ruff accused, 170-
172; Monticello's *Soto* testimony, 220

Newburgh, New York, 82

New Castle, Delaware, 99

New Jersey Attorney General: deal with Slocum, 150; Pagano out, 151-154; no more

New Jersey Attorney General *(cont'd)*
plea bargains, 181; motion to disqualify
Last, 204; *Soto* ruling, effect on, 252-255;
Verniero youngest in state history, 258-
259; Christmas Eve meeting, 262-263;
no credible evidence, 264-265; stalling
DOJ, 268; Jackson meeting with, 284;
State Police review announced, 292-
295; ordered falsification case, 303-304;
Zoubek confronts Verniero, 306; deniability, 307-308; appellate court judges deny motion, 310-311; Interim Report
drafts circulated, 312-314; Interim Report revised, troopers charged, 317-318;
Interim Report unveiled, *Soto* appeal
dropped, 320-321; 34000 plus one legal
matters, 322; Verniero's confirmation to
State Supreme Court, 324-326; Dunlop's
speech, 330-331; profiling cover-up un-
ravels, 334-336; powerful forces within,
338; pressure building on Farmer, 340;
depositions, 343-344; Gilbert testifies,
349; Verniero as malefactor, 353; Verniero's amnesia, 356-364; derelict in duty,
366; articles of impeachment, 370; Farmer ties loose ends, 374

New Jersey Bar Association, 312

New Jersey Law Journal, 143, 327

New Jersey Monthly Magazine, 26, 59, 380

New Jersey Senate Judiciary Committee:
Verniero nomination, 301; Verniero confirmation hearing 324-326; Gormley calls
additional hearing, 336-337; Verniero press
release, 341-342; SJC impeachment hearing, 348-352, 353-364; recommendation
drafted, 365-367, articles of impeachment,
369-370

New Jersey State Police: true crimebusters, 6-
8; founding of, 9-13; Federal court order,
18; the Academy, 19-20; Pagano and Dintino, 22-26; first black trooper 35-37; spying on, 71-72; Ruff complains, 80; WWOR
letter, 98-99; poster boy for, 109-110; drug
dogs, 111-113; anonymous whistleblower,
119-122; Collum and Pagano, 123-126; prima facie case against, 127-128; Without Just
Cause aired, 129-132; Disalvatore shooting, 133-140; humiliation, retaliation, call
for investigation of, 141-144; second Pagano interview, 145-148; Buckman's first
encounter with, 157; Dintino new Superintendent, 164-166; Title 39, valid stops,
169; Ruff accused, 171-172; biggest scandal
in history of, 173-175; Ruff's defense, 186-
187; Ruff terminated, 191-192; Henig fired,
193; Williams replaces Dintino, 210-211;
Whitman denies profiling by, 284-285; no
such thing as profiling, 292-294; Williams
resigns, 298-300; Gilbert's blue binder,305-
306; Interim report drafted,313-314; Dunlop's speech to,330-331; trooper march, 334;
new evidence against, 336; image transformed, 353; organizational failure, 375; *See
also, State of New Jersey v. Soto, et. al.*

New Jersey State Police Academy: pure military, 12; Wilson enters, 52; raised requirements for, 177; Douglas taught course at,
218; Burke nicknamed by classmates at,
269; leaving the, 297; racial profiling routine practice from, 376

New Jersey Supreme Court: Outfit guarding
the, 25; blue-ribbon panel, 176; whispers
about Poritz, 253; first female Justice of,
258; Verniero's nomination to, 292-296;

New Jersey Supreme Court *(cont'd)*
two old lions, 298-303; opposition toward Verniero's nomination to, 310-312; Hogan and Kenna thrown to wolves, 318; nomination hearing, 321-325; Gormley calls for additional hearings, 336-337; extraordinary step, 341; Verniero as malefactor 353; prizefight, 355-364; reputation for excellence, 366-367; impeachment denied, 368-372

New Jersey Turnpike: history of, 5-8; steady increase in drug cases, 70-72; premier anti-drug gladiator, 73; Stubbs stop, 83-84; Blair stop, 85-89; fourth stop in sixteen miles, 95; something wrong on, 97-101; money seized on, 111; Pagano refutes I-team story, 142-143; statistics validated, 147-148; Sweeney most hated on, 190; violator survey, 196-198; searches conducted on, 207; Tezsla testifies, 235-236; Pagano in court, 239; blacks stopped at elevated rates on, 242; aggressive troopers assigned to, 313; Interim report, 319-321; bloody disaster on, 322; profiling along, 336

New York City: crack-fueled wave of violence, 27-32; profile list,67; making it in, 76; horrific drug problem, 97; Turnpike conduit, 147-148; Todd's fortune, 209-210; most influential African-American of, 282; top orthopedist, 290; stained by the blood, 315; Mafia prosecution, 337

New York Daily News, 279

New York Times: failure of local authorities, 10; "Mr. Untouchable", 27; Verniero writes to, 258; silent on profiling, 288; Verniero nomination on shaky ground, 322; Whitman doling political favors, 326; NJ Police

New York Times (cont'd)
withheld data on profiling, 336; Purdy comment, 345; Verniero's diminished authority, 365; NJ Republicans disfunctional family, 370

New York University, 135

New York University's Benjamin Cardoza School of Law, 279

Nicholas, Dr. Stephen, 290

Olmstead v. United States, 250

Operation Pipeline, 227-228

Orlando Sentinel, 315

Oxford Circle, PA, 157-158

Ozzie and Harriet, 159

PRA, *See* Patrol Related Arrest

Pagano, Superintendent Clinton: career beginnings, 22, 24-26; drug-free New Jersey, 30; war on drugs, 43-47; metamorphosis, 49; SPAAD, 50-51; no discrimination in highway enforcement, 56; character witness 59-60; Carr memo to, 75; Coflame memo, 95; standing tall, 97; stacks of cash, 112; first Collum interview, 123-126; Marvin's charges, 127-128; *Without Just Cause* aired, 129-131; Disalvatore shooting, 138; whites majority of arrests, 139; minority rights of less concern, 140; videotaped rebuttal, 142-144; second Collum interview, 145-148; Slocum deal, 149-150; replaced by Dintino 151-156; symbolic slap in face of, 164-166; testifying for Henig, 193-194; Tezsla's *Soto* testimony on, 236; *Soto* testimony, 238-240; constitutional sneer, 242; *Soto* ruling 250; dreadful witness, 254; symbol of glory days, 334

Pagano, Trooper Girbert, 26

Pagano, Trooper Lester, 26

Pagano Report, 212, 240

Parks, Rosa, 159

Paskow, Anne, 65-69, 253-254, 294

Patrol Related Arrest(s), 41-43, 96

Payne, U.S. Representative Donald, 200

PBS Frontline, 29

Pelligra, Lt. Phillip, 189

Perretti, Attorney General Peter, 150, 152

Perskie, Steve, 154-155

Petner, Tom, 136-137

Philadelphia Inquirer, 288, 292

Philadelphia, Pennsylvania, 157, 159

Pitt, William, 168

Police Intelligence Systems in Crime Control: Maintaining a Delicate Balance in a Liberal Democracy, 48

Pollock, Justice Stewart G., 292, 294

Pontefract, 209, 299

Poritz, Dr. Alan B., 253

Poritz, Justice Deborah, 253-254, 258-259, 327, 357

Porroni, Albert, 361, 368

PRA, *See* Patrol Related Arrest(s)

President's Commission on Organized Crime, 49

Princeton, New Jersey, 70

Prouse, see *Delaware v. Prouse*

Purdy, Matthew, 345

Queens, New York, 27

Ransavage, Sharon, 255

Reagan, President Ronald, 29, 49, 217,

Record of Hackensack, See *Bergen Record*

Red Lion Station, 3, 245

Red Ribbon, 45-46, 188, 255, 260-261, 269-270,

Reed, Trooper Anthony, 80-81, 94-95, 142, 170-172, 199

Reinfeld, Joel, 77

Reyes, Danny: 273-275, 278, 290-291, 347, 374-375

Rider, A.D., 10

Robertson, Senator Norman, 366

Rolax, Sherron, 257

Rollins, Ed, 210

Roosevelt, President Theodore, 44

Rover, George, 265-266, 317, 349-352, 357-358

Rubin, Ken, 99

Rudd, Mark, 56

Ruff, Dwanda, 171

Ruff, Elizabeth, 18

Ruff, Trooper Kenneth L., beginnings, 17-21; exposure to profiling, 39-42; slave auction, 79-80; Black Radical, 94-96; *Without Just Cause* aired 131-132; framed, 170-172; victim of smear, 186-187; evaluation, 191-193; prepped to testify, 202-203; *Soto* testimony, 215-216; telling the truth, 223

Rutgers University, 7, 127, 139, 288,

Rutland, Vermont, 241-242, 248

Salem County, New Jersey, 99, 115-116, 371

Salerno, Anthony "Fat Tony," 337

salt and pepper team, 41, 79

Sanders, Trooper Greg, beginnings, 18-21; refusing to play the game, 41-42; at Newark Station, 79-81; branded Black Radical 94-95; *Without Just Cause* aired, 129-131; say pervasive, 141-142; lynch mob, 171-172, advising Ruff, 187; testifying before Congress, 199-200; refusing Buckman, 202; SJC testimony, 370

Scheck, Barry, 279

Schiereck, Sgt. Lawrence, 87

Schwab, Kevin, 77

Schwarzkopf, General H. Norman, 11-12

Schwarzkopf, Superintendent Herbert Norman, 10-13, 35, 151

Schwarzkopf, Julius, 10, 12

Scurka, Gary, 91, 97, 119, 135-136

Secaucus, New Jersey, 76

Sea Girt, New Jersey, 12, 19

Senatore, Trooper Joseph, 257

Sharpton, Reverend Al, 282-284, 293, 315

Shaw, U.S. District Court Judge Robert, 7

Simpson, O.J., 206

SJC, *See* New Jersey Senate Judiciary Committee

Slocum, Alfred, 150

Smars, Johnny, 35

Smith, Sgt. James E., 94, 244-245

Smith, Rolland, 129, 138

Smithson, Judge Andrew, 338, 340, 374

SNAP, *See* State Narcotics Action Plan

Snipes, Wesley, 315

Social and Economic Rights Action Center, 246

SOP F-55, 177, 273

Soto, Pedro Agaury, 180, 206, 217

Soul On Ice, 37

SPAAD, *See* State Police Against Age Discrimination

spotlighting, definition of, 53; examples of, 40, 62, 99 234; Ruff on, 202; Ruff testimony, 215; Cupingood *Soto* testimony to 237; Interim Report, 320

St. Matthew's African Methodist Episcopal Church, 284

Starks, John, 133, 134

State Narcotics Action Plan 30, 43, 66, 69

State of New Jersey v. Pedro Soto, et al.: Judge Lisa, 180-185; Violator's Survey 196-198; shopping an insider, 201-203; Judge Fran-

State of New Jersey v. Pedro Soto, et al. (cont'd) cis assigned, 204-208; opening testimony, 212-216; Fahy, 217-219; continuing testimony, 219-223, Wilson, McCaffrey testify, 226-229; pressure taking its toll, 229-232; Tezsla, Cupingood, Pagano testimony, 236-240; hearing ends, 241-243; Francis rules, 248-251; pondering appeal, 252-255; Verniero appointed NJ Attorney General, 258-259; Justice Department probe, 262-266; status summary, 286-287; approaching moment of truth, 293-294; stalling for time, 296-297; delay appeal, 300; *numbers are not good,* 305-306; appellate court, 309-311; Interim Report, 320-321; Lynch questions political expediency, 325; Francis demotion, 327-328; unraveling cover-up, 335; SJC hearing, 350-351; Verniero testimony, 356-357; Brady obligation, 360; articles of impeachment, 369-370

State Police Against Age Discrimination, 50-51

State Police Pipe & Drum Corps, 165

State v. Kennedy, 58, 196, 250

Steinhagen, Renee, 199, 201

Stephens, Trooper Mark, 245

Sterling, Eric S., 29

Stern, Judge Edwin H., 309-310

Debra Stone: offender profiles unconstitutional, 65-69; petitioned for advice, 253-254; numbers similar to *Soto's,* 286-287; appellate dilemma, 293-294; talking to troopers, 297; on the warpath, 300; falsification case, 303-304; Gilbert's blue binder, 305-306

Students for a Democratic Society, 56, 279

Susswein, Ronald, 65-66, 68-69, 254

Sullivan, Cornelius, 49

Sweeney, Trooper William, 61, 163, 173, 188-190, 194

Taylor, Valerie, 31-33, 99, 153

Team Groundhog, 226

Temple University, 184-185, 272

Tezsla, Major Alexander, 235-236

The Godfather, 219

The Harder They Come, 219-220

The Patty Duke Show, 235

Time Magazine, 29

Times of Trenton, 34

Tomar, Simonoff, Adourian & O'Brien, 179

Toney, McArthur, 55-57

Tornquist, Trooper Gary, 60

Touw, Captain Richard, 254-255

Trenton, New Jersey, 9, 65-66, 301

The Triangle, 43, 47

Trooper of the Year, definition of 45-47; references to: 41, 61, 73-75, 86, 103, 109, 152, 163, 188, 255, 260-261, 269-270, 272-273, 290, 320

Troopers Behind the Badge, 133

Turner, Elijah, 35, 37

Tuxedo Club, 34, 37

Union Hotel, 355

United States Supreme Court, 8, 66, 168, 169, 212

U.S. Justice Department: investigation into NJ State Police opened, 262-263; probe turns into minefield, 264-268; Williams sacrificial lamb, 307; consent decree, 330; SJC hearing testimony, 351-352, Verniero's denials, 356-358, 362

U.S. News & World Report, 29

Vermont Public Defender's Office, 241-242.

Verniero, Supreme Court Justice Peter: meteoric career, 258-259; meeting w/Gilbert, Williams, 262-263; quell threats, 264-265; stalling DOJ, 267-268; Jackson demands meeting with, 284; seeking State Supreme Court nomination, 292-296; Lynch demands confirmation be delayed, 298-302; considering falsification charges 303-304; adopting a posture, 306-308; continuance on *Soto* denied, 309-311; disaster before the Bar, 312-313; bringing falsification charges, 317-318; Interim Report unveiled, 319-321; Dream Team files suit against State, 322-323; Supreme Court confirmation hearing, 324-325; Gormley plans recall, 335-336; bleeding from publicity, 340-342; SJC hearing begins, 348-351; new bad boy, 353; SJC hearing testimony, 355-364; asked for resignation, 365-367; articles of impeachment, 368-372; dodging expulsion, 373

Vince Lombardi Turnpike Service Plaza, 150

Waldie, Trooper Steven, 60

Waldron, Charles E., 173-174, 189, 194

Warren County, N.J., 55, 250

Warren, U.S. Supreme Court Chief Justice Earl, 325, 336

Washington, President George, 5, 135

George Washington Bridge, 124, 129, 131

Washington, D.C., 200

Waugh, Alexander, 262, 350-351, 358

Weber, Scott, 342-344, 348, 361, 368, 373

Weekly Standard, 337

Wenk, Marsha, 56, 250, 251

Wheeler, Douglas, 343-344, 368-369, 371.

Whitman, Governor Christine Todd: short bio, 209-211; Camden City Initiative, 256-257; appointments, 258-259; Jackson, 283-284;

Whitman, Governor Christine Todd *(cont'd)*
Verniero's nomination, 294-295; public relations calamity, 299-300; Buckman before appellate court, 310; wrong about NJ State Police, 313-314; accusations of political expediency, 317-318; Interim Report unveiled, 319-320; demands to withdraw Verniero's nomination, 322; arm twisting and favors, 324-326; photograph goes public, 328; quit Senate race, 329; abdicating Governorship, 333; administration coming to a close, 339; not one achievement, 345; statement in support of Verniero, 367

Whitman, John R., 209

Whitman, Walt, 256

Wilkins, Trooper Roger, 245

Williams, Superintendent Carl: replacing Dintino, 210-211; crying foul, 252; Christmas Eve meeting with Verniero, 262,-263; Gilbert's memo to, 265; coping with DOJ demands, 267; closed door meeting with Jackson, 284; in denial, 293-294; resignation, 298-299; intended fall guy, 307-308; SJC hearing testimony, 353-354

Williams, Jr., U.S. Senator Harrison A., 154

Wilson, Trooper Kenneth, 52-54, 202, 218, 227

Wintner, Jeffrey: throwing in with Buckman, 179-180; brief bio, 204; opening *Soto* hearing, 207; during *Soto* hearing, 213-215, 226-230, 237, 239,-240; at SJC hearing, 356

Without Just Cause: first installment aired, 129; Disalvatore shooting, 133-140; reaction to, 141-144; face on the statistics, 153;

Without Just Cause (cont'd)
Soto opening statement, 207; remarks from admitted into evidence 238; cited in Francis ruling, 250; Dream Team to prove deliberate indifference, 290

Woliver, Sheri, 55-58, 127, 168, 196, 250

Woodley, Christopher, 272, 303

Wright, Burton, 85-87

WWOR-TV: Collum member of I-team, 76-77; looking into profiling, 90-91; investigating the State Police, 97-98; Turnpike interview with Watts, 101; asking every African-American, 106; rumor has it, 129; possibly scuttling series, 136-138; trooper backlash against, 141; swamped with callers, 145; *Soto* opening statement, 207;

Zane, Senator Raymond, 324, 349, 351, 360, 362

Zoubek, Paul: career prosecutor, 286-287; in charge of State Police review, 293-294; position in *Soto*, 297, request for extension, 300; meeting with Verniero, 303-304; Gilbert's blue binder, 305-306; Dunlop's call, 307-308; telephone hearing, 309-311; Interim Report to Governor, 313-314; startling discovery, 317

Zukin, Cliff, 288

Zukowsky, Sgt. Walter, 21, 42, 80, 95-96, 170-172

LaVergne, TN USA
07 December 2010
207780LV00002B/74/P